Realms of Strife

THE MEMOIRS OF

Juan Goytisolo

1957–1982

Translated by Peter Bush

NORTH POINT PRESS

San Francisco 1990

LIBRARY OF CONGRESS CATALOGING-IN-PUBLICATION DATA

Goytisolo, Juan.

   [En los reinos de taifa.   English]

   Realms of strife : the memoirs of Juan Goytisolo 1956-1982 /
translated by Peter Bush.

      p.   cm.

   Translation of: En los reinos de taifa.

   ISBN 0-86547-434-6

   1. Goytisolo, Juan—Biography.   2. Novelists, Spanish—
20th century—Biography.   I. Title.

PQ6613.O79Z46413   1990

863'.64—dc20

[B]   89-25506

Contents

Realms of Strife

The Stealer of Strength

WHEN I MOVED temporarily into Monique's flat on the rue Poissonnière, I was again toying with the idea turned over so often with Castellet and Elena de la Souchère of creating a forum for both the opposition in exile and within Spain to discuss political and literary trends in European culture. My first thought on that 15 September 1956, which would be the start of decades away from Barcelona and Spain, was to suggest to Mascolo the setting up of a committee of French anti-Fascist intellectuals supportive of such an enterprise. Shortly after my arrival, Monique and I were invited to dinner on the rue Saint-Benoît with a group of writers Mascolo had informed of the plan: not only his companion Marguerite Duras and members of the clan but also authors like Edgar Morin and Roland Barthes, whose *Mythologies* I had read avidly in Garrucha weeks before in regular installments in *Les Lettres Nouvelles*. However, to my great consternation, the conversation over dinner centered on the possible success of an assassination attempt on Franco's life. Apparently such a liquidation was feasible in a bullring: one of the guests had been to a bullfight presided over by the dictator and was emphatic he would be an easy target. The police did not suspect tourists: a foreign-looking crack marksman could sit in a nearby box without alarming anyone, shoot and then melt into the crowd, taking advantage of the first moments of confusion. The then secretary to Sartre, Jean Cau, warmed equally to the idea: weeks later, in the course of a political discussion on the rue Poissonnière, he confidently, almost arrogantly, declared that he was capable of organizing single-handedly within a few months the outbreak of revolution in Spain. My idea of a committee did not prosper, despite that first rush of enthusiasm in our after-supper discussions on the rue Saint-Benoît nourished by a generous intake of alcohol. History was in a hurry, the world was entering an eventful era, and the political compass of Mascolo and his friends would immediately swing toward new poles of attraction. The internal crisis of the Soviet system in Poland and Hungary, Nasser's nationalization of the Suez Canal, and the NLF offensive in Algeria hogged the newspaper headlines, and the modest, minor cause of Spain was suddenly of no interest. Mascolo went to Warsaw and returned in a state of great political and emotional excitement, in love with a young Polish lady who lived with him for a while a few months later. Monique and I accompanied them on a long weekend trip to Chartres and Chinon. When we visited him on his return, Wyborowa vodka had replaced dry sherry, and instead of the background flamenco music that followed his holidays in Spain, we now listened to a mournful, almost whining chorus of Slav or Baltic melodies across the staircase landing.

The Budapest rebellion crushed by Soviet tanks shook meanwhile the firmness of our convictions. Monique was still a member of the French CP and I still saw in Paris some of Luis's comrades, members of the Barcelona university group. The spectacle of thousands of demonstrators storming the local office of *L'Humanité* shocked and upset both of us. The police cordoned off the area, and when I went down to the street to see what was happening, one of Reventós and Pallach's comrades-in-arms, the trade unionist Ramón Porqueras, was shouting anti-Soviet slogans. His vehement tone filled me with dismay: the Hungarian events confused me. If, on the one hand, Mascolo, Marguerite Duras, and generally the French writers I knew denounced Russian imperialism and spoke of a second Kronstadt, on the other, my Spanish friends maintained unperturbed that it was a bourgeois uprising and fruit of intricate counterrevolutionary plotting. Octavio Pellissa or one of his comrades went to the press conference given by one of the first refugees from Budapest. He was an obese, decadent individual, laden with rings, complete with French accent learned in childhood from governesses or nurses, the total opposite of those heroic militiamen in the dramatic photographs of the pages of *Paris Match*: a reactionary bastard, they said, whose wealth had been expropriated by the new society and who, not content with saving his ugly skin, dared to criticize from Paris the magnificent conquests of the people. Monique was more exposed than I to the indignation that abounded in intellectual circles, and her faith in the Party evaporated:* I remember accompanying her, as her partner, to a district branch meeting in the side road leading to the Bonne Nouvelle church, next to the steps later filmed by Louis Malle in *Zazie dans le métro*. The agreed agenda items avoided all mention of events in Hungary and, rather than an assembly of revolutionaries, I had the impression I was attending a meeting of the parish council or of Catholic Action devoted to planning or completing routine duties. My reference to Khrushchev's report, published by the bourgeois but not the Communist press, led to an embarrassing silence: although a number of those present were certainly familiar with the report, it had not received the blessing of the leadership and did not officially exist. Monique yielded to the friendly pressure of branch companions and renewed her Party card, but she ceased to participate in activities and gradually distanced herself from the organization.

In the first hectic weeks of my stay in Paris I also met up with Spanish exiles and visitors from the Peninsula who were mostly within the orbit of the Spanish CP: Tuñón de Lara, Antonio Soriano, owner of the Spanish bookshop on the rue de Seine, Eduardo Haro Tecglen, Ricardo Muñoz Suay, Alfonso Sastre and Eva Forest, and Juan Antonio Bardem. A few days after my arrival, Mascolo took me to the office of Maurice Nadeau, editor of *Les Lettres Nouvelles*, so I could tell him about my idea for a Spanish magazine aimed at breaking the tight grip of the censor. This was the first of a series of related initiatives that usually ended, after interminable futile discussions, vetoes, expulsions, and confrontations, with the project being shelved and forgotten, but only after provoking in those involved feelings of anger and hurt pride that were difficult to heal. Although Nadeau generously ap-

---

*Her friends Claude Roy, Roger Vailland, and J-F Rolland deserted the ranks of the CP at that time.

proved the plan, he did not have the means to finance it and advised us to ne-
gotiate with Albert Beguin and Paul Flamand. After my visit to the former,
we accompanied Mascolo and Muñoz Suay to the latter's office. Flamand, at
the time the editor of le Seuil, gave us a courteous welcome. As I was setting
out in general terms the political and literary range of the project, I realized
that my argument, or rather the scheme's viability, was not convincing the
man opposite me. The enterprise as presented to him was political philanthropy pure and simple and of no interest to a responsible publisher. After a
pointless wait of some weeks, I put the fantastic concept to one side and decided to wait for that hypothetical moment to resurrect it when favorable developments within the Peninsula would naturally put the spotlight on Spain.

Around this time—October 1956—I met Eduardo Haro Tecglen in the
Deux Magots café. He was a journalist on the Madrid daily *Informaciones*
and the author, as I would later discover, of an amusing analysis of Spanish
censorship and of the most original theories on the subject of the current
minister of the department, Rafael Arias Salgado, which had just appeared
unsigned in the magazine *Esprit*. With the knowing, mysterious air of one
at the center or in the holy of holies of the organization, Muñoz Suay led me
to understand that Haro was "one of us"—the password or magic phrase
that in years or months to come Party members would whisper in my ear,
suggesting a flattering complicity. One of the first to be endowed with that
halo of concealed, almost sibylline prestige was, to my surprise, Enrique
Llovet, the Spanish general consul. Before we were introduced, I remember
Muñoz Suay and Bardem telling me that "you could talk freely" with him.
With their go-ahead, I set before Llovet the idea of the magazine; but his af-
fable caution discouraged me. A few months later, when I had already abandoned the scheme, he invited Monique and me to his home for dinner, on the
eve of our planned trip to Almería.* His wife, the daughter of Ricardo
Baeza, the writer and translator of Oscar Wilde, defended much more liberal positions than his own and, against the old Trojan-horse Leninist prac-

*On Tuesday, 12 February 1957, according to Monique's diary, to which I shall be referring
whenever I mention a date.

tice of infiltrating the enemy, she was in favor of a public break with the Régime to bring his ambiguous diplomatic role to an abrupt, sensational end. A kind of euphoria we all shared lulled us into believing that Franco's days in power were numbered. In the space of a year, the Party had extended the radius of its clandestine activity into the different branches of the country's cultural life, gaining positions and influence there never again to be reached; but the phenomenon was limited, as facts would soon prove, to a very narrow segment of the intelligentsia and had not spread, as we then believed, to the historic protagonists of the revolution, the proletariat and the peasantry. The momentary rapprochement of the Party to a handful of civil servants and members of the Spanish ruling class was and would be interpreted not just as individual breaks whose centrifugal strength was cast within the framework of the relentless pressure of an unchanging social order, but as a general indication that the inner disintegration of Francoism had reached the centers of power, now convinced of its imminent demise and the advent of a new society in which the Party would naturally play a leading, rallying role. The later, almost Pauline conversions of some children of ministers of the Régime or aristocrats like the Duchess of Medina Sidonia would for years bolster the hopeful but mistaken image of the country as a "volcano on the point of erupting." I don't doubt that this revolutionary subjectivism or voluntarism was necessary to maintain the structure and morale of an organization constantly under attack in its long and often disheartening trek across the desert. Nevertheless, the unwarranted belief in a discourse developed for propaganda or tactical reasons became over time a kind of mirage or self-deception, as I learned to my cost in 1964, during the internal Party crisis that climaxed in the expulsion of my friends Semprún and Claudín. This mystification, of which we were all victims to a greater or lesser extent, was difficult to diagnose in the early stages. Within our small circle the feeling that great changes were in the offing was strengthened daily with new examples and experiences. In one of the consulate offices on the boulevard Malesherbes, Llovet had introduced me to a colleague of his, the vice-consul Rafael Lorente. A generous, impulsive extrovert, endowed at times with that likable, youthful, irresponsible extravagance that is so common in Spain, Ra-

fael displayed great interest in getting to know me. He made several visits
that autumn to the rue Poissonnière to tell me his personal anxieties and political worries: unlike my Spanish friends he was sure that Communism
would not survive Budapest and was trying to organize people like me into
a new party that we would jokingly baptize "the party of caring snobs." One
night he came to ask me a favor: he wanted to be introduced to la Pasionaria,
to converse and have a drink with her. Although I said I didn't know her and
was totally unaware whether she secretly resided in France or the Soviet
Union, I saw he only half believed me. Then under the influence of the cognac or calvados I was pouring him, he told me of his plan to land in Fernando Poo with a handful of friends and proclaim the Republic: if we could
withstand the onslaught of Franco's navy for a few days, we could bring together there both the politicians and government in exile and win diplomatic
recognition from socialist-bloc countries. Although we never spoke of the
subject again nor mentioned his meeting alone with la Pasionaria, I continued to see him for several months until, after receiving another posting, he
decided to abandon his career and, infected by my enthusiasm for Almería,
settle down in the coastal village of Aguas Amargas and devote himself to
the cultivation of his land.

However, Rafael Lorente was a pleasant, unusual exception in the group
of Spaniards surrounding me, all of us steeped in crude, vulgar Marxism, almost always through Politzer's dogmatic simplifications, and a linear conception of history based on so-called scientific observations. Alfonso Sastre
was obsessed by the idea of compromise and hesitated even at that time
about asking to join the Party, but he did not vacillate for long: on his return
to Madrid, after his son's birth, he entered the organization and was soon cat-
apulted onto its central committee. Antonio Soriano and Tuñón de Lara,
with their long but discreet records as militants, did not talk about their political connections and remained tolerant and open. The future publicist and
popularizer of history had just published a book on Spain written jointly
with a Hispanist, Dominique Aubier, whom my French friends carefully
avoided. She would later be known in my adoptive province as the "Dame
de Carboneras," wore an Indian sari and rode on the back of a camel deep in

a cabbalistic reading of Cervantes. She already displayed an exuberant passion for Spain, translated the chroniclers of the Indies and, as I had the opportunity to discover, welcomed visitors to her flat on the rue de Seine in a bullfighter's hat—the cool fount of her stylistic inspiration, she would add. Tuñón and Soriano tolerated the torrent of overpowering rhetoric as best they could, but I was less patient than they and resolved at once to avoid her: once apprised of my plan for a magazine, she had wanted to participate, decide on the content, on who should and should not contribute. Her interference alarmed more than one friend and was probably crucial in my loss of heart and subsequent decision to throw in the towel.

My stubborn loyalty to the idea of a magazine bore fruit many years later, by which time I had already abandoned en route many illusions and pens. Although my early sociability faded with time and the idea of teamwork no longer appealed, I still associated myself with the *Cuadernos de Ruedo Ibérico* enterprise and lent my voice from the start to the *Libre* scheme, knowing that it would never bring me any satisfaction nor really suit my character. As in other areas of my life, I would achieve the objective I had anxiously sought at a moment when it had lost its previous attraction and my interests and taste were heading in a new direction. I would make moves at the wrong time and even against the tide of history, and changes and new developments would catch me without appetite rather than unawares—like the absurd, untimely corpse of Franco, whose death I had ceased to believe in.

What most impresses me as I review, pen in hand, and with the hindsight of thirty years, my first months in France are the different political positions or, more precisely, the varying degrees of political maturity and experience of the Parisian or Spanish friends who appear in these pages: while the latter as Party members or sympathizers lapped up their daily copy of *L'Humanité* and accepted its theses and explanations of the radiant society of the future, the former had already passed through this phase, spoke scornfully or with distaste of the USSR and pursued a complex, sophisticated political line which, although in my view unrealistic and even ridiculous, was nevertheless much more lucid and honest than the color-blindness and moral deafness at which my compatriots and I excelled or would excel. Apart from a few isolated exceptions like Soriano and Muñoz Suay, everybody judged harshly my friendship with those "renegades" and expelled members. My close relationship with the contingent on the rue Saint-Benoît, Roger Sté-phane—whom I would soon meet through Monique—and Elena de la Souchère, aroused the reservations and criticisms of my comrades until the need to resort to the bourgeois media, like *France-Observateur* or *L'Express*, to spread or support their new policy of "national reconciliation" or the cam-paign for amnesty for Franco's political prisoners led them to revise their po-sition and use my connections and influences to further their own interests and aims. But in the period covered by my narrative—including the rever-berations from Khrushchev's report and the invasion of Hungary—the "ir-responsibility," "contradictions," "double game," and "anarchist spirit" of left-wing French writers had attracted like a magnet the criticisms and withering observations of my fellow countrymen. What was behind that morbid preoccupation with human rights in Poland and Hungary? Didn't they notice perchance that the tiny, inevitable imperfections within the new societies of the popular democracies were small potatoes in relation to the so-cial injustices and inequalities in the so-called bourgeois democracies and their lack of broadly based freedoms? By criticizing the USSR, were they not falling into a clumsy, diversionary maneuver directly or indirectly ma-nipulated by the agents of imperialism? The genuine fickleness of the in-telligentsia of the Paris Left Bank, their inclination, rightly satirized by Ge-net, to change causes, if not political allegiance, as they swayed to the breeze of *France-Soir* headlines, often opened the way, it is true, to such attacks and sarcasm: months later, one of the writers I entered into contact with as a re-sult of the committee for solidarity with Spain abandoned that project en-tirely, and, to my great surprise, led a futile, esoteric call to support the Dalai Lama and Buddhist monks in Tibet following the Chinese invasion. How-ever, together with these unconscious comic tics and traits of the *animaux malades de la pétition*, as one of their friends affectionately dubbed them, Mascolo and his colleagues' generosity and desire for justice—opposed both to the Right and the Party, to the moralizing of Camus and to Sartre's fellow traveling—were soon evident in a concrete, risky, and practical form—in sharp and healthy contrast to the Party's ambiguity and caution—if not in relation to Spain, at least in respect to the Algerian war. Among the devotees of Marguerite Duras's flat on the rue Saint-Benoît—Robert Antelme, Louis-René des Forêts, Blanchot, Edgar Morin, etc.—appeared Madeleine Alleins, the wife of a famous doctor and passionate defender of third-world causes: a founding member of one of the clandestine support groups for the NLF like the renowned Jeanson network, the future novelist hid money, propaganda, weapons, and even members of the Algerian resistance in the homes of her trusted friends. A few weeks after my arrival, she came to our place at the suggestion of Mascolo and asked if we would look after the organization's funds for a short period. Monique accepted unhesitatingly and, a few days later, Madeleine reappeared with a big suitcase, which we placed on the top shelf of a pantry next to the front door. For almost a year, our contact dropped in from time to time to collect the amounts of money she needed, the totals of which she spelled out in coded telephone calls to Monique at Gallimard. At such times, I would open the suitcase stuffed with five-thousand-franc notes of the period, put the right quantity in an envelope, and give it to our friend when the doorbell rang punctually. Living as I was on very little money—my only source of income came from the reader's notes I began to write for publishers—I would often lament with Monique, also dazzled by the spectacle of that prodigious Ali Baba's cave, the fact that the treasure belonged to the NLF fighters and had not been mistakenly entrusted to us by an agent of Franco, Trujillo, or Somoza, so we could cheerily spread it around traveling the world in the footsteps of Phileas Fogg.

My first contact with North Africa, through the process of decolonization, was intensified throughout the Algerian war and its hateful repercussions in the metropolis: racial discrimination, persecution of North African immigrants, curfew, murders, and *ratonnades*. Just over three years later, Monique would be one of the first to sign the "manifesto of 121," which encouraged recruits to the expeditionary force to desert and which led to a conviction for her and a dozen writer-friends for "attacking the morale of the army" and "inciting soldiers to disobey the orders of their officers": "Anyone would think I'd been streetwalking in front of a barracks!" she exclaimed in amusement when she received notification from the court. While recalling later the vicissitudes of this period and my subsequent Arab affinities, she would laugh and comment that, although she in no way regretted her signature nor the subsequent complications—summonses, telephone threats, trials—if she could relive that time, she would fight for "my" Algerians with slightly less zeal and enthusiasm.

But I must get back to the strict chronology of my narrative. In January 1957, on our return from a brief, exciting trip to Italy, the French edition of *Juegos de manos* appeared with a well-documented, enlightening introduction by Coindreau. The novelty value of a novel from Francoist Spain after fifteen years' opaque silence aroused immediate, disproportionate interest in critics from *L'Humanité* to *Le Figaro*. Left-wing newspapers and weeklies emphasized, logically enough, the novel's rebellious, nonconformist tone, my implicit but undoubted hostility to official values. In spite of its great defects, limitations, and influences, the book fulfilled an expectation and was welcomed with unstinting enthusiasm: not one of my adult works from *Señas de identidad* to the present would win in any way such wide-scale approval, which clearly indicates the time-serving imponderables of that journalistic pseudocriticism, subject in Paris as elsewhere to a combination of prejudice, fashion, self-interest, and backslapping that distorts its function and changes it into a hollow charade swinging from ecstatic praise to the heaping on of ridicule. If the furor around the novel uncovered me in no uncertain way to the Francoist authorities, it granted me in passing a degree of immunity: to the extent that the Régime aspired to European respectability, it would not do to persecute an author who had built a reputation for himself as a result of cultural activities and works that would not be considered criminal in any democratic country.

On my arrival in Paris, Monique and I had agreed that after three or four months I would return to Spain for a period: just enough time to bring myself up-to-date with the situation in intellectual and university circles and to

visit, without the haste of my previous trip, the villages to the south of Garrucha. On 14 February I boarded the train in Austerlitz station pleased with
myself and naively proud of my book's success. If the external vision of
things predisposed me to optimism and even euphoria, the relentless, implacable flow of facts at once brought me back to reality. After my happy,
stimulating stay on the rue Poissonnière, the return to Pablo Alcover damp-
ened my spirits: decrepit people and things, cold, stingy light, my father's
anxious questions, Grandfather's silence, Eulalia's pathetic smile, diffuse
oppression, painful memories, anguish, anxiety, remorse. The depression
that was insidiously overpowering me in the family hearth filled with skel-
etons from the past was deepened by an event that occurred on the eve of my
arrival: Octavio Pellissa's arrest. His capture endangered the university
group organized by Sacristán, and Luis, who was directly threatened, was
being extremely cautious. I remember that just after my return someone
rang our doorbell very early in the morning, when we were both asleep in
our bedroom at the front of the house. Eulalia peeped into the garden and
came and informed us, with that worried look brought on by our new acquaintances, that a man was asking after us. We were startled by the news
but, belying our apprehension, the visitor turned out to be, not the feared police inspector, but an old friend of mine from Paris, the art critic Arnau Puig,
sent from there by the CP leadership to find out the cause and extent of the
raid in which Pellissa had been arrested. That rather rash and amateur mission to enable my brother to put him in contact with the "cadres" of the organization rightly alarmed Luis: the elementary lack of caution at a time
when he was possibly being watched was not at all in keeping with the need
for the meticulous rigor of clandestine activity. Although Octavio bravely
resisted the "interrogations" and was the only Communist student to be
caught, the police clean-up operation extended on the following days to
every area of opposition, from monarchists and Catalan nationalists to the
socialists of Pallach and Joan Reventós.

In the midst of that oppressive atmosphere, which was both uncertain
and threatening, we tried to lead a normal existence: we dined out with
friends who were less compromised than we were, visited the bars of Escu-

dillers and the Ramblas and returned home in the early morning. But the earlier excitement of my forays into the red-light districts had disappeared: my cheerfulness was forced, I was bored by the nightly sessions with whores and queers in La Venta and El Cádiz: we wearily complied with the empty, tedious ritual. Monique telephoned me daily and our long conversations in French mysteriously disturbed my father. His instinctive, but well-placed, fear of our suspicious carryings-on kept him awake until we were back: as we tiptoed across the passageway, we heard him stirring medicine or yogurt with his spoon, then look for his light switch and without fail ask us the time. Under the pressure of circumstances I abandoned the planned trip to Almería: in case of danger or a new police roundup, I would be unable to help or get information from that remote and isolated province. Monique, for her part, began to be worried by the politicizing of my novel in Paris and, finally persuaded that I would be more useful outside than in, I decided to cut short my visit and rushed back to Paris.

To avoid being exposed at the first police passport control between Massanet and Gerona to the needless danger of inspectors consulting with central police headquarters, I thought of the idea, which now seems childish and ridiculous, of catching the train in Figueras. Jaime Gil de Biedma, whom I sometimes accompanied on his most cautious nocturnal ventures on the Ramblas,* offered to drive me there, and I remember how en route, in the late afternoon sun of 2 March, he brushed against the wheel of a cart he was overtaking and we almost skidded and crashed, either as a result of his jittery nerves at that journey-cum-escape or his absorption in our weighty conversation on Gramscian compromise. After apologizing to the muleteer, we continued the drive to Figueras and said our goodbyes when the train arrived. The passport check proceeded without incident in the down-at-the-heels station of Port Bou: the inspectors stamped mine without comment and minutes later I was on French soil.

The frontier syndrome, which developed on my first journeys outside Spain, gradually diminished with the frequency of trips, as I learned to con-

*See his *Diario del artista seriamenta enfermo*, Barcelona, 1974.

trol my fears, but vanished completely only upon the death of the dictator. In years subsequent to the present stage of my narrative, when I crossed the frontier in potentially riskier circumstances, I did so with greater sangfroid, a mixture of casual indifference, fatalism, and irrational faith in my lucky stars that amazed those around me. The cheeky bravado of such an attitude aroused admiration, as I had noticed in the university militia camp where I spent the first months of my military service, on the day I decided to slope off, come what may, and not go through with the drills or exercises I most detested. However, in neither case was it in fact these qualities, but something more modest: my personal inability to accept the likelihood of punishment, my superstitious faith in a separate destiny. Sustained by both, I acted without considering the risks. To talk then of courage would not reflect the reality of the feelings with which I confronted my journeys in 1960 and '61; nevertheless, if at decisive moments I acted with a calm of which I am proud, my dreams were finally penetrated by the threat implicit in everything related to Spain. The ambiguous nature of my future relationship with Spain could perhaps be explained by the country's early association with a nebulous idea of danger, with a place where one could be arrested for no reason. While my European colleagues walked the world in a state of innocent tranquillity, conscious of exercising an inalienable right, I did so for years in a state of suppressed terror, with the persistent but fortunately mistaken foreboding that, like Luis, I was walking into the lions' den and sacrificing myself to a cannibalistic saturnine deity that implacably devoured its more lucid children. My early experiences at home reinforced the impression of fatally belonging to a nation eternally at war with itself that relentlessly transmitted its savage settling of accounts from one generation to another. Until I was well into my forties, Spain would symbolize for me not a welcoming, benign land receptive or at least indifferent to my labors on behalf of its language and culture, but a hostile arena of rejection threatening punishment from unexpected quarters. It is difficult to erase the scars left by dictatorships and totalitarian régimes. The treatment is long and uncertain: ten years after Franco's death, it is quite revealing in respect to myself that I still feel more at ease in Paris, Marrakesh, New York, or Istanbul than in the cities and places that formed the backdrop, for good or for evil, to the fears and fantasies of my childhood and youth.

On my brief visits to Spain in February and August 1957 I explained to my few journalist friends on the official press Gallimard's publishing plans, namely, our efforts to promote in France the most outstanding novels recently printed in the Peninsula. The list of works under contract included a good dozen authors representative of different postwar narrative trends— Cela, Delibes, Ana María Matute, Sánchez Ferlosio, Fernández Santos, etc.—but this initiative would be predictably met in Madrid with suspicion and mistrust, although less Cain-like countries than ours would have greeted it with praise. Some writers who were not selected and enjoyed posts of responsibility in the official ranks of the Régime began to communicate their anger and pique through the Movement's press. The translation of a proscribed work, *La otra cara* by José Corrales Egea, served as a pretext for the launching of a campaign of slander led by Aparicio, still the General Director of Press, and his colleague from *Pueblo*, Emilio Romero. The departure of the former in 1958 may have opened up new areas of cultural freedom, with the appearance of magazines like *Acento* and the timid, drip-feed surfacing of the name of some banned writer, but it did not substantially change the situation.* The attacks in *Pueblo* and *Arriba* intensified, coinciding with the publication of my manifesto, or statement, by *Ínsula* magazine, "Toward a National Popular Literature": perhaps Emilio Romero was offended by the fact that not a single creation of his own genius figured in the collection I was mounting and so launched an offensive, through his acolytes, against "the rival to Blasco Ibáñez based in France" whose sinister "customs-officer" role prevented, in his view, contact with the real glories of our contemporary literature.

The *Ínsula* manifesto, a product of an insatiable reading of Gramsci and not of my own still modest narrative experience, led to a ripple in the quiet

---

*Aparicio temporarily suspended the publication of *Ínsula* and *Índice*, despite the carefulness of the former and the notorious ambiguity of the latter.

waters through which the magazine used to steer, because of my rather un-
focused and unfair criticisms of Ortega and my obvious, if rather confused,
threading of openly Marxist theses. What surprises me most when I reread
it today is not the revisiting of stale formulas repeated with wearisome insistence by professional "progressives," but the chasm separating the ideas and
slogans set out there and my literary personality and novelistic production:
none of the work of my youth—*Juegos de manos*, *Duelo en el paraíso*, *Fiestas*,
El circo—had fortunately anything in common with the waffly schema for
national popular literature that I propounded, nor did the sensationalist strident promotion of my fiction in Europe and North America harmonize
with the somewhat Barresian Gramscianism that it flaunted. Guillermo de
Torre, in his acid response to the pamphlet, would rightly underline the
weakness of its premise and, without fighting shy of ad hominem arguments, its flagrant lack of coherence. The enfant terrible of the Barcelona
bourgeoisie that my New York publisher, in his raucous publicity material,
compared to the then fashionable Françoise Sagan did not suit the helmet
and armor of the provincial ideologue who assailed the lack of transcendence in decadent, dehumanized experimental literature. Criticism scored
a direct hit when it brought to light the duality of my position or, rather, the
gap between mask and reality: while my work revealed the influence of
Gide, Malraux, Faulkner, and the young southern novelists, my manifesto
implicitly rejected those authors and defended principles and norms at the
other end of the spectrum. Although in my wounded pride I would not admit to the shortcomings and contradictions denounced by my adversary, I
did from then on strive to align my writing with the more or less Marxist
declarations I was parading about: after failing with *La resaca*, my attempt
at a social novel, I followed in the footsteps of Rocco Scotellaro, Vittorini,
and Pavese, trying out, with greater or lesser success, the literary mode of social documentary and short story, from *Campos de Níjar* to *Pueblo en marcha*. With his usual clumsiness, Julián Marías had indirectly attributed my
article to an international conspiracy against Ortega and had evoked in this
respect the specter of "Maoist communes" and, together with the spontaneous reactions of other opponents, allowed me nevertheless to interpret the

polemic as the fruit of a counterattack from the right and thus sidestep the
indispensable debate with myself. That Corrales Egea, Juan Nuño, and
other Marxists came to my defense spared me the need to reflect on the dichotomy of my behavior and hidden moral schizophrenia: numerous intellectuals from the Spanish-speaking world still commonly have the attitude
that they can chase success and take advantage of the benefits of bourgeois
democracies, win scholarships, and teach in North American universities,
and at the same time adopt extremist Jacobin, dogmatic positions in the field
of politics and theory.

As far as I am concerned, the mismatch between life and writing was not
resolved till some years later, when hand-to-hand combat with the latter, the
exploration of new areas of expression and conquest of subjective authenticity, gradually integrated the former in a universe of text: the world conceived as a book ceaselessly written and rewritten, rebelliousness, struggle,
excitement fused in life and script as I was consumed by the delights, white
heat, torments of the composition of *Conde Julián*.

Seven months later I embarked with Monique on the visit to Almería, postponed because of Octavio Pellissa's arrest; we left her daughter in the Valencian village of Beniarjó and paid a return visit to our friends in the pensión
Zamora in Garrucha. In a small four-horsepower Renault we drove round
the villages and communities of the area: Huércal Overa, Cuevas de Al-
manzora, Mojácar, Palomares, and Villaricos. Monique was deeply impressed by the forlorn poverty we saw: she did not share the personal moti-
vation nor secret affinities which drew me to that land, and she was horrified
by the idea of vacationing, sunbathing, enjoying life with the reptilian indifference of a Swedish blonde in a landscape that was luminous and beautiful while harsh and poverty stricken. That was the starting point for our
frequent discussions of the subject: Monique would reproach me from then
on for my aesthetic fascination for places, regions, and landscapes where living conditions inevitably offended anyone with a minimum of social awareness. I was more hardened than she to the spectacle of poverty and strangely
attracted by human qualities and features that have been inexorably swept

away by the leveling commercialization of progress: my attitude was indeed ambiguous. The feelings of immediacy and emotional warmth that I discovered in Almería provoked a painful, bitter, insoluble conflict within me. Moral anguish based on the reality of my experience would then emerge: it was not the superficial by-product of my class guilt or reading of Marx, but the fruit of thoughts that encompassed sympathy and solidarity alike. My desire to denounce the reality was tempered by love and prospective nostalgia for what I was denouncing: the struggle to eradicate the iniquitous situation that predominated in Almería did not exclude the real, if uncomfortable, conviction that the necessary social and economic transformation would sweep away in its path those ingredients of openness, close-knit living, and spontaneity that were the seed of my commitment. I did not allow myself to be paralyzed by this conflict but returned to the province alone, determined to write an eyewitness account. In the future this southern aesthetic would color my interventions in the area and reflect in its light the hidden turmoil or civil war between the realities of beauty and underdevelopment: as I would point out in one of my first exercises in lucidity, we intellectuals who are not single-minded but are made up of variegated, antithetical features struggle for a world that we will perhaps find uninhabitable.

Rather than continue to Sorbas and Carboneras as we had initially planned, we turned off toward Granada and Málaga in pursuit of greater comfort and pleasure. I returned to Almería without Monique in August 1958 and in March 1959 and explored the disturbing region of Níjar on foot, by truck, and by bus, and when I had finished the manuscript of the book in Paris—fusing in one journey for reasons of narrative practicality the incidents, events, and encounters of the different visits—I returned to scrutinize the whole area by car, in order to photograph the places described in the account with the film director Vicente Aranda. My later journeys to the region were in difficult circumstances that did not favor my aims: if, on the one hand, Luis's arrest, the Milan affair, and the furor aroused by the press around our wretched name exposed my apparent freedom of movement as an illusion, on the other hand, the appearance of *Campos de Níjar*, in spite of

the censor's *nihil obstat*, had provoked the angry reaction of the town mayor
and the provincial government authorities. While in 1959 I managed to penetrate incognito the cave district of La Chanca, on the pretext of looking for
the relative of a friend exiled in Grenoble, without raising the suspicions of
the inhabitants or attracting police interest, a year later my presence did not
go undetected and I was forced to take a number of precautions: in the company of Vicente Aranda, I first visited Almería with Simone de Beauvoir
and Nelson Algren and then with the filmmaker Claude Sautet, without
daring to pursue my surveys of Níjar or La Chanca. My fear of compromis-
ing my informants was not at all imaginary, as I would later be able to prove
at the bullrunning in Albacete. However, stripped of its purpose and attractions, my stay in Almería became meaningless. Like the locals, I was imprisoned in a diffuse atmosphere of policed freedom and felt caught with them
in the net. It is difficult to express the bitterness and gloom with which I
would decide not to return, thus depriving myself of the warmth and sense
of belonging that by instinct, and in compensation, I would search out and
find in North Africa.

The writing of *Campos de Níjar* closes a chapter of my narrative in relation to Spain. It is written extremely carefully in order to avoid the attention
of the censor, and the book's technique, structure, and focus can all be explained by reference to censorship: the use of ellipsis, association of ideas,
implicit deductions that may seem obscure to readers used to freedom of
expression but not at all to those long manacled by the censor's iron grip, who
acquire, as Blanco White intelligently pointed out, "the skill of the mute at
communicating with signs." An experienced student in the art of speaking
to the voiceless, I took up the challenge of writing a work full of hidden messages and winks and nudges to the alert reader, without the stalwart functionaries of the Information and Tourism Ministry—information for images to please the tourists—being able to latch onto anything in particular to
justify cutting even a paragraph. Although this was a victory of which I was
then proud, subsequent thoughts persuaded me that it was a double-edged
sword or, in other words, a Pyrrhic victory. To escape the traps and snares of
the censor, I had turned myself into one. Forced to obey the rules of the

game, to act within the limited field of what was possible, I had paid hateful tribute to the guardians of the Régime. As the defenders of this strategy rightly pointed out, the frontier between the banned and tolerated was not fixed and established forever: the mood of the times, persistence of writers, circumstantial changes allowed small advances, the freeing-up of space that had been closed off for a long time, a series of partial if comforting successes. Nevertheless, such an exercise involved the writer in a painful self-mutilation, the devastating effects of which would be later revealed: a continuing imposed respect for dominant norms, fear of one's own ideas, insidious conformism, exhaustion, and sterility. When adapting to the censor's rules, an author cannot be sure of emerging unharmed, of not displaying forevermore the melancholy scars and traces they leave. The idea of marking out the boundaries—of letting the censor get on with his work while I got on with mine, not worrying about his existence—slowly gained ground. Five years' practice in doing what was possible had forced me to swallow too many snakes and, as my friend Fernando Claudín would say in circumstances fairly similar to the ones I describe, everything has a limit, even the consumption of snakes. This liberating decision was obviously going to unleash unbridled attacks on my work and character: after the salvo of accusations and insults orchestrated by the General Director of the Press, don Adolfo Muñoz Alonso, they would ban in Spain everything I wrote up to the death of the dictator.

The absurd power that oppressive governments of right and left endow upon literature—a totally undeserved honor—by preventing its dissemination and putting all manner of obstacles in its way, arouses a curious reflex-thought in opponent practitioners of the art: the belief that a poem, novel, or theatrical work, through the mere fact of its being banned or possibly being banned, has a direct impact on reality and enjoys the miraculous virtue of molding it in its own image; an obviously inept supposition, since the influence of the literary text on the reader's mind is fortuitous and develops slowly over a long period. However, a Party comrade, filled with enthusiasm by *Campos de Níjar*, had tried to convince me on the eve of one of my visits that the account would, and these were more or less his words, "awaken the consciousness of the popular masses in the province"; with unbounded optimism and excitement concerning my powers of enlightenment, he urged me to visit the bookshops and cultural centers in Almería, introduce myself to the clerks or managers, and fruitfully discuss the work's social content. Although I did not share his illusions, I decided to follow his advice, and, once in the city, I went into the bookshop that seemed to have the best-stocked window. In muffled tones, because of the timidity that always overtakes me when I refer to my work, I asked the clerk if she had a copy of *Campos de Níjar*. Her reply, as she raised her eyebrows in an astonished, friendly look, immediately shattered my dream castles. "I'm sorry," she said, "Campos where?"

Apart from my trips to Almería, two political-cultural events in which I participated in one way or another stand out as interesting in the course of that troubled and at times bitter year of 1959: the homage to Machado in Collioure and the Peaceful National Strike of 18 June, which, according to its organizers, ought to have marked the beginning of the end for Franco's dictatorship.

In a pamphlet commemorating the Machado gathering, Claude Couffon generously attributes the initiative to me: "It was the idea of Juan Goytisolo, who at the time lived in Paris, where after the success of M. E. Coindreau's translation of his novel *Juegos de manos*, he was busy bringing Gallimard's Spanish department up-to-date. Machado was God and model of national angst for all the resistance poets of the interior. Goytisolo told me of his plan: to set up an honorary committee and bring together the two Spains in Collioure."* To tell the truth, the suggestion came not from me, but from my Party comrades: Pellissa's friend and mentor, Benigno Cáceres—a small, bespectacled man, strikingly ugly but endowed with real charm and a charismatic personality—had persuaded me of the timeliness and importance of commemorating the twentieth anniversary of the poet's death by gathering anti-Francoist writers and intellectuals of every tendency around his tomb to render homage to his political and literary stature. I became the

*L'Espagne au coeur, Souvenirs à propos d'une Anthologie, Paris, 1982.

spokesman for the idea and with the help of Couffon, Elena de la Souchère, and other friends organized the committee of distinguished names that would back the event: after visiting Bataillon at the Collège de France, I collected, among many others, the signatures of Marcelle Auclair, Cassou, Mauriac, Sarrailh, Queneau, Sartre, Beauvoir, and Tzara while my Party comrades obtained Picasso's and Aragon's. In that first fruitful harvest of famous names—an activity I would excel in for a number of years— I experienced only one refusal and partial failure: the director of the Institut Hispanique on the rue Gay-Lussac, whom I had invited to join the committee, demanded first to see the list of members and suddenly went red with rage: what the devil did Sartre and Simone de Beauvoir have to do with Machado and Spain? Albert Camus, to whom Elena de la Souchère wrote a note beginning *Cher Maître*, informed me through his secretary that he was overwhelmed by the title and that, although he supported the celebration of the poet, did not want to be part of a committee whose makeup he disliked.

On 20 February our contingent of more than a hundred people caught the night train at the Gare d'Austerlitz. On our arrival in Collioure, we met up opposite the Quintana Hotel with our friends from Madrid, Barcelona, Geneva, and elsewhere: Blas de Otero, Gil de Biedma, José Ángel Valente, Costafreda, Barral, Castellet, Caballero Bonald, Senillosa, my brother José Agustín . . . The cortège made its way to the poet's tomb, covered in flowers for the occasion, and don Pablo de Azcárate read out a few words in the tense, emotional silence. After a crowded meal, plied with toasts and references to Machado and Spain, the small throng dispersed. There were embraces, pious wishes, souvenir photos, and farewells. Then, the return journey, in a second-class compartment, with Benigno, Isidoro Balaguer, Octavio Pellissa, discussing for hours art, politics, and literature. I can remember Benigno's passion for the latter and also his gut rejection of Cernuda's homosexuality and Arrabal's first plays. Half Pygmalion and half Tiresias, always surrounded by young militants, Benigno was in many ways a different kind of Communist, and he maintained a lively, attractive personal relationship with me right up to his illness and death.

At the end of May I went to Spain with Monique for the first talks on literature at Formentor, and when they were over I stopped in Torrentbó for a few days with Maurice E. Coindreau before returning to Paris on 9 June. In Barcelona I saw the preparations for the strike organized by the Party, with the often symbolic support of other anti-Francoist organizations: there was an atmosphere of euphoria in opposition circles, and I left with the impression that big changes were on the horizon. In the working-class districts and even on some areas of the Ensanche, strike slogans and the Protest "P" were everywhere: as it was impossible to erase them daily, the police changed the words into a Miró-style scrawl, thus converting Barcelona into an extraordinary capital of abstract graffiti. One manifesto signed by all the opposition—with the notable exception of Llopis's Socialist Party—sent through the mail, stuck on the fronts of buildings, scattered through the streets at night by brave drivers, called for a protest against the Régime's corruption and economic policies, amnesty for those in prison and in exile, the removal of Franco, and free elections. Luis and his friends had actively intervened, with differing means, in that display of propaganda: while some students threw handfuls of leaflets from the top of the El Águila department stores, others, led by Ricardo Bofill, repeated the exploit from the heights of Columbus's statue at the end of the Ramblas. Simultaneously, intellectuals, writers, and establishment personalities who could in no way be tarred with the Communist brush—such as Menéndez Pidal, Marañón, Azorín, and even General Kindelán, head of the Francoist air force during the war— supported the amnesty petition in a letter sent to the Justice Minister and which circulated clandestinely. Although the press and other news media kept a total silence, Radio España Independiente broadcast la Pasionaria's fiery calls from Moscow. Faced with this proliferation of hostile acts, the dictatorship finally set in motion its vast arsenal of weapons of dissuasion: brought to Madrid on the pretext of a routine discussion, the diplomat Julio Cerón, leader of the Popular Liberation Front (FLP), was arrested as he left his airplane in Barajas; a vast preventive raid on intellectual and working-class circles made inroads into the ranks of the Party, FLP, and MSC; the newspapers broke their silence, reacted hysterically to the danger, denouncing the "attempt at communist revolution," and dug out memories and photographs of 1936 that exemplified the crimes and atrocities of the "reds."

The prevailing climate of confrontation finally attracted the attention of the French press. Although from my first day in Paris I had warned my friends on *L'Express* and *France-Observateur* of what was on the way, their response had been lukewarm: nothing ever happened in Spain, for the moment it was best to wait. I was thus completely taken aback when, on the eve of the strike day, Florence Malraux phoned me to see if I would be interested in going to Spain as a correspondent for *L'Express*. I agreed immediately, rushed to collect my ticket from the travel agents, and caught the first plane to Barcelona. I stayed there and in Madrid for scarcely three days, after which I flew back to Paris as dejected as a bullfighter after an unlucky afternoon,* to write the report headlined "P for Protest." It was published with a by-line that read: "*L'Express*'s clandestine reporter in Spain has lived through the 'great day of protest' of the resistance to Franco and signed with the pseudonym of Thomas Lenoir in order to envelop the author in a cloud of ink." I had been eyewitness to the strike's failure—shops and businesses open, public transport chockablock, factories apparently working normally—and strove to go back to its source and provide a rationale. I will not relate now my nosy prowl round the streets near ENASA and España Industrial but will merely reprint a few paragraphs from the article which, although of necessity a piece of superficial journalism, hinted at deeper causes and may interest some readers today.

> The two camps eye each other warily and a foreign observer like myself experiences a singular feeling of suspense on the days leading to the strike. Two contestants: one, the Régime, makes great show of its strength and its cards. Daily newspapers, radio, official media continuously proclaim the first; the second are fear, the army, and the police. But the people around me, all from the opposition, stress the courage and bravery of their side. Had I lived exclusively with them, the date of the 18th would

---

*That is how it would be described by Kindelán and Girbau, who were waiting in the airport for the report of another traveler, the emissary of the University Socialist Grouping.

have seemed a decisive watershed: all clandestine movements communicate this feverish excitement, as if the inner awareness of their weakness pushed their leaders to live in a frenzy of expectation. . . .

The appearance of Barcelona and Madrid, their streets patrolled by the police, the ever more strident tone of the government dailies have a paradoxical calming effect on the strike promoters. The show of strength displayed by the Régime is the mold where they think they see the cast of their own power. Isolated, not knowing each other, broken up in a variety of small groups, they have only one mirror in which to glimpse their reflection: the device arranged against them. Personally, I can discern here a second error common to all clandestine movements: that they measure their imaginary strength against the real forces their adversary is methodically organizing. . . .

The opposition leaders I managed to meet in Madrid all agreed on the failure of the strike. These were their explanations: in previous years, the strike movements in Barcelona, Madrid, Asturias, and the Basque country scored partial victories because they came spontaneously from the rank and file: on this occasion, the order came from above and the day was set by the general staffs of the political groups not in line with the situation in Spain, but as a date they could all agree on. . . . The idea of a national strike was amazingly optimistic. The political illiteracy dominating the Peninsula means that the masses respond only to concrete proposals (the boycott of streetcars, for example) with limited objectives (a reduction in the cost of transport). . . . Fear of layoffs and unemployment—in the period of deep crisis Spain is passing through—has clipped the movement's wings. . . . But above all, beyond tactical reasoning, is the reality of a country that after twenty years of Francoism no longer has the taste for politics. If, paraphrasing Valéry, Fascism is the art of preventing people from doing what interests them, Franco, much more than Hitler, is master of the art.

I am agreeably surprised by the lucidity of this report when read a quarter of a century later, unlike other of my texts of the time, laden with the undigested deadweight of dogma. It was written straight off, without consulting my friends, free of any ideological filter or correctives, and naturally provoked angry exchanges with Party comrades, who branded it as both pessimistic and shortsighted. A few weeks after its publication, I was called by Octavio Pellissa to a meeting with two members of the leadership in a café on the place de la République. Those charged with discussing my conclusions and teaching me a friendly lesson turned out to be Jesús Izcaray and Fernando Claudín, whom I met for the first time. I remember that when we debated the problem of whether the strike could be considered a failure or not, I was impressed by the way he received my comments, a million miles from the confidence of a bringer of truths flaunted by his companion: in a rigorously organized hierarchy, like all those inspired by the Leninist model, the "correct" version of the facts always percolates from the top downwards and never in reverse or from the periphery: as Claudín would reveal to me years later, my comments and arguments really hit the mark inasmuch as he had been able to see the limitations in his work when he traveled secretly to Madrid to prepare the strike. Strangely, I had gone to Pilar and Eduardo Haro Tecglen's flat not knowing that it had served as a hideout for Claudín days before, and this clarified in retrospect the feigned bewilderment of my hosts when I asked them for news of what had happened, totally unaware that the police might have followed me. The Régime's cat-and-mouse game with the opposition fortunately had its lapses: thanks to these, we rodents could run out of danger when the cat was off hunting and momentarily sidestep the mousetrap or piece of cheese that it set out for us from its position of serene omnipotence.

Some three or four years after the date of the events I am now relating, an old Party militant, whose wife typed out my manuscripts, entrusted me with a copy of the record of secret police observations kept by the Valencian Regional Brigade of Social Investigation, which the defense lawyer of one of the recently arrested Communists on trial had got access to and secretly microfilmed in one of the courtrooms. It is an extraordinary, juicily significant document in the taste it gives of the methods, organization, language, and even sometimes surprisingly perceptive cultural references of an adversary who was ubiquitous, implacable, and all-embracing, but unknown and abstract beyond flourishes of power and sudden pounces, a comprehensive portrait of the unequal, quixotic, doomed-to-failure struggle of the clandestine opposition groups whose slightest muffled cry was spied on day and night by a hidden but ever-present network of informers, eavesdroppers, lookouts, and guards whose constant diligence showed up as derisively pathetic the opposition's careful efforts to maintain invisibility. The immediate, almost intimate relations between persecuted and persecutors, crossing and losing each other in bars, cafés, avenues, and on curbs, trace in filigree the image of the cat-and-mouse game I suggested before and bestow a general emblematic importance on that document, which is narrated in an impersonal, objectivized style according to the strictest canons of behaviorist fiction. When I tried to describe in *Señas de identidad* the disproportionate struggle between the police and the friends of my alter ego, Mendiola, the best way I found was to insert the secret police account into the novel itself: a real document integrated into the literary text in the same way that an artist sometimes makes his canvas from materials or substances such as seaweed, shells, bits of rope, and ironware—rather than imitating the external world—and then paints them. The life and vicissitudes of the characters would thus acquire a degree of representativeness in the national context that went beyond the situations and plot reproduced in the book: the epitome of my personal and family history, of that of my friends and acquaintances, and, beyond them, of all the student, intellectual, and worker anti-Francoist militants who fell sooner or later in the police net during years of patient toil and vain hopes, the weaving and unweaving of Penelope's cloth, cobwebs remade and continuously stamped on or swept away by a remote deity at once stubborn and malign.

The persecution, trailing, vigilance, and arrests described in the fourth chapter of the novel faithfully translate my experience in those years. November 1958: the imprisoning of the leaders of the University Socialist Grouping, including Francisco Bustelo, Juan Manuel Kindelán, and the diplomat Vicente Girbau. June 1959: the arrest, trial, and later sentencing of Julio Cerón and the other visible heads of the FLP. The patient siege laid to Communist intellectuals and students in Barcelona became more and more obvious, and any slip or mistake in the Party security machine could automatically unleash the reflex action of the police. From March 1958 there was a worrying increase in the frequency and regularity of Luis's visits to Paris, either alone or with María Antonia. Monique's diary shows he was there in May, October, and at Christmas, when he stayed temporarily with us. I could see that an ugly, strange toilet bag made of fiber or imitation lizard skin, not at all in keeping with his taste or personality, was the hiding place for his messages and postal reports to the Party leadership. From his conversations with Pellissa I deduced that he had seen Carrillo and stepped up his activity and the level of his contacts. I also remember him arriving on the rue Poissonnière on 13 December 1959, on the eve of the journey which, together with Solé Tura, Isidoro Balaguer, and other acquaintances of mine, was to take him to the ill-omened Prague congress while, with Monique and Florence Malraux, I went to visit Genet and Abdallah in Amsterdam and enjoyed with them the spectacle of canals, bridges, museums, fading dusks, barges slow and majestic like alligators, in a precarious state of ecstasy and delight.

A few weeks later, on 7 February, from Barcelona, Barral called Monique in her office at Gallimard: Luis had suddenly fallen ill in what looked like the outbreak of an epidemic and the infection was serious. The news, which I had been dreading, depressed me not only because of the misfortune my brother was suffering at that very moment but also because of the family context in which it took place: that gloomy, spectral, decrepit universe of the Pablo Alcover residence, with the elderly trio—my father, Eulalia, and grandfather—shattered by the catastrophe that had befallen them; my feelings of guilt and remorse at living so far from them, protected from the vision of their anguished, devastating orphanhood. The two images pursued and harrassed me, and I rushed to find Pellissa, and through him the Party, to discover what had happened and get some direction. As Pellissa would tell me hours later, the leadership was not aware of the arrests and for the moment could not take any measures or advise anything until trustworthy reports arrived. Thrown back on my own resources, I worked out a plan of action with Monique and our French friends: to inform the newspapers and weeklies that we had access to of the police operation against a dissident

writer like Luis, whose novel *Las afueras* was about to be published in
French by le Seuil, and to set in motion, as with the homage to Machado, the
collection of well-known signatures, this time in protest. I instinctively
knew that only an outcry, better still, a scandal of international dimensions,
could save Luis and those, like Isidoro Balaguer and the painter Joaquín Pa-
lazuelos, caught with him, from a long stay in prison. From home and from
Monique's office at Gallimard we telephoned or got in contact with a great
number of writers and artists, getting their approval for a statement in which
they expressed their concern about my brother's arrest and demanded he be
allowed to exercise his rights to a defense as recognized in the United Nations Charter. Picasso, Sartre, Paz, Mauriac, Senghor, Genet, Peter Brook,
Gabriel Marcel, Marguerite Duras, Butor, Robbe-Grillet, Queneau, Claude
Simon, Nathalie Sarraute, and other figures signed the letter that was published a few days later in *Le Monde*. In Italy, through Vittorini, we got the
support of Pasolini, Moravia, Carlo Levi, and twenty or so famous names. In
Mexico, Max Aub, Carlos Fuentes, and the members of the 1959 Spanish
Movement organized meetings and the collection of signatures. Thanks to
my friends in Caracas and the magazine *Marcha*, I also got condemnations
from many writers in Venezuela and Latin America.

Realizing the prejudice and suspicious nature of the bourgeois media at
the slightest whiff of Communism, I tried to separate out the presentation
of the case of Luis and his friends from their participation in the Prague congress. Jacques Grignon Dumoulin, a *Le Monde* journalist specializing in
Spanish affairs, wrote an article in which, following my suggestions and at
my insistence, he described and interpreted the arrests as a warning from the
authorities to intellectuals judged to be "lukewarm and hostile to the Régime"; such an abrupt measure, he added, led one to believe that, despite its
evolution in the field of diplomacy, the Francoist government had "not lost
internally a single drop of its intolerance." Other similar commentaries appeared in *L'Express* and *France-Observateur*, giving fresh impetus to the collection of signatures and displays of solidarity.

The news I had of Luis through José Agustín was not encouraging. After
being transferred from police headquarters to the Model Prison in Barce-

lona, he was sent within a few weeks to Carabanchel, which made regular visits difficult. At home the atmosphere was oppressive, and father gave his sui generis version of the facts to whomever would listen to him, insisting on our history as a right-wing family and our strict religious upbringing: the target of poisonous reproaches from one or another of my aunts, he defended himself as best he could and protested our innocence. One day he phoned me in Paris: he had received a visit from a police inspector, a real gentleman, as polite as you could wish for, who had given him comforting news of Luis; it was not a serious matter and could be resolved, he told him, but from the outside I was politicizing things with signatures and articles that could only harm Luis and make his problems worse. In trembling tones my father begged me to stop the French press from talking about Luis, and he put forward the defensive arguments that, as I would discover much later, he used in a petition sent to the authorities. Although I did not then possess my present experience of dictatorships, forever caught in the dilemma of silencing dissidence by coercion yet presenting a façade of respectability to the outside world, it was my intuition that silence was the best accomplice of oppressive systems and that only a repeated denunciation of their abuses could finally put an end to them—an intuition that was strengthened by this incident. If the police had dispatched one of their functionaries to our house to get father to put pressure on me to be quiet, this was an indication that my activity was upsetting them and should consequently be pursued. That demonstration *a contrariis* of the effects of mobilization abroad for the release of Luis was further reinforced when the press silence on the subject was broken and the daily *Pueblo*, organ of the so-called Vertical Unions edited by Emilio Romero, revealed its annoyance in two editorials, "The French Fashions of Young Spanish Writers" (29 February 1960) and "Distortion" (15 March 1960).

The anonymous author of these articles was surprised by the strange devotion of the French press to the fledgling author of *Las afueras* and denounced the vogue for Spanish literature that was translated not as a measure of its value but as "evidence of opposition to present-day Spain"; then, with an obvious allusion to me, he continued: "there is even a customs post, which is very difficult to avoid, that hands out licenses, and the customs official bears the same surname as the young writer recently canonized." Two weeks later, in response to a brief note in *L'Express* inspired by me, although I was not responsible for the sensationalist illustration, the *Pueblo* editorialist took up the cudgels again, justifying the newspaper's interest in our surname to the extent, he said, that it enjoyed "favorable treatment from some foreign press, not so much for the literary activities with which their authors cause a stir in the bookshops as for their political activities, which are more likely to give them a stir in the police stations." On 24 March I replied in the French weekly* to the accusations of Emilio Romero's daily, with a defense of the realism of the Spanish novel, a defense that in hindsight does not seem entirely off-track.

A few days later, taking advantage of the right to reply recognized in the press law passed by the Régime, José Agustín and I sent two notes to *Pueblo*'s editor, while forty-odd colleagues from Madrid and Barcelona in an open letter, which would be published only outside the country, protested against the style of political denunciation used in the paper's attacks, expressed their human and professional solidarity with me, demanded the publication of my reply, and described my literary activity at Gallimard as "truly favorable for the publication of our literature abroad." After several weeks' silence, the spokesman of the Vertical Unions devoted a double page to the affair, including our letters and a fresh extensive onslaught on my political position and cultural activities ("The Young Wave and Other Matters," 22 April 1960): the editorialist's clichés and personal attacks—I don't know if it was Romero himself—anticipated those that would be used in massive doses a year later by the press, radio, and television. Four days after the publication

---

*"*Pueblo* and literature." The text, also published in Mexico with the rather provocative headline "Spanish novelists' realism irritates Francisco Franco's inquisitors" says among other things: "In a society in which social relationships are deeply unreal, realism is a necessity. From morning till night the Spanish intellectual thinks he is living in a dreamworld. Everything around him contributes to uprooting him from the time in which he is alive, until he finally feels like an inhabitant of another planet, dropped by mistake into his country. This uprooting creates a vacuum that must be filled, and which each individual fills in his own manner. For writers in Spain, reality is the only escape."

of this unusual controversy, aired by Romero in a pamphlet translated into French to teach *L'Express* a lesson at the expense of union funds, I traveled with Monique to Spain, where the second literary get-together at Formentor was about to be celebrated in somewhat Kafkaesque circumstances.

Contrary to what one might at first think, judging from the verbal acrimony of the attacks on me, my alleged dossier as a resistance fighter against Francoism can lay claim to neither torture nor arrest. If we discard the time I was interrogated by the Albacete civil guard during the bullrunning in Elche de la Sierra, my only stay in a police station, in August 1958, was apolitical, fortuitous, and far from heroic: I was caught with Jaime Gil de Biedma and a friend of his in a police clean-up raid on the Barrio Chino, and we spent a sleepless night in a badly lit dingy room, with a selection of individuals—drunks, pimps, hustlers, and even a handsome blond youth accused of the outrageous crime of "going with French women"—while we waited for the van to take us to headquarters on the Vía Layetana, to be classified indelibly as louts and set free a few hours later—obviously without anyone realizing who we were or trying to exploit the incident—thanks to the successful intervention of Jaime's father. It was scarcely an exemplary episode, and if I aspired to an official hagiography or a preening self-portrait, I should put it carefully aside rather than shine an inopportune spotlight on it at a point in my narrative when my public acts lend or could lend themselves easily and unintentionally to idolizing eulogy!

Nevertheless, when we landed in Barcelona airport on Sunday, 26 April and handed our passports to the police, the officer in charge of the control disappeared with mine into an office, probably to consult with his superiors. Monique, who was right behind me in the line, bravely stuck her head round the half-opened door and smiled at the inspector who was phoning headquarters, my passport in his hand. Is something the matter? she asked innocently. No, nothing was the matter, and my passport was returned to me without explanation or apology. As we commented on the episode while waiting in the transit lounge for our connecting flight to Palma, the functionary picked out by Monique came up to us and, as if apologizing for being caught in the act, said that he followed my work very closely and would like to welcome me: after politely asking permission to sit at our table, he ordered drinks from the waiter, asked after Luis and the polemic with *Pueblo*, and debated novels and literature with me until the loudspeakers summoned us to the departure gate, where we met up in a cheerful, excited mood with the other writers and publishers who were also leaving for Formentor.

During the literary discussions and group sessions devoted to the future international prize, we circulated a petition on behalf of Luis, which was signed by all those in attendance. The presence of well-known writers and personalities gave me a temporary immunity that I could use and did use quite unashamedly. With a political instinct and judgment that now amaze me—maturity or mere exhaustion would later make me clumsier and cruder—I adapted my tactics to the space for maneuver allowed by the circumstances, without resorting to rash acts or false moves. Lacking, as I do, any Christian propensity to self-sacrifice, I surrounded myself with defensive walls and parapets. The best way to avoid the misfortune that befell Luis was to present the enemy with the dilemma of having to resort to drastic measures harmful to its image or having to tolerate pinpricks without loss of composure, and to do so in such a way that the balance would logically swing toward the latter. Although I harbor not the slightest doubt that the supporters of a hard line within the Régime wished to teach me a good lesson, I did not give them the opportunity, for the negative factors such action would bring outweighed any possible advantages.

Back in Barcelona after the congress, we spent a night in our old haunt at the Cosmos after a nostalgic walk along the Ramblas. Then, like some unhappy guilty prodigal son, I paid a visit to the house on Pablo Alcover. Luis's enforced absence had clearly precipitated the degeneration of people and things, and the picture presented by the aged trio filled me with both anguish and consternation. Father spoke obsessively about a supposed Communist trap set for Luis, Grandfather said nothing, and Eulalia inscrutably stroked the suede coat and presents we brought her from Paris. Before leaving for Majorca, Monique and I had agreed that when she resumed work at Gallimard I would stay on for a few weeks in Spain in order to visit Luis in jail, finish off the inquiries we had planned on his behalf, and travel to Andalusia with Simone de Beauvoir. On 8 May I bid her farewell at the airport and, after a stressful, restless night at home, beset by most disturbing nightmares, as I mention in a later letter, I traveled to Madrid, where I had agreed to meet up with Florence Malraux three days later. I can remember my visit to Carabanchel: the line of prisoners' relatives, where I came across the poet Gabriel Celaya's wife, carrying a parcel of food for one of his brothers, and saw the mother of Luis and Javier Solana, two future Socialist leaders; the conversation with my brother through two iron grilles; he looked calm, if sickly, as a result of the hunger strike he had participated in; my feeling of impotence and emptiness when the bell rang and we were obliged to break off the exchange.

On 13 May I collected Florence at Barajas and stayed with her in an old-fashioned but comfortable suite in the Hotel Victoria, the balconies of which looked out on the plaza del Ángel. The daughter of the writer, who was at the time Minister of Culture in General De Gaulle's government, had met Luis in Formentor the previous year and with a show of generous affection toward Monique and ourselves that I shall never forget, she agreed to my idea of coming to Madrid to ask her country's embassy to intervene on my brother's behalf. Florence's stay was hectic and short: my memories of it are limited to a variegated succession of snapshots and minor details. For twenty-four hours we rushed in the rain from the Prado to the mansion on the calle Serrano where she was received by the ambassador just before a dismal dinner with a group of friends. The diplomat promised to make a discreet approach to the Ministry for Foreign Affairs, and his words inspired in us a cautious but wary optimism. On the day of her departure she briefly met Simone de Beauvoir and Nelson Algren, and I accompanied her to Barajas in an emotional state of gratitude difficult to express.

We were to leave Madrid two days later to allow the recent arrivals quick visits to monuments and places of interest in the city. Forgetting Sartre and Castor's horror of shellfish I took the latter and her companion to dinner in the Hogar Gallego, where the vision of pink carapaces and retractable lobster limbs, crabs, and prawns took her to an isolated corner far from the aquariums and baskets where the owner proudly exhibited his exquisite delicacies. Either that evening or the following one I also organized a small dinner with my Party comrades. As everyone wanted to meet de Beauvoir and the number of possible guests was rising alarmingly, my colleagues adopted the heroic but misguided decision to leave their wives behind in order not to overwhelm her with the uncomfortable pressures of a formal banquet. What a crass, unforgivable mistake!: we had hardly sat down in our private room in a restaurant next to the Plaza Mayor when one of those present mentioned his wife's tremendous interest in *Le Deuxième Sexe*. What! He was married and had come by himself? Castor looked at me and asked if they were all married. I said they were with one or two exceptions. "But for heaven's sake," she exclaimed, "you call yourselves antifascists and then leave your wives at home as if they were your servants. That's really incredible!" Neither the embarrassed excuses or explanations of the diners nor their later instructive descriptions and analyses of the situation in Spain managed to dispel entirely the bad effect of their well-intentioned macho behavior. With the professional, Cartesian, relentless plainspokenness that characterized her, the writer told me afterwards that although my friends had made a favorable impression at the political level, their immaturity regarding the position of women and relations between the sexes confirmed her fears that the struggle against the residues of patriarchal society would be particularly difficult and arduous for us.

It is not my intention to narrate the twists and turns of the journey that took the three of us and Vicente Aranda to Granada, Almería, Almuñécar, and Málaga for eight to ten days. Simone de Beauvoir describes them briefly in the last volume of her memoirs and with greater humor and powers of imagination—sometimes bordering on the whimsical and the absurd. Nelson Algren drew a series of portraits or vignettes of the journey to be published months afterwards by a North American magazine. Without wishing to draw any conclusions, I will just make one simple observation: the passion minutely described in *Les Mandarins* seemed to be water under the bridge and while accompanying Algren out of a kind of friendly fidelity, Castor was living mentally with the author of *L'Être et le Néant*, to whom she continuously referred when she saw or heard something interesting, adding the inevitable comment, "Oh, I must tell Sartre about that!"

After saying goodbye in Málaga—and while they went on to Sevilla— I went back to Madrid with Aranda. The parents of my sister-in-law's brother, Luis Carandell, had offered me hospitality in their flat on the calle Libertad and it was there on 28 May that I was surprised by the good news of my brother's release just as I was getting ready to visit him in Carabanchel. I can't remember exactly whether my cousin, the notary Juan Berchmans Vallet, went and collected Luis at the prison door or whether my brother and I met up with him later to thank him for his constant, valuable help. But I have not forgotten that long mutual exchange of information in our room at the Carandells' nor the visit and congratulations of Señora Solana, whose son was still in jail. To avoid showing openly that they had given in to the pro- test campaign centered around the figure of Luis, the authorities also re- leased the less-committed participants in the Prague congress, including Is- idoro Balaguer, while others arrested with him on the same charge spent months and even years behind bars, in a convincing illustration of the rule according to which silence has been, is, and will be the greatest accomplice of the abuses and crimes of dictatorships. I retain only one of the stories and anecdotes recounted at the time to us by our Madrid friends: that of the nov- elist who stretched back in his armchair at the Café Gijón, after reading aloud one of the reports or lead articles about my brother, and stigmatized, in the hollow resonant tones of an ex-bureaucrat or retired officer, antipa- triotic behavior in "those times rent with polemical tensions" and, infected by the virulent affirmations of the editorial writer, he endorsed them with all the power of his hoarse authority: "It is quite plain his activities verged on those of a common criminal."

After accompanying Luis to Barcelona and his jubilant reunion with the family and María Antonia, I returned to Paris on 8 June.

The euphoria created by our modest victory had strengthened my deter- mination to continue the struggle and increased my confidence in the pos- sibility of an imminent radical change in Spanish society, along the lines of the "democratic, antifeudal, anticapitalist transformation" at the heart of the Party's program. A fortnight after my return to Paris, Monique and I were back in Spain with Carole, Florence Malraux, the filmmaker Claude Sautet, and other friends: ensconced in the family mansion at Torrentbó, we were visited by Luis and María Antonia, Ricardo Bofill, Castellet, Barral, Gil de Biedma, and other writers and intellectuals who would soon make up the so-called *gauche divine*; we would often meet up with them in Barcelona and, after dinner in the Amaya or the Barceloneta areas, we tramped around Escudillers and the Barrio Chino, visited El Cádiz and La Venta, perhaps hoping for my catastrophist perspectives to be confirmed in the dirt and poverty of that setting. Unaware of the lung infection he had contracted in prison, Luis seemed possessed by a violent desire to live and make up for lost time; my malingering crisis with Monique and the tension of those last months had equally intensified my capacity for late-night drinking and other diversions. The drinking habit, which all three brothers suffered at one stage or another in our lives, was violently at odds with the fanatical anti-alcoholism my father had inculcated in us from childhood. In my case, it revealed a feeling of growing exasperation at my own contradictions and personal inability to develop or resolve them. The dichotomy between bourgeois lifestyle and Communist ideas, love and sexual urges—the sudden, devastating lashes of which I suffered on occasion on those nighttime forays—could only be overcome, I thought, in a wave of revolutionary action when it would lose all its raison d'être. As I waited for the earthquake and the flowering of the new morality from the ruins, I tolerated with increasing difficulty the stubborn blindness of reality to the omens of cataclysm. In these years my letters to Monique, both from Spain and Cuba, reflect an irrepressible impatience with a development that—as a result of what had happened on the island since the fall of Batista—seemed just around the corner. What an illusion! The slow but deep transformation of Spanish society which began at that time would catch me and many others totally unawares. I can remember my last visit to Almería in September 1960 with Aranda and Sautet and our chance encounter with a group of French actors

and filmmakers dazzled by the beauty of the landscape and its future possibilities: the newcomers spoke of hotel complexes, film studios, installations
worthy of a new Cinecittà or mini-Hollywood. Was that the change you had
bet on? Could material well-being and progress be disassociated from the
conquest of freedom and justice? Apprehensive, anxious, in inner turmoil,
you left that land—so poor yet coveted, exhausted, but appealing, rich in attributes and nonetheless abandoned—and only returned sixteen years later,
when transformed into a completely different being: anonymous like any
other foreigner, stealthily visiting the countryside you had dreamed of, hoping to come across familiar faces or friends, and only hearing, as in the fable,
the dogs' accusing bark.

The discovery of Luis's illness and his symbolic withdrawal to Viladrau,
the drawbacks and stress of the last trips to Spain had dashed your plans to
spend Christmas at home. As you were going to Italy two months later for
the launching of one of your books, you decided to postpone your visit for a
few weeks and fly to Barcelona from there. On 11 February 1961 you were
in Rome and after a number of days promoting your book and meeting
writer-friends, you went to Milan, where Feltrinelli was organizing a cultural soirée at the Teatrino del Corso. His literary adviser, Valerio Riva, had
supported your idea of illustrating the theme of La resaca—the plot of
which was set in the Barcelona shantytowns inhabited by gypsies and An-
dalusians—by showing a documentary about emigration, filmed without
permission with a 16-mm camera by two acquaintances studying with Ricardo Bofill at the Geneva School of Architecture. Following your guide-
lines, the filmmakers, Paolo Brunatto and Jacinto Esteva Grewe, had been to
numerous villages and districts of Murcia, Almería, and Granada, photo-
graphed half-depopulated rural areas and then interviewed in Switzerland
some immigrants from those areas; other sequences showed the shacks and
caves that then made up a good slice of the industrial belt of your city. The
film, Notes sur l'émigration, was rather amateurish and fell prey to historical
and social simplification, but Riva agreed with you that it contained scenes
and images of interest and deserved to be shown. To round off the soirée, the

publishers had programmed a recital of Spanish songs, with a more or less political content, that had been popular in Italian anti-Fascist circles ever since the time of the civil war.

On 18 February, after Riva's brief introduction and a few words from you on the novel, the film was shown in the small crowded room. It had hardly started when you heard two muffled explosions and the room was suddenly filled with smoke. There were moments of panic, those present ran to the exit, and a voice started shouting, "Someone's been hit." In a flash, and everything happened amazingly quickly, two nurses miraculously appeared from nowhere with their support equipment and stretcher, and took the would-be victim outside wrapped in a blanket. Although it was a ridiculous scene, no one thought to stop them or to follow them out to the ambulance. While you recovered from the shock and the spectators returned to their seats certain it was a Fascist provocation, Brunatto and Esteva Grewe emerged angrily from the projection room: taking advantage of the confusion, someone had removed the rolls of film and quickly run off. The setting off of firecrackers and appearance of the stretcher-bearers then became perfectly clear: the men responsible for the theft had completed their mission with professional skill and efficiency. The following day the Italian press related what had happened in banner headlines and put the crime down to Milanese Fascists, closely linked to their Spanish counterparts: a police investigation of the former would lead on 3 March to the arrest of four individuals, a former blackshirt and three members of the parachute brigade well-known for their involvement in extreme right-wing circles of the city. You were able only years later to establish the real identity of the intruders, which was, however, hinted at by the fact that the stolen copy was shown soon afterwards in Spain. Anxious to avoid any diplomatic repercussions, the local authorities were quick to bury the matter; the interrogation of those arrested bore no fruit and they were soon released.

The incident and, especially, the reactions in the Italian press made you immediately fear possible reverberations in Spain. Your worries, communicated by telephone to Monique and a couple of friends in Barcelona, were quickly confirmed. On 22 February the whole range of Peninsular media published an EFE agency dispatch about the episode, insidiously linking it to an FAI terrorist attack on the Spanish consulate in Geneva and the celebration of "an act of anti-Spanish propaganda" chaired by Waldo Frank and Álvarez del Vayo in the Barbizon-Plaza Theater in New York. While some newspapers wrote about this triple attack in fairly subdued tones, *Arriba*, the Movement's official organ, gave it front-page prominence: "CNT-FAI, Álvarez del Vayo, Waldo Frank, Goytisolo: a new model of Molotov cocktail against Spain" and the *Pueblo* headline splashed over three columns: "J. G. tries to screen a lying, insulting documentary on Spain; a group of spectators protest and throw smoke bombs." The EFE statement underlined the Communist character of the Milan "mass-meeting," indirectly attributed to you authorship of the incriminating documentary, pretended that the firecrackers had been thrown by honest, upright Italian patriots. "The Communist press"—it concluded—"has been upset by the incident, rails against the disappearance of the film during the melee, to the point of stating that it was all a provocation by agents from the Spanish consulate." At about the same time, a lead article in *El Español*, probably written by its editor, Juan Aparicio, came out against your vile campaign of "defamation" in Europe and an ineffable report from the Rome correspondent of *El Diario de Barcelona*, "J. G.'s Latest Pirouette," accused you of publicly intervening, "with cool and collected tactics, not to challenge Spain's régime politically but to slander your own Fatherland"; after dubbing you "the gangster of the photo or film camera," the writer lambasted the "sour cocktail of Soviet-style words, images, and songs, which insulted Spain on the pretext of introducing a book by a Spaniard living it up abroad and paraded around by the Communist Parties."

But that astonishing flood of slurs and attacks in print was only the beginning. On 28 February, José Agustín telephoned you and said that the film stolen in Milan had been shown the night before on Spanish television, together with a thunderous reply from José Antonio Torreblanca that described you as an impostor, mercenary, and other charming roles. In fact, as you discovered straightaway, it was a cut and doctored version of the film with a sound track and commentary that in places differed from the original.

As the copy that had been shown seriously distorted the content and intentions of the film, you dispatched registered letters to EFE and those in charge of television, invoking the right to correct the impression given. But your protests, this time, remained unpublished. Spanish television's showing of Esteva Grewe and Brunatto's film was to unleash a strident pack of hunting dogs after a silenced prey. Rereading today the press clippings you have preserved,* and from which you composed the soliloquy of Voices in your first adult novel, is enough to bring on a laughing fit; a quarter of a century ago you had mixed feelings of devastation, sadness, and incredulity. Sometimes the accumulation of denigrating terms and absurd accusations is so exaggerated that it borders on the grotesque and seems like a caricature or parody ("That series of acts of aggression against the Iberian Peninsula is dominated by the participation of that 'fellow traveler' and young gigolo, J. G., who has set up in Paris"); at other times the emphatic style, rather familiar to your journalist's ear, recalls its deliberate insertion or parody in the body of *Señas de identidad* ("Resident more years in France than in Spain, with habits that are more French than Spanish, even as far as his mistress goes . . . he gives them what they ask for. Turning out scenes of poor suburbs is exceedingly easy. A few extras, dressed up as policemen, can 'beat up a worker,' strip a little boy, cover him in coal dust and sit him on a heap of manure—this is within the reach of any unscrupulous hack. But whoever does this reveals such a moral stature that it is better not to mention him, although it would only require two substantives and a preposition"). The top prize in this wretched contest should perhaps go to Manuel Aznar, the editor of *La Vanguardia*, for his lead article on 16 March 1961 "Feltrinelli, or the Festival of Insults," a real monument to demagogy, hypocrisy, and grandiloquence that, unable to appear in the eventual edition of *Historia universal de la infamia*, also received its just reward by being included in your book. However, it is a long list of examples, and you will break off here so as not to take advantage of your readers.

You would then discover that spite nestling within the heart, "the terrible Spaniard's eternal bile" so beautifully evoked by Cernuda. The insults that

*The fullest collection of clippings is in the archive of my papers at Boston University.

then poured out and their impact on your family—your father's visits and worried letters to newspaper editors, quixotically intent on saving the family's good name—will leave a bitter aftertaste in the mouth but on the rebound will grant you a kind of immunity, by transforming you into the prickly writer you are today, insensitive and hardened to the never-ending succession of insults and vicious taunts. To tell the truth, your reaction to what happened in Milan symbolically prefigured your relationship with the secular customs of the tribe: everything that came later—ostracizing, scandal-mongering, and vindictive jibes—would have the tired look of déjà vu. What had been singled out decades or centuries before by other sharp-shooters and dissidents was duly proved in your case: those who attack in Spain one day from the right attack later from the left while waiting for the opportunity to repeat the attack from the right—and the victims are always the same. This showed you early on—and it would be a discovery of prime importance—that your people will praise or reward only dead writers or works. Those who preserve their lives are a source of concern and arouse that indirect form of praise lurking behind the treacherous form of an insult. The disgust and horror you would provoke in the future only echoed, sometimes literally, expressions and turns of phrase coined years ago and which have no impact on you; reading them inside out, following the Poet's gloomy advice, as higher forms of praise, you would derive a sense of pride from them. Your apprenticeship in the customs and laws of the tribe would be completed only years later; but the lesson you received then would be a warning or threat whose imprint will never fade.

While the Francoist press boasted of the honesty of its news service by offering your countrymen on Spanish television a film documentary "aimed at deceiving the naive"—but being very careful not to explain how your so-called creation had reached them—there was no reply to the questions formulated by the Italian newspapers. There was no doubt that the Spanish authorities had intervened in the affair; the riddle would have remained shrouded in mist had not the blustering indiscretions of one of the protagonists later and unknowingly furnished you with the key. In the autumn of 1965, during your first fertile and contagious stay in Tangier, Eduardo Haro

Tecglen, who had moved to the city when appointed editor of the now defunct daily *España*, revealed to you that in the course of a dinner attended by the general consul in Tetuan, the latter had glorified his peculiar involvement in the affair to the rest of the guests; according to his account, the perpetrators of the aggression against the gathering in the Teatrino del Corso entrusted him with the copy of the film and, following instructions from Madrid, he ensured it reached the right destination by way of the diplomatic pouch. Such praiseworthy behavior had won him the warm congratulations of his superiors, and the former Spanish vice-consul in Milan still trembled with excitement as he recalled the amusing, action-packed episodes of this James Bondish thriller . . .

Although this man's sad role in a police plot whose ramifications helped to embitter the final years of your father's life would justify the pillorying of his name, the bullet with which he suddenly ended his days in Argentina moves you to have mercy. A faithful servant to a system of which he was both creation and instrument, he finally and tragically set himself up as his own implacable judge. The holy terror suicide inspires within you demands respect; grant him silence, and leave him in peace.

The aim of that violent campaign seemed obvious: by presenting the Milan anti-Francoist cultural event as a gathering of "reds" and linking my participation in it to terrorist activities backed by "international Marxism," the authorities wanted to scare me and force me into voluntary exile. My ambiguous dissident status, eyewitness accounts of trips to the Peninsula, pro-Communist sympathies, and connections with the French press had finally riled the high priests of the Régime, who were confronted with the dilemma of arresting me or of continuing to tolerate behavior whose example could spread and contaminate other writers and artists. I was the victim of a flood of insults and veiled threats with which they tried to shut me out, turn me into a remote, innocuous outlaw. I was sure of this and adopted a poker-player's tactic: misleading my opponent with a false show of strength, to persuade him that I was setting a trap by returning in order to be arrested. During Luis's imprisonment the previous year I had traveled to Spain swathed in a protective band of well-known personalities, but this time I decided to go back quite openly, with the feigned lack of care or awareness of someone cheerfully stepping into the lions' den. Seeing that my demands for the truth to be published remained unanswered, I had recourse once again to the good, selfless offices of my cousin, the notary Juan Berchmans Vallet: with his customary calm and common sense he advised me on a trustworthy lawyer, completely outside politics, who under his guidance would accuse the all-powerful General Director of the Press of slander. It seemed an absurd undertaking, and the possibility of bringing the case before the courts was clearly very slim indeed; however, the manner of my attack drew my enemy's attention from my main aim: to return with impunity to Spain. On 21 April, a week before Monique's visit to the Formentor literary talks, I went by plane to Madrid, where I was met at Barajas airport by my cousin. I cleared the police entry procedures without incident. That same night, Juan Berchmans Vallet had set up a meeting with my lawyer to plan a successful strategy on the eve of my scheduled visit to the Ministry. I can remember very clearly arriving there in the morning and the vast mural in the entrance hall with the images of the archangel's annunciation to Mary. If, as Umberto Eco pointed out in his day, the amount of information transmitted by a communicative unit depends on its degree of probability and, the less this is, the greater will be the unit's informative content, the Francoist Ministry of Information could not knowingly have chosen a better symbol: the chubby, blond, salutiferous envoy of the Lord transmitting the improbable communicative unit to the blushing Virgin and, consequently, the most substantial information about the unexpected benefits of the visit of a dove whose plump white sheen keeps the pious spectator of the fresco in an understandable state of confusion between the Holy Ghost invoked by the opulent Mahalia Jackson and the colorful advertisement for Avecrem will not fade from my memory and will surface in the pages of *Conde Julián*.

The General Director of the Press, the philosopher and professor don Adolfo Muñoz Alonso—who in those blessed times would gloriously represent Spain in all the international congresses on thought and knowledge: a profound and illuminating contribution, whose lasting effects deserve some day to be calmly glossed—received us with unaccustomed speed. Gesturing affably, he was an unctuous man, sure of possessing the Truth and conscious of his importance. On his table he had a voluminous dossier of foreign-press articles devoted, he said, to my political activities. He added that he was aware of everything: my attitude of continuous hostility to the Régime and the values it embodied could not be more patent or open. Acting as I did outside the framework of legality, I should not be surprised by the violent reactions of condemnation aroused by my wretched behavior. He understood, he made clear, young people's political preoccupations; but these should be directed along the available channels. He turned to one of his secretaries—a bespectacled young man busily going to and fro from his office—and introduced me to the writer Jaime Capmany, an example to be followed: He also has his worries but expresses them responsibly and constructively, rather than trading as you do on the fair name of Spain. If, he concluded, you are upset by the harsh, biting tone of some replies and attacks in the press, it is your fault: to keep silent on insults to the Fatherland would be to display a lack of courage and to reward immorality. He listened in silence as my lawyer, my cousin Juan Berchmans, and I set out our views. It was a complex, serious matter, he finally replied, and required time for reflection. After an exchange of opinions as to the legality or illegality of my actions, he told us to return to his office on the following day.

At the appointed time we went back to the ministry, and Professor Muñoz Alonso gave me a welcoming smile: "Last night," he told me, "you were very much in my prayers." I must confess that I blushed maidenlike at that confidence, as unexpected as the amorous approach of some heavenly creature. I stared at the wall, carpet, or ceiling, incapable of articulating a response. The professor's angelic sophistry had suddenly lifted me to a confused limbo of unreality where I gently hovered throughout the laborious interview. The text of my letter, drawn up with the help of my cousin and the lawyer, did not belie my hostility to Francoism as our distinguished thinker intended after consulting his pillow; it simply established the bare truth of the facts. After exchanges in which I made no pertinent intervention from the perch of my sudden nirvana, the General Director of the Press agreed to a brief note of clarification to the effect that my involvement "in the cultural event celebrated in Milan" was purely literary and I had not assumed in the course of the same any "insulting, indecent, or contemptuous attitude toward the Spanish régime." This comment would be published in *Arriba* and *La Vanguardia* and, in return, I would withdraw my slander charge against the Ministry of Information. We parted amicably and, as agreed, my letter appeared immediately in the two newspapers. As for Professor Muñoz Alonso, absorbed in his many-sided official tasks and distilled Augustinian perceptions, I am unsure whether he had time to think of me and devote any prayers to me as he generously promised when we said goodbye. He became the flaming torch of Hispanic thought and died fifteen years later from exhaustion or sadness, when his Benefactor went into decline and made a definitive exit.

I continued my travels through Spain despite my transformation into that character in Chamisso stripped of all shadow—an unattached citizen, condemned to silence, held in moral quarantine, watched over meticulously, if discreetly, by the authorities. I would be forced to prolong for some time my leprous or ghostly eyewitness presence out of fear of a leap into the void—cutting the umbilical cord that tied me to the tribe, feelings of solidarity and patriotism soon to be alien to me—how was I going to act in support of others if, as I would gradually discover, I had hardly any sympathy toward myself, toward the official character I embodied? In May 1961 I participated in the Formentor literary gatherings, although my name does not appear in any of the reports, while Jaime Salinas, then the secretary to the international jury that awarded the prize to Beckett and Borges, would be visited by two inspectors with a keen interest in the words and deeds of Feltrinelli and my humble self; for the penultimate time until Franco's death, Monique and I went on holiday to Torrentbó in July, accompanied by Florence Malraux and our friends from Barcelona; between the seventh and twenty-eighth of September I traveled to Albacete with Aranda and Ricardo Bofill, captivated by the dark splendor of the Yeste mountains and the fascinating brutality of the bullfighting festivals of the area; in April 1962, on my return from my exciting stay in Cuba, I attended, like the Commendatore's statue, the international Formentor meetings—under attack from some newspapers as a "hotbed of communists"—and the Barcelona Publishers' Congress—during which, with exemplary irony and boldness, a small Portuguese publisher would denounce the ravages of censorship in our unhappy Peninsula: there I learned, from the foreign press and radio, of the slow but irresistible spread of the Asturian miners' strike to neighboring regions and the first contagious outbreaks in the city's industrial belt.

I returned to Paris on 12 May, but ten days later I was back in Spain. The breadth of the strike movement and the challenge it posed to the Régime suddenly rekindled my illusions that the final struggle was at hand. Sent by *France-Observateur* to report on events, I visited working-class districts in Madrid and Barcelona, though I was unable to reach Asturias as initially planned because of Interior Minister Camilo Alonso Vega's proclamation of a state of emergency in the province. I had few contacts with the political leaders of the strike: caution was the order of the day and most of them slept away from home. Even so, I can remember López Salinas taking me to a terrace on the Castellana where Federico Sánchez was waiting for us, totally at ease in his role as the carefree bourgeois with time on his hands: his incredible rash calm at a moment when he was the man in Spain most wanted by the police impressed me inasmuch as it perfectly matched his legendary reputation as an elusive, mocking Scarlet Pimpernel. The political climate of the period is described fairly accurately in my report "A travers l'Espagne en grève," which was published on 31 May 1962 with a note that "the writer must remain anonymous since he is still in Spain." I reproduced some paragraphs word for word in *Señas de identidad*—the visit to the cemetery of Francoist martyrs in Paracuellos del Jarama. Others, read with hindsight, reflect the ambiguity and contradictions between the bare depiction of the facts and the corrective "ideologized" interpretation:

> Although it is true that the strike began spontaneously and for strictly trade-union reasons, the movement's development immediately revealed the existence of a political coordination and focus. . . . If, as the failure of the Day of National Reconciliation on 5 May 1958 and the Peaceful Na-

tional Strike of 18 June 1959 testify, the Communist Party lacks the necessary strength to initiate a strike of its own, it has now shown that it wields enough influence to channel the protest of the masses, thanks to discipline and experience acquired over twenty years of clandestine activity. . . . Confronted by the orderly calm of the strikers, the government alternates between policies of force and appeasement, with a lack of decision that reveals the profound crisis in its institutions and structures. . . . With an eye on foreign powers, it strives to benefit from the situation by portraying the present movement as proof of that "democratization" necessary for Francoist Spain's entry into the Common Market. It is easy to foresee that Spanish diplomacy will develop this line during the months to come. The plan to legalize purely trade-union strikes is already a first step on this path. . . . A train has just set off and Ridruejo is advising the bourgeoisie to get on board before it is too late.* The supporters of a liberal government run the risk of being overtaken by events if they do not assume their proper responsibilities at once.

But to this reasonable statement, which I can support today, I appended conclusions that only revealed my impatience and gut hostility to the painfully protracted if predictable Europeanist solution:

> Gradually abandoned by its supporters, the State seems more isolated than ever. In any case—as is confirmed by the attitude of the youth—its days are numbered. . . . The Régime has entered a stage of disintegration and, after slumbering for twenty-three years, the country is on the eve of enormous changes.

Nevertheless, after some significant concessions from the employers, the impact and drift of which would become clear only years later, the social unrest declined. I was disappointed and, after holidaying with Monique and her daughter in Capri—where we met up with Semprún and his wife, guests of Mario Alicatta, then the editor of *L'Unità*—I returned to Spain on 11 September to complete my research into the May '36 events in Yeste and be present at the fierce, compensatory bullrunning ceremony. Along with Ricardo

*A reference to a well-known interview with the poet that had appeared the week before in *Le Figaro*.

Bofill and Vicente Aranda, I visited the dam and the shores of the reservoir that caused the tragedy, I followed the forest paths and byways where the peasants were massacred, I climbed the stockades and crossed squares and alleys where one of the beasts would drag me twenty years later, I chatted at length to a local about what had happened there before and after the war, I dallied till late at night around the stalls and sideshows of the fair until I finally came across a pair of civil guards stationed in an alley next to the inn, waiting for us to arrive. The nighttime interrogation—Why had we gone there? Why was I interested in talking to the fellow with the criminal record so well-known for his opposition to the Régime? Who had introduced him to me, and in what circumstances?—took place in a doorway, almost in pitch-dark, as if they were trying to intimidate us. Although it did not go any further and we were allowed to leave after showing them our papers, the incident did have its repercussions: the intrusion of some "well-heeled reds" from Barcelona was noted with fear and hostility in the village. As I recently discovered when I returned to the fiestas in Elche de la Sierra, my casual conversation with the victimized socialist had been spied upon by two pillars of society—a veterinary surgeon and a chemist who have since died—who not only spread their story around the café but stretched their patriotic refinement to the point of denouncing me to the civil guards. Only one guest at the inn—an emaciated, bald-headed, middle-aged individual of ascetic Castilian mien—dared smile at us and begin a friendly conversation with me about that latest piece of village gossip. After carefully sounding out my ideas, he pointed at Bofill's red car, I remember, and asked if my friend was of moneyed stock. "Well," I said, "he's a member of the bourgeoisie." "National or monopolist?" The national bourgeoisie, I assured him. From that identificatory tag, as clearly as if he had shown his Party card, I soon guessed that the place where he told me he had lived with a really smart painter from Paris was prison and that the artist's name was Pepe Ortega. "How do you know?" he exclaimed in amazement. "The way you talk is your visiting card," I replied. This militant—one of those people who looked as if he were called Ramiro, Prudencio, or Casto—had a toy stall at the fairground, and there we bid him farewell when we left the village, just as he was broadcasting the merits of a pretty articulated doll over his homemade loudspeaker from his perch in his modest stand.

That incident frustrated my attempt to continue on-the-spot research and brought to a definitive close my wanderings through the southeast of Spain, to which I had tardily discovered a sense of affinity or belonging and whose poverty and oppression I intended to highlight. From then on, when I returned to Spain I would do so reluctantly and under compulsion, in a gradual state of disaffection from a country on the road to progress but morally and politically stagnant, perkily healthy but stubbornly mute. Like many Spaniards my age, I had prepared myself for something that never happened and for a time experienced a strong sense of being cheated. The actual prospects were as obvious as they were unpleasant: the Régime would last as long as the hateful figure of its creator. The year after this gloomy conclusion, I would seek out consolation in Cuba in the shape of the flame of a miraculous revolution promising justice and freedom. A *fuite en avant* from Spain and myself that finally led to a change in my writing: a change of skin, an end to posturing, gradual purification, a purging of a surly, inhospitable identity.

In 1962, where your narrative is lurching in fits and starts, your political activism intensified and spread from the strictly Spanish field to new, more exciting revolutionary challenges. It coincided with a period of literary fame that bore no relation to the real merits and stature of your work—the undoubted fruit of your convenient and profitable position as a fellow traveler—and was at the same time, as you will subsequently try to show, the unhappiest period in your life. The unresolved problems of your sexual identity, the precarious nature of your links to Monique, the stifled, corrosive impression of being sucked down by your contradictions, further and further from any way out, had gradually led you to neurosis and alcohol, brief interludes of euphoric excitement, spiraling cycles of depression and suicidal obsessions. Your enthusiasm for the Cuban epic followed not only from your welcoming there a kind of settling of accounts with the execrable past of your ancestors but also from its value as a prophetic new dawn of the social revolution that was to transform your life Rimbaud-style. The victorious struggle of a handful of men over the supposed inertia of Hispanic peoples and their traditional fatalism constituted in your eyes irrefutable proof that things could change radically in your country, providing imagination and daring were combined with strength of will and spirit of sacrifice.

Although it was the most spectacular, the example of Cuba was not unique: in the heart of Paris, where you were living, the Algerian people daily showed that the cause of justice and dignity could triumph over brute force. Curfews, arrests, covered-up murders, torture, threats, outrages had not succeeded in daunting the tens of thousands of immigrants who arose miraculously at midnight from the métro stations of Saint-Michel, Opéra, or Concorde, in a calm, serious, clear-minded provocation. Excited, full of indignant loathing for the *white skins*, you were present when they were rounded up and arrested, when they were driven by truncheon into the prison vans without offering the slightest resistance or when lined up in compact battalions on the place de l'Étoile, which suddenly had gone all yellow, they stood firm, like ghostly sleepwalkers, marked out by the crude brushstrokes of the gyrating police spotlights. Your feelings of immediacy and intense involvement were not only a response to your natural sympathy for the underdogs or to political motives. They were also inextricably intertwined with a hidden, intimate detail—you were dazzled by the physical beauty of the immigrants. As their faces gradually matched those that appeared fleetingly but clearly in your innermost dreams and fantasies, that feeling turned to passion: close by, though still forbidden, the masculine world that rushed blindingly into your life was awaiting the opportune moment to strike and throw you headlong.

A peculiar mixture of anguish and personal dissatisfaction, frustrated revolutionary desire and solidarity with a human and cultural landscape that would soon fascinate you, impregnates the pages of the books and articles you wrote at this time. While you then strove to sift things through and separate out the critical vision from the reality of your mental scenario and libido, your essay "Spain and Europe" painfully reflects the tensions, turmoil, sublimated instincts, and opposing demands with which you were then struggling. The dark, opaque, censored shadows on the surface of the text finally contaminated it with insidious irrationality, and through the fallacious warp of Marxist ideology there emerged in places the thread of a somnambulist revolutionary fantasy. Straddling the outside world and subjective authenticity, your critique was at the very least confused and incoherent. The lack of an unsullied relationship with yourself was thus inevitably translated into a sullied relationship with the world and everybody else.

The article was written, if you remember correctly, at the request of Simone de Beauvoir or some other member of the editorial board of *Les Temps Modernes*, and was intended as a response to an essay by Enrique Ruiz García that had appeared a few months before: after carefully weighing the pros and cons of Spain's entry into the Common Market, he concluded that it would imply historical progress for the nation and in the long term there was no alternative but to take up the challenge. Although his analysis did not conceal the problems that this eventuality would pose to the different layers of Spanish society from a liberal, democratizing perspective, it clashed head-on with the Party's political conceptions, which were trapped in the ostensible dilemma of the perverse status quo of Francoism or the antifeudal, antimonopolist democratic revolution required by the growing pauperization of the masses. You aligned yourself externally with the positions of your friends, and your text sketched in broad outline the history of the failures of Europeanizing Spanish liberalism only to draw the somewhat paradoxical conclusion that, in the light of recent anticolonial and anti-imperialist experience, Europe represented the dead past and the third world, a luxuriant, brilliant future:

> For more than a century and a half, the progressive Spanish intelligentsia tried to suppress the Pyrenees and the barriers that cut us off from Europe, and the conservatism of our ruling classes ruined their efforts. Now, when the old gravediggers are proposing union, we must not fall in the trap that this is a hidden concession, nor be lulled by their hollow rhetoric. Our response should be quite simple: "Too late." . . . Today we should turn our gaze toward Cuba and the peoples of America, Asia, and Africa who are fighting for their freedom and independence. Europe now sym-

bolizes, historically, the past, stagnation. It is now perhaps time to Africanize, as Unamuno would say, and turn the stale irony of that phrase "Africa begins at the Pyrenees" into the slogan for our banner.

If the facts entirely justified your expression of solidarity with the world exploited and oppressed by the "civilized nations," it was a real aberration to identify Spain with that world, and it clearly revealed your unfortunate propensity at the time to convert your impatience into a law of history and take your desires for reality. The deep crisis you were experiencing, still hidden under the disguise of political compromise and revolutionary ecstasy was, however, transparent in a few lines whose painful sincerity stood out from the gray prosaic magma of your confused feelings and ideas: "The reader must pray understand that to write in Spain is to weep and that there is no worse punishment than to face our reality without blinders or excuses. The intellectual in Spain is the victim of a profound neurosis. Larra's despair pursues him like a specter, and how can you escape it if every day is gray? Forgive us then our homicidal instincts. It is difficult to live and always keep calm."

In a fragile, morbid, turbulent mood you went to Sicily with Monique for a few weeks' rest and were caught there by the October crisis—the Khrushchev-Kennedy confrontation over the missiles—that put the world on the brink of war. Your moral conviction that the Castroite revolution embodied the values of justice and freedom which you defended drove you to abruptly break off the holiday and return to Paris. A few hours later you sped to the Cuban embassy to offer your services to the Revolution, ready to fly to Havana on the first plane to break the blockade. At a time when the future could not be more uncertain and foreign guests and sympathizers were rushing to abandon the island (including a Communist poet with a world-wide reputation), your decision seemed adventurist, if not rash. Nevertheless, you reached it without fear or hesitation. For the first and only time in your life, you took the risk of losing it on behalf of a worthy cause: you would reach the besieged Cuba after an interminable journey with stops, delays, searches, and friskings in various airports, in a clumsy old jalopy closely inspected by American fighter planes. You landed in Rancho Boyeros and, dressed in a uniform provided by Carlos Franqui, spent the night on an air-base bristling with useless Soviet artillery; later, with a number of Army officers and chiefs, you followed the "clean-up" operations in Escambray. In retrospect, you still warm to that ingenuous reaction which you do not disown: it was so similar to the feeling that led poets and writers of the stature of Cernuda, Spender, and Auden to place themselves at the disposition of the Spanish Republic at the very moment the ideals that sustained it were yielding to the double-flanked attack of Fascism and Stalinism. However, the apocalyptic vision of life and unconscious desire to solve your problems in a suicidal act of self-immolation seem now overly dramatic and exaggerated—you fell into a pathetic fallacy that is now upsetting and embarrassing. Although sincere, your gesture was excessive and theatrically avoided the debate with yourself and with your own reality. Your stay in Cuba, justified by your work as a scriptwriter for the Institute of Cinematic Art and Techniques, was rich in political and personal experiences but did not on this occasion fulfill your enthusiastic expectations: the gradual degeneration of the revolutionary process, the anxieties of the writers and intellectuals you met, the first rats bearing the message of the plague that would years later ravage any kind of nonconformism and unseemly behavior—these were too visible for you not to see them. Full of doubts as to the viability and desirability of the Cuban model for Spanish society, you went back to Europe to confront a harsh but pertinent response to the vagaries of your third-world proposals.

Francisco Fernández Santos's article "Spain, Europe, and the Third World," written for the *Tribuna Socialista*, rebutted the conclusions in your article and laid bare its defects, distortions, and illogicalities. Santos argued that the Europe we faced was many-sided and ambiguous: a left-wing intellectual's opinion on Europe's colonial policy toward the third world was one thing, and the question of the structural impact of the entry of Spain in general, and of the Francoist régime in particular, was something of quite a different order.

But, isn't Spain African enough in the worst sense of the word? . . . How can anyone seriously think that a policy based on Africanization (sup-

posing that one can be formulated at all coherently, which I doubt) would
not be greeted with wry amazement by the Spanish people? Can one
predicate as a goal for that people precisely that which they are trying to
get away from? I think it quite clear that in today's world, oppressed as
they are by the feudal-capitalist dictatorship, the popular masses of Spain
have no other solution, no other more real or practical pole of attraction
than Europe. Europe's advanced capitalist countries appear in the eyes of
the Spanish like a nearby, tangible, tempting reality to which ever greater
numbers have access. In such conditions . . . a real move toward Europe
is *in practice* a revolutionary project.

Your opponent's well-constructed arguments and sharp tone wounded
your vanity and self-pride. Hurriedly, you wrote a riposte in which you drew
out and clarified some of the confused points in the previous essay, while insisting that alongside the concrete European solution, which was undoubtedly popular and seductive for a majority of Spaniards, others did exist,
which, as in the case of Cuba, had imposed the dialectical surprise of a new
reality, despite their difficult, minority character. In fact, you felt very uncomfortable defending yourself against Fernández Santos's criticisms, since
you were forced to take up in public Jacobin positions that you were gradually ceasing to believe in under the twin experience and influence of the Cuban police-state bureaucracy and the evident flourishing of your own
bourgeoisie. To understand your sudden volte-face months later, one would
have to realize that it had been gestating ever since your second visit to Havana, and it was only the wretched polemic which enmeshed you that forced
you to keep it hidden and display a circumstantial radicalism to the gallery.

Fernández Santos put his finger on it when he defined your attitude as the
typical "pseudorebellious or revolutionary escapism" of a bourgeois with a
bad conscience; but he was less accurate when he noted signs of moral opportunism and political careerism. The controversy began as a straightforward conflict of ideas and finished very Hispanically in an acerbic exchange
of personal invective and contemptuous animosity. If the *genus irritabile va-
tum* you exhibited soon disappeared, along with your attachment to the literary world, the lesson you learned then both exorcised and initiated you. An

essay containing practical proposals had to be clear and could not be contaminated by compensatory fantasies or filtered through your libido. Henceforth, though you would express opinions and ideas in your articles, the irrational component at the heart of literature—that purely poetic truth that loses all meaning and may even seem an aberration once transposed to the sphere of reality—would nevermore pour over into the empirical world or treacherously transgress its Maldororian boundaries.

As a result of a dinner at Gisèle Halimi's house with Jorge Semprún and Teresa de Azcárate, Monique and I began to see a lot of the mythical, elusive "Federico Sánchez." Until then, my dealings with him had been limited to my almost always silent participation in the cultural seminars held in the studio of the sculptor Baltasar Lobo. With the distant, superior tone of seriousness endowed by his position, Sánchez would interject succinctly in the discussions or conversations, as if he had an urgent appointment at the other end of town and was internally appalled by that dreadful waste of time and words: sideways glances at his watch, professional condescension toward the creaking Hispanic verbal diarrhea, a forced smile as he got up and brought to an end the archaic Leninist dialogue. Although no one had told me about the Semprún identity of Federico Sánchez, I soon put two and two together. Monique shared my fascination for this character and his Janus-like face: unlike those leaden, stodgy comrades in exile, whose never-ending nostalgia for Spain sounded over the years like an old unbearable scratched record, Jorge was cultured, seductive, and brilliantly fluent; he moved like a fish in water through the French intellectual world and matched his bravery as a man of action with a hidden passion for literature. As I soon discovered, he was writing *Le Long Voyage* in bursts, but jealously guarded the secret of that activity alien and, in truth, opposed to the responsibilities and funereal solemnity of a "cadre." It was only months later, during my second stay in Cuba, that Monique managed to loosen his tongue about his mysterious manuscript: she did not give up till he lent it to her. It was a splendid novel, she wrote to me at once in Havana, full of enthusiasm. Behind the trappings of an ideologue and urban Robin Hood, Jorge suddenly appeared as an im-

portant ambitious writer: two or three months later, the international Formentor jury would reward his book, while the paparazzi hurried to spread
the sensational news that the prize had gone to public enemy number one of
Franco's police.

Jorge's companion in the CP leadership, Fernando Claudín, in spite of
his long stay in the USSR and a curious, and at first sight disturbing, phy-
siognomy that I hesitate to describe as Russian or Soviet, came over at a personal level as someone sincere and open, interested in artistic and cultural
problems and at a Patagonian or Australian distance from the monolithic
narrow-mindedness that was such a distinguishing feature of his coreligion-
ists. He and his wife Carmen would often come to have dinner with the Semprúns on the rue Poissonnière: used to the harsh rigors and caution of clandestine life on the Paris industrial belt, they were stimulated and attracted by
the free, disorderly bohemian atmosphere that they encountered at our
place. For the first time in my life, I had dealings with Communists—what's
more, Party leaders—with whom I felt naturally at ease; I did not experience
that unpleasant sensation of conversing or laughing with the representative
of an iron-cast assemblage that, like all religious sects in possession of the
truth, endows its membership with a sacramental hue and transforms their
faces at times into rigid, unfathomable masks. Consequently, when they
both told me that they were going to take over responsibility for the Party's
cultural magazine and asked me to join the editorial board, I unreservedly
accepted their invitation: despite my reptilian inability to digest doctrinal
oxen and their ephemeral external manifestations, the open, antidogmatic
line defended by my friends was entirely at one with my taste and temperament. Claudín's long essay on the plastic arts would be proof of the new
path taken by *Realidad*: in the eyes of a Western reader, this essay merely established arguments and facts that were now beyond dispute, but they constituted a truly subversive manifesto in the Soviet bloc and its territorial and
ideological dependencies; moreover, the essay had appeared in the official
journal of a sister party and was, to boot, the work of a member of the executive committee. Claudín's heterodox theses had an immediate and dramatic impact on the closed, self-sufficient world of dogma: Alfredo Gue-

vara, the director of the Cuban ICAIC, was then in the thick of a bitter polemic with the figureheads of the old Popular Socialist Party on the issue of his showing of "bourgeois" and "decadent" films, and he had the essay reprinted *pro domo* in Cuba as an opportune ideological shelter. Rumblings of scandalized sour protest began to rise from the ranks of the Spanish party and, although silenced for the moment by the rank and file's sacred respect for authority and hierarchy, they would soon be exploited by Carrillo and his faithful in the political and doctrinal destruction of his colleague on the day their differences came out into the open.

Our friendship with the Sempruns and the Claudins strengthened throughout 1963: the prolonged, cruel death agony of Monique's mother at a time when my relationship with her was at its lowest ebb; our impotence in the face of the parody of a trial accorded to Julián Grimau and his legal murder, when Monique and I ran at midnight to the Secours Populaire building where Jorge, Carrillo, and other leaders and well-known members of the CP waited in vain for a miraculous papal intervention to suspend the sentence; the pleasure and happiness when Jorge's novel won the prize—all this had brought me politically and humanly closer to both Semprún and Claudín, despite my frequent depressions and anguished internal crises. Their sure and subtle vision of Spain and the democratic possibilities opened up by the rapid evolution of our society had an obvious influence on my own views as I rejected my theoretical daydreams and illusions that were on the edge of reality. At the end of December I began to write an article in which, from less subjective, hobbled, rickety premises, I posed once more the problem of Spain's relationship with Europe. It was a decisive question for me, not only for reasons of a strictly political order but also because of its personal and literary resonances. Although I had believed in the possibility of a violent, radical change in Spanish society, I had put my pen at the disposition of such an objective in a sometimes elementary and didactic manner. My nationalist, patriotic attitude in those years derived from the mistaken conviction that a Spanish revolution was a desirable alternative and close at hand: but my fervor evaporated when I saw clearly that the country was becoming modern and bourgeois under the Franco régime and that the latter would last as long as Franco. As I concluded years later when analyzing this change, the Spain that took wing around 1960, owing to the favorable European conjuncture and the peaceful invasion by millions of tourists, could no longer fan the amorous flame of its intellectuals nor the burning mysticism of commitment: "This in no way means," I wrote, "that the latter cease to take any reasonable or practical interest in their country's destiny: what I mean is that their passion, when it exists, is directed toward other climes."* Comparing the situation in Spain in the sixties with that of Britain at the beginning of the nineteenth century—when political freedoms had been gained, religious conflicts resolved, and the country was thrust into a savage industrial revolution that destroyed both the physical and moral landscape, the national problem ceased to inspire writers and artists—I noted that if the latter still intervened in English social and political life their hearts beat for other causes, as happened even in July 1936, when the Spanish civil war began. The caboose of Europe, our country was losing the dramatic contrasts and features of its picturesque backwardness without yet acquiring the moral and material advantages of the richer nations. The struggle for political and trade-union freedoms, the elimination of social injustice, the abolition of censorship was to continue; but such goals were hard pressed to provoke the depth of feeling created, for example, by the cause of Palestine or Vietnam. The image of Spain already was, and would continue to become, closer to the image of other European countries, and just as no left-wing French intellectual could be stirred by France, nor Dutch or English intellectuals by Holland or England, thus our attachment to a Spain that was neither fantastic nor revolutionary lost its raison d'être. It was necessary to bury the hatchet of anachronistic nationalism and adapt to reality. This metamorphosis affected the writer's strategy and the very nature of his discourse: there was a different mental target. When renouncing the values underlying my previous "committed" literature, I did so naturally aware that I belonged not to a weak or persecuted culture but to one that was vast, rich, and dynamic, as Spanish culture is in the dual compass of Spain and South America. The act of casting off oppressive, sterile identity markers opened the way to a plural literary space that had no frontiers; banned by Francoism, my

*Interview with Julio Ortega reprinted years later in *Disidencias*, Barcelona, 1977.

books could seek refuge in Mexico or Buenos Aires. From now on, the language and only the language would be my real country.

Enlivened by my new certainties, I tried to set them out in a clear, concise, and convincing manner. Thanks to its repression of the working class, maintenance of old production relations in the agricultural sector, and surrender of Falangist rhetoric to the interests of the monopolies, the Régime had laid the basis for modern capitalist accumulation: though, on the one hand, the success of the stabilization plan offered the bourgeoisie unanticipated prospects and gave it a confidence and security it previously lacked, on the other hand, massive emigration to Europe and a spectacular increase in demand within the domestic labor market placed the Spanish working class in an advantageous situation; in this framework its program of demands was more like that of French or Italian workers toward their countries' employing class than that of the peninsular proletariat ten years earlier, which confronted defenseless the harsh monolithic state supported by a frightened and constrained bourgeoisie. The two-way traffic of tourists and migrant workers was to sweep aside traditional mentalities tied to traditional modes of production. Through both, the Spanish people discovered the economic values of "advanced" societies and mimetically adapted their behavior and aspirations to Calvinist principles of modernity. Only Republicans in exile and especially, although I never mentioned the fact, the Communist Party, maintained the relevance of an analysis that was progressively less connected to reality: Francoism would collapse not through the revolutionary struggle of the masses but as the victim of a social dynamic that would empty it of any substance and convert it into a useless, hollow shell:

> The fact that the path of evolution is not the one predicted in 1951, 1956, or 1961 is insufficient reason to reject it or act as if it did not exist. Analyses and programs must fit the facts, and not vice versa. There is no doubt that the change requires extremely painful rethinking on moral, political, social, economic, and even aesthetic fronts, but we must have the intelligence and courage to accept the challenge.

The seductive and somewhat romantic vision of the heroic Spain of '36 has been replaced by a reality that is ambiguous, trivial, and unpleasant. A train has taken off after twenty years of immobility and, caught unawares, the parties and intellectuals of the left have been left on the platform. But it is futile to deny the reality of the train or to pull the rear carriage by rope in the opposite direction. The problem is, on the contrary, how to board the moving train and accelerate its speed as fast as possible.*

My article was ready in January 1964 and I showed a draft to Semprún and Claudín: I remember that they both expressed their disagreements and differences, suggested small changes and clarifications, argued with me over particular points and questions of emphasis. This exchange of opinions had a very marginal effect on the final version; contrary to what was said later, it was in no way crucial. Although I had taken the article to *L'Express* at the beginning of the year, the text was only printed three months later: the editor-in-chief had sought a significant date for publication and had reached the conclusion that 1 April would be the most suitable, the twenty-fifth anniversary of Franco's victory. The length of the essay and its reflective character, detached from the details of day-to-day events, meant that there could be such a delay without any loss of immediacy. In the period between my handing it over and its publication, the theoretical and strategic disagreements between Semprún and Claudín and their companions in the Party leadership, already revealed in a "cadre" training course held near Arras in the summer of 1963, provoked a series of discussions between them and the Carrillo-led majority. I was totally on the periphery of all this, and my two friends did not break the silence imposed by their secret character; nevertheless, from laconic allusions to the existence of problems, I sensed they were worried and anxious. As I later discovered, a first round of conversations with executive committee members resident in France had not brought agreement. Forced to formulate their criticisms as plainly and simply as possible, Claudín and Semprún agreed to a request to present them in writing and argue them through weeks later with their colleagues in the

*The perception of structural change within Spain is quite transparent at the time in the *Carta de España* by Jaime Gil de Biedma, which is in *El pie de la letra*, as well as in José Ángel Valente's beautiful and incisive poems, like "Melancolía del destierro" and "Ramblas de julio, 1964."

presence of la Pasionaria. The meetings of the *Realidad* editorial board were temporarily suspended and Claudín dedicated all his usual calm and energy to explaining and defending his positions. At the end of March they were both traveling to Prague, and at a dinner for the three couples on the rue Poissonnière they said their farewells like actors well-versed in their roles and the unhappy conclusion of the drama: in fine fettle with a touch of melancholy resignation. Spanish readers would find out years later, upon the publication of the *Autobiografía de Federico Sánchez*, what happened in that decisive plenary. While the harsh and bloody confrontation was waged, I was in Paris, a million miles away from the gathering storm. On 2 April my article "On ne meurt plus à Madrid" came out in *L'Express*, with a striking intro on the "decisive change" in Spain over recent years. Two or three days afterwards, I was visited by a writer-friend newly arrived from Madrid who had just been told in very hostile terms of the content of my essay. Although he had not yet read it, he informed me he was worried about my possible revisionist and bourgeoisified positions. Rather upset by his warning, I told him to look at the essay before issuing a condemnation, since I doubted it was as negative as it had been described to him. I added that I had shown it to Semprún and Claudín and that apart from a few minor differences and reservations they had not felt it to be defeatist or out-of-focus. My colleague promised to read it carefully and discuss the content with me before returning to Spain. There was no such conversation, but a telephone call from Gregorio López Raimundo, whom I knew only by sight, to tell me he urgently wanted to see me. I agreed to meet him that afternoon at home, intrigued by his visit and the speed with which it had been arranged, and we had hardly exchanged polite greetings when he asked if it were true that I had shown the *L'Express* article to his two colleagues. I said I had, but only on a personal or friendly level, as I might have done with any other Party acquaintance, like Sastre or Teresa de Azcárate. I was insistent that they had formulated some objections which I had not always taken into consideration and, consequently, responsibility for the text was mine alone. López Raimundo made no secret that this was a serious matter: he said it was part of a much wider assault on the political line of the Party. It was his duty to inform his companions in the leadership of the content of our interview: he or one of his colleagues would call me later to discuss the problem.

On their return from Prague, my two friends described the broad outlines of the plenary meeting in the old castle of the kings of Bohemia and their expulsion from the executive committee. I related to them my interview with López Raimundo and his interest in their possible link with my article in *L'Express*, but they did not pay too much attention to the matter given the circumstances in which they found themselves, subject to that character assassination or process of discredit and moral death that corresponds to revisionism within the purest Stalinist tradition. Their previous experience of Party methods of eliminating, even physically, Trotskyists and dissidents, conferred upon them the cheerful bravura of those on death row for whom all is lost except their self-respect. My concern over the business with *L'Express* was, however, justified. A fresh phone call, this time from Juan Gómez, warned me of his impending visit. Teresa de Azcárate's husband, at the time the Party's leading expert on economic questions, angrily asked me if I had really told López Raimundo that his wife knew of the article. I made it clear I had not: López Raimundo, suffering from slight deafness, had misheard me. Slightly calmer, Juan Gómez went to the heart of the matter: whether or not the two dissidents had helped me write it, the article was full of serious errors, it directly attacked the Party, and it was to be refuted in the pages of *Realidad*. The task of composing the reply had fallen to him and, as he solemnly hinted, it was going to be very tough-minded. As the French version of the article had suffered a number of cuts and contained a few mistakes, I handed him the Spanish original, recently published in Mexico. Juan Gómez politely said goodbye, but not before he had suggested that it would be helpful if I met Carrillo in order to clarify fully my role in what he obviously judged to be a burgeoning, well-orchestrated conspiracy.

But Moscow, Rome, or Santiago had pronounced without considering my testimony or protests. On 19 April the CP leadership called a meeting in a hall belonging to the Communist council of Stains, where Carrillo, who had no legal status in France, spoke for the first time in public; he denounced a sinister plot against the Party, in a speech full of cryptic allusions and veiled attacks on the two absent comrades, of which the only clue visible to the uninformed membership led straight to me: the revisionists and capitulators hidden away in the ranks of the party could henceforth, if they so wished, communicate through the pages of *L'Express* but not through *Realidad*! As Semprún and Claudín told me—several present at the meeting informed them of the drift of the speech—Carrillo had decided to air the polemic within the leadership before the rank and file, and used my article as a weapon against them, accusing them of disgraceful responsibility. Unable or unwilling still to mention their names, he centered his attacks on my article, thus converting it into a butt for all censors, a punching ball upon which blows would rain for weeks and months.

Though not entirely surprised by such behavior, I was upset by the cynicism, contempt for truth, and lack of respect for people that it revealed—attitudes so similar to those that prospered in the beleaguered camp of the Régime. They trampled with abandon on the elementary rules of democracy and free discussion; the struggle of ideas was transformed into a petty-minded interrogation, the aim of which was to destroy the enemy or present him as the devil. As Francesc Vicens later informed me—he was a member of the editorial board of *Realidad*—the board's next meeting was convened behind the backs of the three lepers and, without condescending to explain such striking absenteeism, Juan Gómez announced that the editorial in the third issue would be devoted to attacking my ill-starred article. Vicens and others present intervened to suggest that since I was part of the committee, I should be invited to debate the question with the rest of them. Their proposal did not pass, although backed by a majority, and those who supported the measure were dismissed from *Realidad* without a second thought. However, the show had only just begun and, while the crisis between the Carrillo leadership and the expelled comrades developed and deepened, my astonishment grew apace. One fine day I discovered that my ideas were being "discussed" at all cell meetings, as an hors d'oeuvre to a meatier, more treacherous attack on my friends' positions. As the two Catalan Communist Party members, labor lawyer August Gil and former architecture student Javier Martín Malo, explained in a long interview published by the weekly maga-

zine *Mundo* on 3 April 1978, both were summoned at the end of May 1964
to a clandestine meeting of the Barcelona committee to which they belonged: there, the messenger from the Paris leadership, Josep Serradell, alias
"Román," brought them up-to-date on Claudín and Semprún's expulsion
from the executive committee and their suspension from the central committee for their "right-wing," "defeatist," "anti-Leninist," and "social democratic" stances: "As the only definitive proof, Román read us an article by
Goytisolo in which he more or less said that Spanish capitalism was in a
growth phase and that, in that context of economic development, all illusions about the collapse of Francoism were pure utopianism. . . . What is
incredible is that J. G. was not even a Communist militant, but a personal
friend of Claudín and Semprún. However, he made out that they had used
him to publicize their theses." A corollary of this conspiratorial paranoia, so
rooted in clandestine organizations, would be Román's secret report, the
content and code of which Vicens deciphered for me when he brought his
archive to Spain: aware of my presence in Catalonia—my last holidays in
Torrentbó just before my father's death—Serradell warned the membership of this fact and advised them "to keep an eye" on me. The repetitions of
history are sometimes grotesque, and drama turns to farce: after the Régime's written attacks and police vigilance, I found the similar situations and
attitudes that I was now experiencing particularly enlightening and exemplary.

One cannot today read Juan Gómez's long-awaited reply without blushing on his behalf: the leading Party authority on economics manipulated and
doctored the data with the wiles of a puppeteer to demonstrate that, behind
the appearance of progress, Spain was still lagging behind the rest of Europe, the Régime was in an irremediable state of decay, and it would be "finally" swept away by a sharpening of the class struggle. Unfortunately his
delirious fantasies of victories and catastrophes were not unique: they impregnated all the Communist Party commentaries and declarations. Coinciding with my article in *L'Express*, a *Treball* editorial ("Twenty-five Peaceful Years?") described the situation in these terms: "While the working class
and people reach this anniversary confident of a not-too-distant future of

freedom—the process of the liquidation of the Franco régime has never been so clear as over the past year—the dictatorship celebrates its quarter of a century of victory with the sound of funeral rather than victory marches." In that rarefied, self-satisfied world, to have recourse to the language of facts was like speaking to a brick wall; Semprún and Claudín's daring in doing just that constituted a crime of lèse-optimism and the consequences were quite predictable.

If those months were painful for me, they were even more so for my expelled friends, especially for Claudín and his family. While Jorge had a series of cards in his favor—legal residence in France and a promising literary career—Fernando was out in the cold, with no documents, money, or work. Slandered, placed in moral quarantine, the object of intense pressure to leave France and accept the "generous offer" of retirement or eternal rest in the Eastern bloc—from the attempt to evict him from his tiny flat in La Courneuve and leave him in the street to physical intimidation that forced him to temporarily leave home and live in a Parisian *chambre de bonne* in hiding from both the French police and his own comrades—Claudín resisted those trials without losing his sangfroid, patience, or sense of humor. Years later, when surveying Blanco White's pages on the inquisitorial methods of the Church—its stratagems, tricks, and ploys to cow or eliminate heretics— I was shaken by the parallel between his historical sketch and the recent chronicle of my friends. The use of ad hominem arguments, the desire to deprive the enemy of all rights, the absolute contempt for ethical norms and justice that I then discovered filled me henceforth with a healthy skepticism for the would-be democratic ideals of an organization that did not flinch from the use of force or slander against its own members. The future society envisaged by the Party's public face could only with difficulty spring from such an array of blows below the belt, grudges, lack of scruples, thirst for power, spy-itis, and irrationality. I have not been surprised or saddened by events in Spain since the blessed legalization of the CP—that grotesque tableau of schisms, splits, expulsions, accusations which would end, *risum teneatis*, in the buffeting and fall through the trapdoor of Carrillo himself, in a burlesque atmosphere of farcical exaggeration complete with hairpulling and insults worthy of street urchins or fishwives. After the anathematizing of Claudín and Semprún, whenever I heard righteous, well-meaning criticisms of my movement away from "real socialism" and its rose-tinted promises of happiness, I would keep my ironic amusement to myself. Accusations of bourgeois individualism would bounce off a hide toughened by experience. Without bitterness or rancor, and at the cost of a few pens and a few scratches, I had earned this privilege with the sweat of my brow: the right to smile inwardly.

The systematic denigration over those months was water off a duck's back. After the downpour that followed the inglorious Milan episode, I was aware of both the harshness of my country and the splendor of my own isolation. There was no sense in replying to Juan Gómez's editorial and getting entangled in a fresh polemic. An internal struggle of the left, in its precarious besieged state, could benefit only the supporters of the Régime: in a mood of exceptional levity and relief, I resolved to abandon my fumbling apprenticeship as a politician and leave the subject until the hypothetical day of Franco's death.

You lived for eleven years physically and morally cut off from your country, outside its historical development, the master of a vast void: your name disappeared from the newspapers and your work—printed in Paris, Mexico, or Buenos Aires—was strictly banned. This ostracism nevertheless favored your decision to be yourself, to defend your truth and scale of values against the norms and rituals of the tribe: to put a halt to the insistent pressure of the stealer of strength. From now on, you would express political opinions on Santo Domingo, Czechoslovakia, or Palestine, but not on Spain. You were no longer enthralled by its predictable evolution under Francoism. You occasionally crossed through on your way to Oran, Oujda, or Tangier; a fleeting impression of a hotel, an inn, a stopping place; a blot on the map. Disaffection, indifference, distance, which at extreme moments would nourish your dream of becoming Maltese, of attaining by whatever means the sought-after papers of a stateless citizen: far from your own sleeping-beauty society, the great country of mutes deafened by their long, noisy silence. An obstinate, neurotic denial of your land, an instinctive desire to run away if your neighbors loudly expressed themselves in your tongue, inexplicable unease when you bumped into fellow countrymen who addressed not you but your tiresome double: you shamefully deny your identity and respond to the intruder in a strange abrupt language. The violent rejection of a world, which, with significant ambivalence, you compensate for by a growing passion for its history and culture: you ravenously devour the classics, reread Asín and Américo Castro, are dazzled by and appropriate Blanco White. The unforgettable experience of translating yourself as you translate him, without in the end knowing if he really existed or was a distant incarnation of yourself. You realize that his struggle and moral trajectory were the same because the oppressive régime with which he struggled stretched down to the one you knew. Like him, you transformed punishment into a state of grace. You lightly assume to your own advantage the burden imposed by your destiny: an airborne species, a carnation in the wind open to other climates and stimuli. Seminal stays in North Africa, journeys to the Sahara, carefree wandering through Istanbul, slow river descent to dark Nubian splendors. An apprenticeship in the novelties and hazards of the role of the visiting professor: fertile proximity to the university world, fascination for the melting pot of New York. You share out your life between Paris, Manhattan, and Tangier without the pain of nostalgia for the Peninsula.

An illusory impression, as reality saw fit to demonstrate.

In September 1975 you had flown to the United States, to give one of your usual courses in Pittsburgh, where you heard the news of the trial, sentencing, and execution of the Basque militants. The image of the moribund dictator delivering his grotesque speech reminded you of the drama of Inés de Castro that you had seen in the cinema as a child: her corpse solemnly reinstated on the throne, dressed in the attributes of authority, she too received the silent homage of her courtiers, who were bewitched by the symbol of motionless power that inertia seemed to perpetuate beyond death. Violently repelled by the spectacle, wishing to see the drama filed away forever with its whole troupe of heroes and extras in the library of your classics, you understood that your indifference was a fiction and that the old feeling of shame for everything that the official Spain of the time stood for would stay with you to the grave. Isolated in the stone, metal, and cement landscape of the Golden Triangle, for several weeks you hung on the television news, a prey to the anger and impotence that you had thought gone forever. From Monique's telephone call telling you the news—later denied—of his death until it was over, you remembered your Spanish childhood and youth as if you had been present at the death agony of someone who was really the monstrous head of your family. The certainty of at last being orphaned by the man whose shadow had hovered over you ever since the devastating blast of the civil war rekindled the imperious desire to write about him, to clarify once and for all the nature of that relationship beyond and above the one tying you to a merely putative father. On the night of 20 November you prepared the draft of the text you read days later in the Library of Congress in Washington, as your puny if invigorating revenge on that unvenerable institution that had so much contributed to keeping him in power in your lifetime: a text that, while avoiding direct mention of his name (*In memoriam F. F. B. 1892–1975*), claimed the vile reality of his paternity and would be (though you were unaware of it at the time) the seed or kernel of this incursion into the minefield of autobiography.

The Slippers of Empedocles

MY NAME APPEARED after Cervantes in the list of most-translated Spanish writers published under the auspices of UNESCO in an annual survey of world literary activity relating to 1963. Rather than being flattered by this fact, I was filled first with anxiety and then with despair. What had I done to deserve it? Success so at odds with my feeble, unsubstantial work could only be the result of a combination of circumstances and misconceptions that in one way or another converged on my person. Had the opportunist, much-abused identification of my name with the cause of Spanish democracy and my minor position of privilege in the world of journalism and publishing perhaps created an easily exportable image of the young committed writer that faithfully fitted the clichés and stereotypes of our country? The phenomenon entirely omitted specific literary factors: it developed exclusively from the world of publishing. As one of my critics wrote at the time—expressing, in truth, my own feelings of unease—wasn't I "an amazingly distended balloon" that would be duly deflated "till it reached its rightful size"?

An amazingly distended balloon, like the *hot air* man that Larra describes in such masterly fashion in one of his essays: the likeness of the portrait astounded me. But distended by whom and how? A well-oiled chain of cause and effect had turned me in the space of five years into one of the official standard-bearers of progressive causes in the Hispanic world, welcomed both by the party propaganda machines and an intelligentsia an-

chored to the myths of Romantic Spain and its unhappy civil war. While the
Slovak, Ukrainian, Norwegian, or Finnish versions of my work piled up on
the shelves of my library, the rue Poissonnière was an obligatory meeting
place for all involved in projects or cultural encounters concerning the Peninsula. My friendship with the editors of *L'Express*, *France-Observateur*, and
Les Temps Modernes allowed me a small patch of political and literary influence that I unashamedly cultivated for a time. A mixture of Marxist sectarianism, desire to be in the spotlight, and petty feelings of rivalry led me to act
rather ingloriously, like those social climbers in the world of the press and
publishing whose Shakespearian passions and Machiavellian ruses I would
have occasion to experience many years later. Perhaps, like a handful of writers whom I now detest, I had built a precocious, flamboyant literary career
on the back of the historical misfortunes of my own people? In such circumstances the exalting of the work of a patriotic author fighting against the
abuses of a hateful régime is the same as defending the cause of justice, and
vice versa. It is, of course, a simplistic and deceptive equation, but extremely
beneficial for the poet or novelist who unscrupulously adopts it. One can
criticize an individual who publishes his writing, but not a people in struggle
and even less a whole continent. The amazingly distended balloon, voice of
the anger, dreams, and hopes of two hundred million beings, would float
miraculously above good and evil.

Smug pride, narcissistic complacency, the conceit of a peacock? The arrogance existed and it was palpable: imbalance between being and image,
external persona and the ego lurking behind, the approachable worldly novelist and his insomniac, depressive support, the "normal" husband and the
one gradually taken over by violent, sumptuous, martial nocturnal fantasies.
A delicate if persistent feeling of precarious uncertainty—just like the one
we experienced when we dreamed, for example, of dancing with the carefree agility of a Fred Astaire only to remember in semiconsciousness our real
country-yokel awkwardness—increased the distance and alienation I felt
from myself. The *other's* vanity, his political enthusiasms, worldly ways,
moral opportunism, pettiness, and pride oppressed me and were difficult to
live with. My political zeal began to weaken as I established that outside the

realm of theory Marxist ideals were gathering rust and looking not just miserable, but tarnished and dishonorable as well. Didn't my participation in meetings, projects, discussions, and congresses constitute an enormous waste of time and an exhausting squandering of energies? Did the dinners and engagements with writers, journalists, and publishing people really suit Monique's character and mine, our growing desire to retreat and to be near each other? Had we set out on a course that did not agree with us and demanded an effort that was not matched by the satisfaction obtained in return? These and other questions posed over two or three years pointed me in the direction of a decision, and finally bore fruit: it was necessary to puncture once and for all the distended balloon and reduce it to fairer, more human proportions.

The decision to wage war on my image was firmly taken, but the skirmishes in the battle extended over years and results were late in coming. Even now I have not succeeded in entirely erasing it from the minds of people who met me then and, in spite of my efforts at eviction, small echoes or traces remain within myself. Of all the struggles I have fought against personal inclinations that I abhor, this has perhaps been the most unpleasant and harshest. How could I free myself from this young double, at first sight so blessed by fortune but whose ideas, tastes, and ambitions had ceased to be mine and even repelled me? The patient labor of separating myself out from him has not always been crowned with success. The bursting of the balloon required a series of rejections and transformations that turned my life upside down. To do this, I had to sabotage my modest, but envied, position in the world of publishing in exchange for another doubtful, risky, difficult life in literature; I had to find an economic alternative to my income as a writer; defend lost or unpopular causes against those that were profitable or fashionable; live in isolation and cultivate enemies; stop conceiving of the vocation as a career and the novelist or poet as spokesman for the national interest. Only time and its inevitable cortège of mishaps and mistakes would allow me to assemble a few analects on which I would try to model my behavior: a minor victory but one that would in the future clarify with nodular precision my past confused relationships with myself and with everybody else.

F ROM A CERTAIN *age, one learns to strip oneself of all that is secondary or incidental in order to bind oneself to the areas of experience which apportion greater pleasure and emotion: writing, sex, and love will henceforth be the deepest and most authentic configurations of your territory: all else is a poor substitute that an elemental principle of purely selfish economy advises you to do without and which you will do without entirely: as you will see from your own example, whoever aspires to become a public figure sacrifices his most intimate truth to an image, an external profile: literary favor is a chance and subtle matter and it usually takes vengeance on those who rush in search of recognition by distancing itself and then abandoning them: from your publishing watchtower you will witness over the years numerous examples of literary and moral erosion: that process of self-advertisement by the writer who, because of unfaithfulness to the most genuine sources of his being, finally loses, unawares, his pristine state of grace.*

A FEW WEEKS AFTER my arrival in Paris, Mascolo asked me to help him clear the backlog of work by reading and selecting from the manuscripts in Spanish that were gathering dust in his office at Gallimard. Although it was badly paid work, it had the incentive for me of strengthening my relationship with Monique and her colleagues, while putting me in contact with writers I admired or had heard of when I was at university. The effect of that friendly proximity on a provincial greenhorn like myself was both stimulating and damaging. If, on the one hand, it brought me close to the work of the novelists, poets, essayists, or dramatists whom I often saw in the entrance hall to Gallimard, on the other, it flattered my youthful pride to move among them, to accept their condescending and undeserved familiarity. An interloper in the *sancta sanctorum* of the Parisian intelligentsia, I, like many others, would have yielded to the glamour of literary society—that universe so long-windedly described by Proust's novelistic genius—if it had not been in my case opportunely counterbalanced by my political militancy and Monique's healthy rigor. My association with her and the Mascolo gang drew me into a very well defined group whose trenchant attitudes to Stalinism and writers designated as right-wing discouraged me from any personal excursion outside those carefully traced boundaries. Although their intransigence did not reach the extremes of Debord and his minuscule Situationist International, it did, however, rival that of Breton and his followers. In the peremptory style so typical of Rive Gauche circles, the mere enunciation of their ideas and positions automatically implied the ridiculing and rejection of those of their opponent. While Camus symbolized in their eyes hollow, abstract moralizing, Aragon embodied the image of the perfect, total *salaud*. Even Sartre, with whom they nevertheless shared some affinities, slid, according to them, into opportunism toward the Party, as if to compensate by his flirtation with Stalinism for his past apoliticism in respect to the Nazis. His famous essay on the reappearance of Stalin's ghost with the entry of Soviet tanks into Hungary had not resolved the point of contention with my friends: the adjective "Sartrian" always retained on their lips a reproving, pejorative resonance.

Consequently, Camus's attitude toward me was cold and distant, although he had a keen interest in Spain and sustained an honorable attitude toward the Régime, to the point of turning his back on UNESCO when a representative of Franco joined that organization. I occasionally bumped into him on the stairs or in the corridors at Gallimard, and I was rather disappointed when he just nodded politely in my direction. Living as I did with Monique, and consequently linked to the Mascolo clan, he mentally included me in the group that had aligned itself with Sartre during the polemic around *L'Homme révolté*. As Monique told me later—when her ideas had developed and she willingly admitted her past injustices toward Camus—the latter had gone into the office where she and other members of the Gallimard staff had just read aloud and underlined in pencil the harshest sections of Sartre's reply to his open letter to *Les Temps Modernes*, and he asked whether they had the latest issue of the magazine in which he, apparently, came under attack. Camus picked up the copy that lay visibly on the table and glanced at the pages marked by her while those present kept an embarrassed silence. The painful run through Sartre's text—a read that, according to numerous accounts, deeply affected Camus—was thus associated in his memory with the initial context in which it took place. From then on, the author of *La Peste* drew a dividing line between the people surrounding him: faced with a majority that supported Sartre's brilliant but often mistaken arguments, he took refuge in a warm nucleus of faithful friends.

During this period, Monique and I regularly visited the flat on the rue Saint-Benoît where Mascolo and Marguerite Duras lived on a knife-edge after their breakup. In an atmosphere that gradually filled with smoke and suppressed tensions, we talked into the early hours of literature and politics with Edgar and Violette Morin, Robert Antelme, André Frenaud, and

Louis-René des Forêts. I can remember Marguerite's intense, impassioned, fascinating voice, that subtle magic she communicates to the characters in her novels and plays, the deliberate high drama she brings to the pettiest discussions. We drank a lot, and although we did not entirely share the group's past affinities, they gave us a most generous welcome. After my recent probing of the work of Genet and Violette Leduc, I passed a fine-tooth comb through our friend's poetic world: guided by Monique, the editors of Seix Barral were quick to sign Marguerite up and translate her works into Spanish. Later on, the success of her baptismal incursion into the cinema—the script of *Hiroshima mon amour*, directed by Alain Resnais—would accentuate with charming spontaneity her unquenchable tendency to narcissistic egocentrism. One day when we had debated in turn the relative merits of her books, plays, and cinematic enterprises, one of the guests, as we started our desserts, timidly deflected the conversation toward the latest events in Algeria, and Marguerite retreated into an aloof silence before exclaiming: "Well, since you're having a technical conversation, I'm off!"

I met the novelist Elio Vittorini, the only member of the clan not resident in Paris and on the periphery of the group, when I traveled with Monique to Venice in January 1957 and we spent a few days in Milan. It is impossible to forget that attic where the writer lived on the Viale Gorizia—a gray avenue some distance from downtown, running alongside a gloomy, dull canal. Vittorini's face radiated a captivating sense of beauty; his serious features, gray hair and mustache, the gaze that penetrated his interlocutor with an inquisitive warmth; that embarrassed, unsophisticated smile of his which revealed, in spite of his sharp wit, the roughness of his background: an extraordinary combination of strength and intelligence, wild appearance and gentle domesticity, seduced whoever had the opportunity to chat with him at home, while in the company of his wife and Sicilian friends he talked, laughed, or played an animated game of cards, just as in his native village. By his side, Ginetta shared in his delicate, fierce majesty: tall, serene, noble-featured, her voice had an incantatory power curiously related to Marguerite's. Basking in the glow of their startling beauty, Elio and Ginetta presented the image of an emblematic Castilian couple, lion and lioness resting peacefully; I have not seen, nor shall I ever see again, such a perfect luminous combination of male and female. Ginetta and Elio welcomed us with open arms: they had known Monique ever since her divorce and were obviously pleased to see her with me so happy and full of vitality. Vittorini had traveled through Spain two summers before and was interested in speaking to a Spaniard of my age about the situation in the country and the future of Francoism. Later his literary work would exercise a momentary influence on mine: when he read the Spanish text of *Campos de Níjar* he suggested the idea of extending it with a slight narrative plot and, in the light of his experiment in *Il Sempione strizza l'occhio al Frejus*, I wrote the fictional documentary *La Chanca*, the Spanish edition of which I dedicated posthumously to him. On our return from Venice, we visited his house again like old friends. Ginetta honored us with her gastronomic specialities, and Elio conversed with a genial simplicity rare in the tinsel circus of those infected by literary madness. His death, eight years later, profoundly saddened both of us; of all the writers I have met beyond the confines of my own language, Vittorini was, alongside Genet, the one who inspired me as a person with most respect and appreciation.

While I was getting to know the Mascolo crowd, Monique introduced me, through her doctor, to a group of writers and artists more or less linked by their roots to the Surrealists. Doctor Théodore Frankel had been one of the founders of this movement and appears in the paintings of the time with Breton, Crevel, and Aragon discreetly in the background. Monique used to lunch with him once a week; he would occasionally invite us both to dine with his old friends. Frankel was a bachelor and inveterate womanizer, whose devouring flame of passion for the companion of a famous writer had, in a legend difficult to verify, impelled him to pursue his rival all over Paris with an avenging or justice-seeking revolver: the crime was never consummated and, after a time, frustrated sharpshooter and would-be victim made their peace and saw each other again without any resentment. At these dinners I met Alberto Giacometti, Georges Bataille, Michel Leiris, and other creative artists. Unfortunately, the narrowness of the ideological space I inhabited also reduced the span of my own literary interests and projects: the writers on the edge of the mainstream, the successors to Gide's humanism and Malraux's historic compromise, sometimes seduced me with an attractiveness I deemed to be unhealthy and which I strove to resist. My models were, and continued to be for some time, Sartre and Camus: Artaud, Bataille, and Michaux were thus consigned to the purgatory of the illicit and impermissible until, freed from the straitjacket of my literary-political theories, I could unashamedly surrender to the magnetic pull of my own taste. Although my quintessentially Hispanic resistance or mistrust of new trends from outside—at the opposite extreme of the *plus parisien*–than-the-Parisians-themselves syndrome that frequently befell writers and artists from Latin America—meant I avoided the trap that snared some of them, of worship of all things Gallic, it also made it difficult to approach the work of some writers with whom I conversed quite unprofitably. Giacometti's overwhelming vitality and radiant ugliness, thrust by his genius to a new aesthetic dimension, created a startling, unforgettable contrast to Bataille's pale, apparently bloodless face, the blue of whose eyes reminded me of Grandfather. From the shelter of his thick, bushy eyebrows, Doctor Frankel, with the hieratic patience of a fawn, could not take his eyes off his latest girlfriend or mistress.

My relationship with Raymond Queneau, whom Monique had known for some years, was more original and unexpected. A building-worker—whose life story I included in a report on emigration published in *Tribuna Socialista*—came from the community of Valencian immigrants, relatives, friends or neighbors of our housekeeper and her husband, whom we would visit on the odd Sunday in their Rueil-Malmaison shacks. José was in his way interested in politics and spoke admiringly of an overseer in the building firm that employed him. A refugee from the Spanish civil war, Jadraque was, José said, a pleasure to talk to, and José often visited him in the hospital, where he was recovering from an accident at work. Jadraque was still youthful in appearance, ruddy, well-built, attracted by culture, and endowed with a subtle sarcastic sense of humor. As a member of the CNT or FAI he had suffered the trial of French internment camps and had joined the anti-Nazi resistance before adapting to the grayness of life in exile by getting the job of overseer in the firm that employed some of my Valencian friends. Jadraque quite rightly lamented their political ignorance and lack of interest in trade unions: his vision of Francoist Spain was bitter and lucid; he did not share the others' fantasies of an imminent return home. Convinced that the Régime had castrated young people, he sought refuge in the classics of acratic thought and discussed Marx's authoritarian tendencies with me. I remember how one day out of the blue he mentioned Queneau and asked if I knew him. I told him that Monique met him daily at Gallimard. "I also see him a lot," Jadraque commented; "his novels are very amusing." The reasons for this unsuspected relationship became clearer days later. Jadraque cohabited with the housekeeper of Queneau, who was very fond of him. As my compatriot had mentioned me to him, the author of *Les Dimanches de la vie* told Monique he wanted to meet me and invited us to supper in his Neuilly flat. Behind his easy smile and defensive irony, Queneau seemed an affectionate, timid man, full of secret crannies and corners, with a gently exuberant character and a heterogeneous, limitless culture. His unusual literary exploration, which I gradually assimilated as I got to know him, seems now unique and seminal. An anarchist in ideas and temperament, the writer treated Jadraque almost paternally. My links with him, which owed nothing to the literary world of Paris, had been the best route to the secluded space of his private life.

This peculiar bottom-up relationship, through our housekeeper's friends or fellow countrymen who had migrated to France after the frosts had ruined Valencian agriculture for a time, would provide me for a period with an unanticipated vision of some aspects and habits of the indigenous intellectual bourgeoisie. After placing a good number of them on the sites of Jadraque's firm and in the homes of writers and journalists more or less known to Monique, on Sundays our flat became a meeting place where the newcomers from the district of Gandía could noisily swap stories of their respective employers. Thus, quite undeliberately, we discovered that a famous literary critic on *Le Figaro* padlocked his refrigerator when he went away on the weekends or that a renowned author made her Spanish *bonne* eat her leftovers. This indirect, involuntary prying—which would have delighted

someone more into gossip than I was—nevertheless revealed the existence
of a sordid penny-pinching that until then I had thought the exclusive property of our underdeveloped lugubrious middle class.

Just as a villager from the Bierzo or the Batuecas miraculously introduced
into a harem would gradually shed his wonderment and adapt naturally
with a few doses of ennui to the delights of his dream made flesh, so my sudden admission to the Olympus of the great had the predictable consequence
of quickly curing me of the provincial desire to scale its peaks. Monique had
established friendly ties not only with French writers published by Gallimard but also, thanks to her good knowledge of English, with foreign authors of the stature of Faulkner. The day I met her, the latter was talking to
her in her office and laughed when he learned that she was leaving him for a
few minutes to say hello to a young Spaniard of "Belmontian" appearance.
The friendship of Monique and her ex-husband with the author of *Wild
Palms* dated back to the time when he passed through Paris after being
awarded the Nobel Prize.* She and the novelist had been writing intermittently to one another ever since: in flight from the relentless pursuit of the
professional Faulknerians, he would forewarn Monique of his private visits
to France. When Carole was born in 1952, Faulkner asked to be godfather
and insisted on giving her as a present a silver cup engraved with his name
and an inscription; in the rush to return home, he did not have time to order
it and entrusted the right money to Monique, who instead of spending it on
that showy, rather absurd present, preferred to lavish it on something more
interesting and substantial. Months later, when she learned of the godfather's sudden arrival, she would be forced to hastily buy another cup and dent
it to remove its new, unused look: it was a deception that Monique herself
would uncover to Faulkner when he came to see his goddaughter. At the
start of our relationship, she had asked me if I wanted to meet him, but my
absolute ignorance of English at the time would have forced me to play the
role of the dumb guest or spoil the conversation with a painful exercise in
translation and persuaded me sensibly to reject the offer. Nevertheless, even

*Monique published a piece evoking her friendship, "Une apparition," in the issue of *Le
Magazine Littéraire* devoted to Faulkner.

apart from the cases when my reticence obeyed an objective situation of inferiority, my sudden, dizzy nearness to the big names of the day made me soon understand that, with the exception of singular examples of communication, as with Genet, the role of peeping tom bored me and was at odds with the inclinations and preferences of my real character.

Thus, when on 1 August 1959, Monique, Florence Malraux, and I crossed paths with Hemingway in the bullring in Málaga, at a bullfight with Diego Puerta, Manolo Segura, and Gregorio Sánchez, I gave a lukewarm welcome to their decision, especially that of Monique, romantically in love with Spain as a result of her youthful reading of *Death in the Afternoon*, to accost the writer as he left the arena; I just followed them on an adventure, the ramifications of which would spread, as in a serial story, to a family dinner with an unpredictable ending on one of my stays in New York as a visiting professor, a number of years after the novelist's suicide.

You were in a middle row and he was a quarter of the ring away at the most visible point of the front row, in his shirt-sleeves and wearing a peaked cap to ward off the sun. Forgetting past rancors, the press had given wide publicity to his presence and spectators recognized him, *toreros* dedicated their performance to him, and to the applause of onlookers he drank, arm held high, a jet of wine from a leather bag someone had handed him. He was following Ordóñez in his *mano a mano* with Dominguín around the bullrings of the Peninsula: the period described in *The Dangerous Summer*.

You lost sight of him at the end of the fight, but Monique would not give up: you found him in the bar of the city's best hotel. You headed without haste to the now defunct Miramar and asked after him. Tell him André Malraux's daughter wants to see him. The ploy bore immediate fruit: within a few minutes, the writer appeared in the lobby and gave you a warm welcome. He talked in a strange mixture of English, French, and Spanish and introduced you to his retinue: from the old acquaintance from Pamplona portrayed in *Fiesta* to the wife of a degenerate and alcoholic Peruvian millionaire. He spoke to Florence about her father and the civil war as if wanting to justify his return to the country. It was a pleasant evening that ended in bear hugs. You don't remember now if Valerie Danby-Smith was among those present.

The day after, Hemingway departed to meet up with Ordóñez and you had to return to Paris, now that the holidays were over. However, the writer noted down your address and promised to tell you if he was going to France. At the end of September, he kept his word, forewarned Monique of his visit to the Midi and generously sent three train tickets to Nîmes. You had the opportunity to see him there for a couple of days totally living up to his reputation, surrounded by his faithful followers—Ordóñez, Domingo Dominguín, Valerie, the Franco-Peruvian millionairess: discussing bulls and joking about Shakespeare with Ordóñez, drinking nonstop from midmorning an exquisite Tavel rosé. His affectionate, almost father-daughter relationship with Valerie channeled his dissipated energy: although no conventional beauty, Valerie was a very young, subtly delightful Irish woman who, months earlier, had gone to interview him in his hotel and had accompanied him on his travels ever since. The novelist and storywriter you admired in your youth had become a living monument to himself: that Papa Hemingway that anyone on the make could treat familiarly and whose literary rigor and moral alertness had shipwrecked in a sea of publicity and self-interested flattery.

While you journeyed to Spain with Dominguín and Ordóñez, Monique and Florence would see him again on the Auteuil racecourse, and in his Parisian lair at the Ritz. Monique received several letters that winter from the United States written in his most idiosyncratic trilingual patter: Hemingway seemed depressed and touched at length in one of them on the question of suicide. After a year's silence, during which one or two letters from Monique met with no response, you heard on the radio the news of the shot with which he killed himself on 2 July 1961, just after you had driven across the Franco-Spanish frontier, on your way to Torrentbó.

Over the next ten years you had indirect news of Valerie: the unexpected marriage to Brendan Behan, his alcoholic death agony, her widowhood. In 1974, after an article on *Conde Julián* appeared in the *New York Times*, the newspaper sent you a letter in which she affectionately described past meetings and gave you her address and telephone number. You got in contact with her and she invited you to dinner. On the agreed night, you reached the door to her apartment building only to realize that you knew neither the number nor letter of her apartment. In the conversation she mentioned that she had remarried, but you did not know what the hell her husband's surname was. You looked in vain for a Danby-Smith on the list by the entry phone: there wasn't one. When you were just about to go call her from a telephone booth, you spotted on the list the existence of a Hemingway: an odd coincidence or had she been legally adopted by the writer before his suicide? You rang the bell: her voice answered. Moments later you were in the small apartment where Valerie and her two sons welcomed you. The elder was called Brendan and was her first husband's. The second, a tiny lad, seemed to belong to the other one, whose absence she apologized for: Gregory finished his consultancy very late and would perhaps arrive after dinner. During the meal you recalled friends held in common, yet the mysterious husband made no appearance. When he finally came and you were introduced, you began to put two and two together and establish the real nature of the situation: one of the sons from Hemingway's second or third marriage was a doctor and was in fact named Gregory. As the plot unraveled and you mentally reconstructed Valerie's extraordinary life story, her husband poured himself a straight glass of whiskey, showed you the manuscript of a book that, he said, he had just written about his father, separated out twenty or so pages and handed them over to you. You settled down in an armchair and, while he downed glass after glass until he had emptied the bottle, you skimmed over, first in surprise, then with unease, finally, with fascination, some sections where, according to your host, Hemingway had boasted to him that he had precipitated his mother's death by a brutal telephone call to the hospital where she was convalescing from a serious heart attack: *I got her*, or words to that effect. Gregory seemed to be waiting anxiously for your verdict and, trapped in that unforeseen situation, you felt a curious impression of unreality thicken: was this scene real or was it a dream? You felt him staring at you, you listened to him muttering about the suicide. Valerie, his wife, remained impassive: she cleared away the plates, talked lovingly to her children. You don't know what you managed to say to Gregory about the manuscript, nor can you remember how you bid farewell to the couple. You can see yourself back in the street, returned to the nocturnal bustle of the city, about to be swallowed up by the powerful jaws of a subway station, threading together the absurd chain of events that had led you there from a chance encounter in the Málaga bullring.

REGRETTABLY, IN THE *literary circles you know best,
writers have a very marked tendency to take themselves
more seriously than their own work: as you said years ago in* Conde Julián, *genius
is confused with appearance and appearance is the key to genius: the greater the
genius, the greater the appearance; the greater the appearance, the greater the genius: since then the situation has worsened both in and outside Spain: while the
number of clowns proliferates, the number of authors who take their work seriously, instead of lovingly putting on airs, seems to be in steady decline.*

*The writer's physical presence obstructs a proper evaluation of his work by in-
troducing factors outside specific literary criteria: the living author, if he is a smart
operator, throws dust in the eyes of those who are looking at him and seeks positions
of fame and prestige far beyond his real merits: consequently, when one of these
live wires dies he seems to deflate, as you deflated yourself, and falls rapidly into
oblivion: having been exalted to excess, he is now brought down with excessive dis-
regard: only the unfashionable never goes out of fashion: as the surrealists said, any
triumphant idea or person is fatally on the road to ruin.*

*The attacks directed at a writer are very often the proof that his work exists, that
it wounds the moral or aesthetic convictions of the reader-critic and, subsequently,
they provoke his reaction: in short, they enter a dynamic relationship with him:
you yourself see them usually as a paying of respects and, fortunately, there is no
lack of professional swashbucklers: an innovative work stirs up a defensive response from those who feel threatened or under attack from its power or novelty:
the phenomenon is as real today as in the day of Góngora.*

*The novel that avoids the easy well-trodden paths inevitably creates a tension,
collides against the unformulated expectations of readers: the latter are suddenly*

faced with a code they are not used to, and this code poses a challenge: if that is accepted and the reader penetrates the meaning of the new artistic system, the victorious hand-to-hand combat with the text is itself the prize: the reader's active enjoyment.

If your books were one day welcomed with unanimous praise, that would show they had become harmless, facile, and anodyne, very quickly they would have lost their power to repel and their vitality.

In general terms, writers divide into two classes: those who conceive of literature as a career and those who don't: the first can be easily recognized from their behavior, which follows a strategy of advancement halfway between Macchiavelli and von Clausewitz: they look for glory and jobs, praise those who praise them, read those who read them, practice a barter form of economy, are professional congress attenders and introducers, they serve all governments, climb doggedly to the peaks of the Establishment.

For your part, rightly or wrongly, you believe that the author's labor demands in a free, permissive society do not concern you: you have defended and are ready to uphold the economic and union rights of any trade or job with the exception of that of writers and artists: the activity of the latter is, in your opinion, the result of a vocation that is at once a state of grace and damnation itself: if you are a writer because you cannot be anything else, writing is an essential part of your life, as might be, for example, your family background, your native tongue, your sexual orientation: to professionalize yourself as a writer would be for you as incongruous and ridiculous as doing so because you are male, expatriate, bisexual, or morally a gypsy.

You do not propose to live from your pen: your position in this respect is the exact opposite of the career writers: you do not write to earn a living, but earn a living in order to write: from nourishment, literature is transmuted into an obsessive vice: an incurable form of addiction: however, as it has recently provided you with a decent income, your literary addiction is today self-sufficient and, thanks to the distribution of your books, you have moved from the category of a mere addict to that of peddler or dealer.

T HE ATTENTION PAID to Spain by French publishers has almost always been mean, out-of-focus, and intermittent. Apart from the special case of García Lorca, glorified *ab initio* by the publication of his complete works, neither the most representative authors of the 1898 Generation nor of successive pre- and postwar generations were given even average exposure in the 1950s, nor were they the object of selective, accurate translation. If critics and readers in the neighboring country are still unaware in general of a novel of the stature of *La regenta*, why should one be surprised that more than a quarter of a century ago, they only knew a handful of works, already sometimes out of print and unobtainable, by Baroja, Unamuno, Machado, Valle-Inclán, and Ortega? I can remember how when the first of these died, just after my arrival, I was telephoned by several newspapers and literary magazines asking after "that Spanish novelist whose funeral Hemingway attended." Later on, when Buñuel's film *Nazarín* received its première, a refined Gallic reviewer would spawn an ineffable paragraph graciously granting Galdós Mexican nationality. This traditional contempt for or lack of interest in what is written beyond the Pyrenees—so similar to our own in relation to Portugal and the Arab world—had been reinforced by the fairly widespread conviction that Spanish culture had died with the war. Francoism had converted Spain into a barren waste; no fruit, however wizened, could spring up there. The writers in exile—novelists like Barea and Sender, poets like Alberti and Guillén—attracted a small sympathetic audience beyond the circles of Hispanists but, in spite of the propaganda activity of the Communist Parties on behalf of their members, martyrs, or sympathizers—from Antonio Machado to Miguel Hernández—the mental barrier erected around the Peninsula stood its ground:

Max Aub was translated only in the last years of his life, and when Cernuda died, not even the poetry magazines gave him an obituary.

When I began to read books for Mascolo, Gallimard's only permanent reader of Spanish was Roger Caillois, the editor of the series *La croix du Sud*, devoted to South American narrative. As a refugee in Buenos Aires, like Gombrowicz, during the Nazi occupation, Caillois had connected with the group around the magazine *Sur* and had the honor of introducing Borges's work into France. In contrast, his knowledge of modern Spanish literature was vague and behind the times; as he himself admitted to me, he had no recent serious information on the slow resurgence of letters in the Peninsula. Maurice-Edgard Coindreau's discovery of the new writers encouraged Claude Gallimard to consult with me on the matter and, in agreement with Coindreau, we drew up a list of works that were in our opinion worth translating. Over a decade, they published more than twenty novels of unequal value, representative of the literary panorama within Spain. Although, as I shall later examine, ideology and personal friendship influenced the choice, the latter also took Coindreau's tastes into account, and if anything it suffered from being too easygoing: not all the authors included reached an acceptable level, but certainly the country had nothing else to offer. The only significant regrettable absence from the picture is that of Martín-Santos: his novel reached me late and, when I read it, it had already been contracted by le Seuil. The translated works almost all received favorable comments in the press; however, with two or three exceptions, they all failed commercially. When Monique resigned from her post and I accompanied her to Saint-Tropez, Gallimard's interest in the matter declined. Quite rightly, the new readership was turning toward the growing Latin American boom, and although I intervened sporadically in favor of authors who would soon be famous, like Carlos Fuentes or Cabrera Infante, and contributed to the publication of Valle-Inclán, Cernuda, Max Aub, and Mercè Rodoreda, my opinion ceased to be decisive. The atmosphere at the publishers had changed in my absence and even though I continued my links there for some years, the eclipse of some well-known faces and meddling by the woman who was Cortázar's companion made me feel vaguely distanced and detached from my old haunt. Long before my friendship with Sarduy brought me to the literary haven of le Seuil, visits to the publishing house where I met Monique and Genet, and which so influenced an important stage in my life, began to seem forced and uncomfortable: prisoner of an image prior to my change of skin, I was forced to assume a role there that was no longer mine. Rid of this double or "inopportune guest," I would realize to my relief, when *Juan sin tierra* was rejected, that, for good or for evil, I had definitively ceased to belong to that world.

Although your function as a consultant was more than modest, the importance attributed to it by the Francoist press when they nicknamed you the customs officer, and the relations you wove at the time with those in charge of the cultural pages of various left-wing newspapers and magazines, finally did grant you, willy-nilly, a small patch of power. While you had plenty of scope to select works for translation in line with your literary tastes, political sentiments, and personal affinities, the fact that you could rely on good friends on *Le Monde, Les Temps Modernes,* or *Les Lettres Françaises,* and that you could make yourself at home in the offices of *France-Observateur* and *L'Express,* placed you in the advantageous position, so common in literary circles, whatever the epoch or climate, from which to obtain reviews and critical articles based less on the value of the work than on godfatherly influence and exchange of services. The compliments that today greet *urbi et orbi* the offspring or progeny of those with some sort of influence, or those from whom the flatterer expects a favor, bring a smile to all who, voluntarily or not, put themselves outside the system and don't aspire to climb the ladder. Nevertheless, in the first phases of your life, you took them at face value, at the risk of changing yourself by this attraction into one of those self-sufficient barrels brimming at the edge, always ready to bring their light from under the bushel. As the years passed, only self-criticism and experience would show you that, on Parnassus, one thing is what people think, another what they say, quite another what they write and publish. There is an enormous distance between these limits, and there are authors whom nobody admires in their thoughts and very few in what they say, yet in the press and media they are literally covered in flowers. Others, on the contrary, like Cernuda up to his death, are secretly admired, but nobody or almost nobody expresses this admiration in writing. As you will later be amused to conclude, a work's real impact, whether it is Clarín's or Américo Castro's, is measured by the attacks—the more vicious, the more personalized they are—that the author arouses in his life and, in a more underhand, hypocritical fashion, by the resounding silence of the professional eulogists and adulators.

The old invigorating air of Spain!

As the consultant to Gallimard on the list of Spanish novels included in the publisher's catalogue, the task often befell me of guiding their authors' steps through the undergrowth, tracks, and byways of the indigenous cultural jungle: interviews, press conferences, encounters with Hispanists, and the other usual ways of getting publicity. My role was reduced to telephoning journalists and critics who might eventually be interested, arranging a meeting with my fellow countrymen, and translating the questions and answers if, as often happened, they knew no French.

In the spring of 1958, to coincide with the launching of *La colmena*, we had a visit from the author. Camilo José Cela already belonged to the pantheon of Spanish literature; the creator of such works as *Pascual Duarte* and *Viaje a la Alcarria* merited my esteem, and his entry into Spain's Royal Academy had conferred upon him, as he crossed the threshold of maturity, the support and respect of official circles. For two or three days I introduced him to the main editors at the publishers, escorted him to interviews arranged by the press service, acted as a transmission shaft for self-important or awe-inspiring specialists and fervent groups of admirers. After a while he modestly, quite plainly, told me of his great desire to meet Sartre.

I confess that his request surprised me—however I wracked my brain, I could not imagine what might be the link or point of contact between the two men—but I yielded to his friendly insistence and telephoned the philosopher's secretary. The latter gave us an appointment a few days later in Sartre's old home on the corner of the rue Bonaparte and the place Saint-

Germain-des-Prés, which he would later be forced to abandon by the threats and attacks of the thugs and crusaders of *L'Algérie Française*. I gave Cela the message and my colleague asked me rather uncomfortably if he could take Sartre a bottle of cognac. I thought that it was a present and agreed, adding, if I remember rightly, that the author of *La nausée* was following an alcohol-free diet on account of his arterial hypertension. Oh, it's not for him to drink, Cela explained: I want him to sign it; when Hemingway was in Spain, he also signed it for me. I told him that that type of gesture in no way fitted Sartre's style and that he had better let the bottle rest in peace. Cela demurred to my arguments and didn't mention the matter again. Some time passed and, although I still did not understand the motive behind the interview, I was telephoned by a compatriot whose name I have forgotten. Mr. Cela, he said, has asked me to contact you in order to arrange for me to take some photos of his meeting with Sartre. I was bowled over and replied curtly that there was to be a meeting of the two writers, but that he had not been invited to attend: knowing as I did Sartre's suspicious attitude toward journalists, I did not want to see myself implicated in an episode that would upset him and that he would hold me responsible for.

Without these decorative frieses and architraves, the would-be tête-à-tête of the great turned out to be a stale limp affair. I accompanied Cela and our common friend Eugenio Suárez to the flat and translated as best I could an exemplary dialogue of the deaf, with its dodges, feints, and blows on target. At the start, Sartre seemed interested in finding out about the real position of the writer under Franco, the nature of his literary and political problems, his struggle against censorship, but his conversation partner deflected these issues with jokes and anecdotes, some of which were humorous in Spanish but inevitably lost their spark in translation, although I strove to catch the humor in French. After several laborious exercises in "sonorous inanity," Sartre hinted that the interview was at an end and we said goodbye to him. He always found Cela's reasons for seeking this exchange rather mysterious. Aware of Sansueña and its rites, I was not amazed by the episode: the tribal remnants in the literary world, evoked so lucidly by Cernuda in his poem on Dámaso Alonso, are an integral part of our folklore, and anyone who, out of idiosyncrasy or temperament, does not wear them for the gallery would appear antipathetic and sulky in the eyes of its televiewing citizens—a rare specimen from a solitary, unsociable subspecies, probably on the path to extinction.

The same motives that nourished my presumption as *chef de file* of the new Spanish generation contributed in a pettier way to the growth of my *cacique* inclinations under the disguise of an ideological, political cause. Even though my reader's reports for Gallimard were usually fair-minded and took the literary value of the works into consideration, I undoubtedly showed greater indulgence toward the writers of my generation who were Party members or fellow travelers than toward those who were on the right. That is to a certain extent normal, and I do not reproach myself. But my zeal as the guardian of Spanish anti-Francoist orthodoxy displayed, if not at the publishers, in the publications and media where I had influence now seems, of course with hindsight, regrettable and dubious.

I remember how Arrabal, furiously assailed at the time by Benigno and my friends in the Party, had managed to get to Sartre, through Nadeau, one of his first plays, which was to appear in their magazine with an introduction by the philosopher. The news made me really bad-tempered, as if an intruder had invaded my territory and his talent might overshadow my own; alongside my commentary, it similarly scandalized my companions in struggle. Following their advice, I went very democratically to Simone de Beauvoir to prevent the "outrage": Arrabal, I told her, was a reactionary idealist and repudiated our struggle; if Sartre promoted him, that would confuse many people and would, in any case, damage the anti-Francoist cause. As a result, Sartre did not write the prologue and my friends and I unblushingly savored our mean victory. Only when I cast off, among other things, the feeling of sordid rivalry of those who conceive of literature as a dogfight and the aftertaste of the arbitrary Manichaeism of the Spanish media, did I realize my ephemeral but sad role as a censor. As I tried to express in *Señas de iden-tidad*, the ideological and cultural police were a perfect match for the peculiar code of the tribe. Five centuries of inquisition and denunciation had shaped the structure of the psyche and, to a greater or lesser extent, the inquisitor, informer, and spy had insidiously infiltrated everyone's mind. The institution forged by the New State in the midst of the civil war would thus engender a kind of cancerous growth, courts issuing sentences under different signs. I was ashamed to discover later that the difference between the paid censors and those of us who acted spontaneously was a mere question of detail.

A s you never *tire of stating, the only moral imperative for the writer, against which there is no recourse, is to return to the literary-linguistic community to which he belongs a fresh, personal style of writing different from what previously existed and which he inherited when setting out on his task: to work on what is given, to follow accepted models is to be condemned to impoverished insignificance, however much applause the writer gets from the public: the work of whoever does not innovate might as well not exist, for its disappearance would not affect the development of his culture at all.*

The giving of narrative or poetic form to the general ideas of the time—freedom, justice, progress, racial and sexual equality, etc.—lacks artistic interest if the author, as he does so, does not simultaneously set them a trap, charge them with gunpowder or dynamite: all ideas, even the most respectable ones, are double-edged, and a writer who ignores this works on a photograph of reality rather than on reality.

The enterprise of a novelist, as conceived by you, is an adventure: to say what has yet not been said; explore the potentialities of language; launch oneself into the conquest of new areas of expression, of those few meters of land that, as Carlos Fuentes said, the Dutch reclaim patiently from the sea: the writing of a novel is a leap into the unknown: to land in a place unsuspected by the writer when he flings himself into the void without safety net or parachute; when a technique has been mastered or you have reached the end of an experiment, they must be abandoned for the search for what is still unknown: in the field of art and literature, a hundred birds in the hand are worth less than the one that—to our torture and delight— continues flying, inspired, mobile, light-winged.

Literature extends the field of our vision and experience, is opposed to all that

reduces or anaesthetizes our perceptive potential, conditions us culturally, ideo-
logically, and sexually, brainwashes us and dulls our senses: the counterdiscourse
against discourse: against the inevitable incorporation of what is new and repel-
lent, the parody of what has become conventionalized or respected with sheepish
deference: like Bouvard and Pécuchet, literature draws up an inventory of the
commonplaces of the day and mockingly revivifies the universal map of idiocy.

O
UR ASSOCIATION AS a couple with literary life—
conversations, meetings, dinners, etc.—embraces
the period between my arrival on the rue Poissonnière and our move to the
Midi at the end of 1964. From the diagnosis of Monique's mother's cancer to
the cannibalistic digestion of her death, a reading of the diary in which Monique briefly noted the days' events reveals a rapid succession of professional
or social dates with publishers, intellectuals, and journalists, as if the drama
and internal pain she was suffering had forced her to seek refuge in a whirlwind of lunches and receptions. This agitation, covering up the real anguish
of a death agony lived like a process of emotional catharsis, described with
restraint in *Une Drôle de voix*, coincided with a personal crisis within myself
and in my links with her and with an unsettling sense of alienation and detachment in respect to our milieu: a furtive awareness of being an impostor,
a result of not matching up to the role you were playing; the tedium of nighttime living, only tolerable thanks to the use and abuse of alcohol. My recent
political disappointments and the bitter certainty that I had created a work
that had perhaps satisfied my civic responsibilities but fell totally outside that
dense, purifying, initiatory zone forged by literature was now joined by the
sudden realization of my homosexuality and the distressing clandestine nature of relationships, which I will describe later. The combined essence of all
this could be summed up in one word: weariness. Weariness with the bustle
of literary publishing, political militancy, functional writing, my ambiguous
image and usurped respectability. So I felt more and more sharply and
clearly the need to concentrate my physical, intellectual, and emotional energies in those areas I deemed vital and to throw all else overboard.

In a passage in the last volume of her memoirs, Simone de Beauvoir mentions the fact that a dinner with Sartre on the rue Poissonnière restored their enthusiasm for parties. Two years later, these would be regular events throughout Monique's distressed countdown. I can remember one when, overwhelmed by the weight of the tensions of my incipient schizophrenia, I crept out for some fresh air, to the great annoyance of our guests: French and American publishers, the Semprúns, and Simone Signoret had talked or danced into the early hours and, unable to assume the host's mantle, I kept a rude but eagle eye on the clock, as I waited for the moment of liberation when I could stretch out in bed. However it was, our crowded dinner parties began to try my nerves with sometimes lasting effects: my portentous ability to absent myself, by putting a million miles between me and everyone else, developed at that time and would sharpen over the years till it became part of my character and hardened my thick skin. It probably began as a defense against others' interfering in my deepest reality, and it allowed me to maintain an albeit flawed façade of correct social behavior, without being torn from the secret pull of the binomial that ruled my life. Fleeting, futile words, subdued smiles, convoluted discussions: "reality" was only the cortex that could be destroyed in a moment by a fertile, incandescent metaphor or the imaginary representation of a body. The stunning, palpable universe evoked lit up the nocturnal opaqueness of the ritual—like a silent, brilliant flash of sheet lightning. Only the woven texture of literature could create that sudden burst of splendor which illuminated the world. When you read Góngora's *Soledades*—the fierce, seering glimpse of those fighters "restrained by mutual knots / like hard elms entwined by vines"—the ophidian lasciviousness of the phrase and copulation of word-made-flesh revealed to me the transmutation of Góngora's daily anguish in the still of his poetry: his generative ability to harness, in polysemic harmony, sexuality and writing.

Reduced to a gradually residual presence—did my friends at the time notice the radical nature of the change? my mental flights in midconversation, the signs of a hardly hidden impatience at the prolonging of an evening, the evasive expression on my absentminded or sealed face? Something of my state of mind must have filtered through, since the distancing and abandon were soon reciprocal. In autumn 1964 the rue Poissonnière dinner parties became less frequent, and when we returned after eighteen months away, some of the regulars had forgotten them entirely: the nucleus of friends was significantly reduced without the magnet of influence in publishing. From then on, in the company of Monique and a few others, I would rake the forbidden ground for all that had remained wild and implicit.

The terrain I was slowly penetrating demanded complete rejection of all that did not connect with it. The alienation was further accelerated by an awareness of pathetically wasting time on things that were of no interest and on people who were of no importance to me. My new conception of literature demanded absolute surrender, the total erasing of my previous universe. A change of life, a change of writing. The creative pride developed while you composed *Conde Julián* would darken henceforth the glow of your conceit. As I would later see formulated in Flaubert, I would not from then on be sufficiently modest to be flattered by rewards or fame.

Monique's decision to break with Gallimard, Paris, and our sociability fell on me like an April shower. Although it created difficulties for the secret bond tying me to Mohamed, it enabled me to escape from a stifling atmosphere where day after day my alienation intensified. Travel, isolation, a new departure in literature and life were worth more than Paris and all its glory. Monique's grief at her mother's death fitted in with my desire to move well away. United in our sadness and need for a change of scene as we had not been for some time, we packed our bags with almost ecstatic feelings of relief for the pacific backdrop of provincial existence in Saint-Tropez.

Sometimes when she left her Gallimard office, Monique and I would meet alone or with others involved in her work, in the comfortable, quiet underground bar of the neighboring Pont Royal Hotel. The design of the place, the sensitive distribution of luxurious, comfortable armchairs, and the dimmed lighting created an intimate, secluded atmosphere, suitable for whispered confidences and exchanges. The clientele was mainly intellectual, with the regulars keeping at a respectful distance from each other, each group to its own corner or den. I had often seen him there, dressed with distinguished simplicity—a polo-necked jersey and English tweed jacket—

and the jagged tufts of hair and unmistakable face that appear in the rare photos of him. He used to sit a long way from the bar and the stairs, at the other end of the small lounge, with a rather younger woman or some translator. His shyness, reserve, evident fear of interference from others established around him a kind of inviolable sacred space, like the one opened up in the street by a blind man's white cane. The impossibility of invading it and stamping like some simpleton on the frontier of his invulnerable modesty turned the mere thought of approaching him into a sacrilegious act. The writer and his female friend conversed isolated in their transparent bubble. Although I knew and admired his work, I respected, like everybody else, the integrity of his territory. It was Samuel Beckett.

I thought of Beckett, precisely of Beckett, in my room at the Free Havana Hotel the day I was visited by another colleague. The poet Yevgeny Yevtushenko had been living there for some time in the room adjacent to mine: he had fallen into relative semidisgrace through some whim of Khrushchev and had been sent to Cuba to a kind of gilded exile, and he awaited impatiently, champing at the bit, for the moment to make peace with his leader and once more lay his prolific muse at the service of the official creed. Fond of notoriety and flattering attention, he was hard pressed to tolerate his stay in a place where his work and person were unknown. Informed by friends on the daily paper *Revolución* that I was a neighbor, he appeared at my bedroom door one night, very tall, fair-haired, with childish features, and tiny blue eyes that after a few minutes' examination revealed a curious similarity with those bifocal lenses, made for seeing far and near: naively Siberian above and cunning and mischievous below, or perhaps vice versa. Yevtushenko spoke in broken English and Spanish, and in his picturesque gabble explained to me that our respective fame predestined us to earthly or sempiternal friendship. He wrote, so he told me, dozens of poems in the solitude of his room, deprived of the comforting presence of an audience, the deference of his admirers, the din of applause: the ozone that allowed him to breathe. After various pauses and the odd linguistic quid pro quo, he suddenly disappeared into his room to reappear with a bundle of sheets of paper, the first fruits of his poetic impulse. He said he was going to read them to me; I firmly rejected his offer: I understood not a word of Russian. No matter, he retorted, you look, you listen. He adopted the theatrical pose of a bolero bard: it was a grotesque scene that I quickly cut short. I explained how I didn't have an ear for other languages and how I hated recitals ever since I had seen Berta Singerman; when his poems were translated into Spanish, I would be tremendously interested in reading them. Visibly upset, the poet made a change of plan: he wanted to go with me to some dance hall and drink a few iced daiquiris. I cannot remember exactly whether we went first to the Red Saloon at the Capri Hotel or directly went into a noisy bar, where he was apparently a regular, as he was immediately accosted by a beautiful mulatto and began to entertain me with an energetic, almost acrobatic exhibition of the twist lit up by the swirling glare of a rainbow strobe. I left him engrossed in the contemplation of his own spectacle and made my exit. But the taiga minstrel was stubborn and would not take a hint. Days later he returned to my room, this time poemless, and looked at me with the wan gaze of an orphan child: You don't admire me, why not? I must have smiled as I told him that you could not have admiration by decree. If you understood my poetry, he assured me, you would admire me. Unfortunately for him, that was not so, and my thick Hispanic skin tortured and filled him with despair.

When we left Cuba, he to the official rallying cry of his anti-Chinese muse in the pages of *Izvestia* or *Pravda* and I to a much more obscure life in Paris, I thought we would not meet again. However, on 8 February 1963, during the terminal stage of Monique's mother's cancer, we had a telephone call from our friend K. S. Karol, at the time on the editorial board of *L'Express*, headed by Jean Daniel. Yevtushenko was in Paris and wanted to see me. In our state of mind at the time, the idea of a nighttime spree with him seemed most opportune; it would momentarily distract Monique from her anguish and we could enjoy the man's grandiloquence. I am still unaware of the reasons for his second, and visibly unfruitful encounter with me: as I later discovered through the indiscretions of another journalist, the bard's greatest aspiration—intoxicated by the same provincial, servile spirit that impelled his colleague and rival Voznesensky to write poems to the glory of

Jacqueline Kennedy—then centered on rubbing shoulders with De Gaulle and Brigitte Bardot.

Whatever the motives behind his friendly persistence, we went with K. S. Karol to meet him at the Louvre Hotel and, escorted by a female functionary from the Soviet Embassy, we went as he desired to a show at the Crazy Horse. The striptease acts were ingenious and attractive: at one moment of the performance there was an amusing parody of a kind of military parade. Some girls in combat jackets, belts, and boots comically took the stage and Rouget de Lisle's popular tunes were given a burlesque airing. Unexpectedly, to everyone's amazement, the poet got up, stood to attention as stiff as a brush, to the full length of his undeniably Siberian one meter ninety, in a laudable demonstration of respect for the sacrosanct national anthem. People mumbled, smiled, and coughed: What was behind that attack of patriotism? Perhaps it was part of the show? The rest of the evening was less colorful and although, as a result of Monique's bad advice, it ended hours later, much to the bard's dismay, with brazen transvestites at the Carrousel, the image of Yevtushenko doing his Eiffel Tower act while the smiling girls stripped to the tune of the *Marseillaise* attains that degree of exemplary representativeness when anecdotal and general combine to sum up the spectacular romantic conception of the demiurge poet complete with the slippers of Empedocles. Don Yevgeny or Beckett, don Camilo or Cernuda, don Ernesto or Lezama: authenticity and myth, critical passion and egotism, moral knowledge and emblematic projection. Two opposing conceptions of literature and life: the sober acceptance of both or the theatrical, clownish accoutrements of the seer on the flies of kitsch and expansive word-weariness.

Monique recounted this anecdote to you.

On her return from Corfu, she was waiting in the sun of Athens airport for the plane that was going to take her to Paris. The loudspeakers announced the arrival of the Air France flight, and as she was absentmindedly looking at the runway and the preparations of the staff around the recently becalmed machine, she suddenly noticed a round of frenetic activity. A dozen journalists and photographers ran to the steps and crowded around the bottom waiting for a celebrity. The passengers slowly emerged from the doorway and, soon, she spotted the unmistakable silhouette of the Sartre–Simone de Beauvoir couple. The writers walked down the steps onto the runway and walked through the hungry pack of paparazzi without anyone noticing their presence or paying them any attention. Seconds later, a kiss-throwing, hat-waving Eddie Constantine would be the target of an ecstatic welcome and, for someone witnessing the scene and its different actors, one really difficult to forget.

My Lailat-ul-Qadr fell one 8 October, perhaps in the sacred month of Ramadan, on the night I first went to the place where I now write these lines and met both Monique and Genet, two people who in different ways decisively influenced my life, an encounter like a new dawn. I owe my later development mainly to them, to their efforts to drag me from the suffocating narrowness of my milieu. Genet's appearances and eclipses over two decades showed me a new moral territory: after the closed confines of the bourgeois world of the Barcelona district of Bonanova, with its family ghosts and emotional devastation, I will gradually, cautiously penetrate, led by their hand, that fertile space, stripped of notions of country, state, doctrine, or respectability, of my medina-commonland in la Bonne Nouvelle.

CHAPTER III

The Poet's Territory

A FEW WEEKS before revising these pages, I had on one day two or three telephone calls from a man with a vaguely foreign accent who wanted urgently to talk to Monique. When she returned home and took the phone, the stranger anxiously besieged her with questions about Genet. Where was he? Had something happened to him? Who could get him his address? Monique explained how we had had little news of him for some time and that only indirectly: all she could advise was to write to his publishers. But her interlocutor seemed upset and would not give up. Neither he nor his wife understood what had happened: the day before, Genet had lunched with them and asked them to telephone him without fail the day after; however, in the hotel where he was staying they said he had paid his bill and left without leaving a message. It was impossible he had forgotten his date with them; perhaps he had suffered some upset; perhaps . . .

The man's sad disarray was nothing new to us: it reproduced a Genetian situation that we had known for decades. After living with this man and his wife for a few days or weeks, granting them the fortuitous gift of his presence, Genet had suddenly disappeared from their lives, from the friendly haven where he had camped down and fleetingly felt at ease. Suddenly abandoned for no apparent reason, deprived of his exuberance and state of grace, this stranger was unable to comprehend that the writer's momentary wellbeing, the impression that he was being integrated into the heart of a family, had probably been the cause of his flight and exile. His name and his wife's would thus be added to the long list of those seduced by Genet's personality and intelligence, then brutally abandoned by the side of a path that upped and downed, turned sharply, forked and changed direction. Bewildered and incredulous, he would gradually, bitterly realize that Genet had ceased to exist for them except in the hypothetical case that in the future he might have recourse to their services or find himself forced to ask a favor of them.

It was 8 October 1955 precisely. Monique Lange, whom I had met a few days before in the entrance to Gallimard, had invited me to have supper in her flat on the rue Poissonnière, adding at once, fearing, as she later confessed to me, that her warm and beautiful smile would not be sufficient motive for me to accept her hospitality: "Jean Genet is coming as well. Do you know him?"*

Yes, I knew him from his books or, rather, the last of his books published at the time, *Journal du voleur*, which a friend had lent me two years before on my first brief stay in Paris. The reading of that book had an enormous moral and literary effect on me. The author's strange, personal, fascinating style accompanied an introduction to a world totally unknown to me; something I had sensed darkly from adolescence but that my upbringing and prejudices had prevented me from verifying. I can remember the person who gave me the grubby copy of the work once pointing out an individual in his thirties, looking defiant and insolent, heading for the café terrace exactly opposite ours—it was called and I think it's still called La Pérgola, next to the Mabillon métro station—and muttering knowingly: "That's Genet's friend." Days later, when I returned the book, he asked me whether I had masturbated as I read it. I said I hadn't, and he looked taken aback, a mixture of disappointment and incredulity. He said, "I did dozens of times. Every time I read it, I jerk myself off."

I have never liked this kind of confidence and I cut short the conversation. As Genet told me years afterwards, he found nothing more irritating than the inopportune homage to the pornographic virtues of his work: he gave no credit to the opinion of homosexuals and appreciated only the praise of those outside the ghetto described by him, who took his novels for what they

*See *Forbidden Territory*, pages 220–21.

were, that is, an autonomous world, a language, a voice. As for the so-called friend singled out by my initiator into the novels, it must have been Java or René, considering the date. "But neither of them used to go around Saint-Germain-des-Prés," Genet observed when I mentioned the incident to him, "both of them were pimping in Montmartre or robbing queers in lavatories or in the Bois de Boulogne."

Ten days after our first encounter on the rue Poissonnière, I went with Monique to see him. Genet was ill from something or other, and she took him a bag of food and medicine. We climbed up to a small studio on the rue Pasquier, where he welcomed us from his bed. Other visitors soon arrived: Madeleine Chapsal and Jean Cau, then secretary to Sartre and later the faithful spokesman for the fears and phobias of the right.

The daily papers carried more and more disturbing stories of the repression in Algeria, and Genet had the idea of celebrating in his way the forthcoming All Saints' Day. He had prepared a statement addressed to those visiting the graves of their loved ones, to be handed out at the cemetery gate. Genet looked for his glasses on the bedside table, stuck them on, and with that inimitable voice—grave, serious, full of intense, restrained anger—read the reproachful statement, which, with great poetic violence, urged the recipients to think of the other dead, those who fell daily, mown down by the criminal bullets of *their* army and *their* police: old people; children; women; humble, illiterate peasants . . .

I was moved by the text, but Jean Cau immediately poured out a bucket of cold water: the tone is too aggressive, he said, and its effect would be counterproductive. He then proposed drawing up another in more measured, practical language, the usual sort for that kind of manifesto. While he discussed the phrasing with the visitors now packing into the studio, I noticed that Genet seemed completely to lose interest in the conversation, as if the action planned to fit the political line of a respectful, always defensive opposition did not concern him.

The text was never given out and, as Monique wrote me in Barcelona, where I returned a few days afterwards, Genet's proposed act of poetic agitation was never realized.

A year went by. Monique regularly informed me of her contacts with the poet and meanwhile I read all of his work in the last months of my military service. When that was over, I returned to Paris with Monique and settled down with her on the rue Poissonnière.

Genet dropped in without warning—Monique's flat was a kind of canteen for him—and although I wanted to talk to him about his writing, I soon noticed that he was appalled by the prospect. Used to the preening vanity of the Hispanic literati, I was surprised by his attitude. Genet imposed an unbridgeable distance between himself and his work, avoided like the plague those who admired it for the right or wrong reasons, and assumed the aloof detachment of a Rimbaud trafficking on the desolate steppes of Harar. When he later asked for my opinion, he did so with modest self-restraint, without the customary layers of aggression and irony with which he defended himself against untimely veneration or inquisitiveness.

Among those who similarly turned up from time to time was René, whom Monique had known from the period when he saw a lot of the poet and was seeking a modus vivendi by stealing from homosexuals at night in the usual pick-up areas. That friendly relationship, punctuated by comic incidents, has been amusingly portrayed in Monique's first novel, *Les Poissons-chats*. René was in his thirties at the time; he was tall, stout, and coarse, and his rough, ungainly face immediately revealed his past life as a petty criminal; he was now married, with two children, and cleaned bedspreads, sofas, and armchairs in people's homes, which allowed him to earn an honest penny as well as to lay numerous servant girls and housewives whenever the opportunity arose. As a way in, he would insistently inquire as to the origin of stains unresponsive to his energetic therapy, dryly discard confused and heated hypotheses, and gradually center suspicions on the spermatic origin of the libation. His visits to the rue Poissonnière obeyed as much the desire to remember old times with Monique as the aim to bed down Hélène, the domestic help who lived with us and took Monique's daughter to school.

Hélène talked sixteen to the dozen, wore too much makeup, and went out dancing every night. From her extravagant stories we gathered that she was in with some pimp, since she had been invited to work as a beautician in Ca-

sablanca; she was a single parent and had entrusted her three children to Social Security. Her continual verbal diarrhea irritated Genet: while she served
out the food, he ordered wax pellets for his ears. One day, at his wits' end with
her chatter, he exclaimed: "For God's sake! Aren't you able to express even
one general idea?"

Some of the encounters during those months have been preserved thanks to
Monique's little diary.

We went with Genet to the quai de Conti, where he was to attend Jean
Cocteau's entry into the Academy: it was the first and last official event I ever
saw him go to. He was visibly annoyed by the ceremony and went reluctantly to talk with his colleagues, apologizing to us and furious with himself.
He did not belong to their physical, moral, or literary world: Genet, in the
guests' gallery at the Institute, was a falcon mistakenly let into an assembly of
peacocks. What he would see and hear there fed all he held in contempt: feelings of disgust, a desire to throw up.

Cocteau had made a decisive contribution to getting Genet out of jail
twelve years earlier and he felt a debt toward him. However, Genet avoided
personal contact whenever he could; he was offended by Cocteau's worldly
ways and exhibitionism. When the author of *Les Enfants terribles* died, Genet spoke to me about him and the superficiality of his work quite mercilessly, but without rancor.

At another time, the diary briefly notes a "Genet–Violette Leduc dinner in a
Chinese restaurant," which I don't remember at all.

Violette Leduc had just left the psychiatric sanatorium where, thanks to
Simone de Beauvoir's generosity, she had recovered from one of her half-
real, half-imagined attacks of madness and depression. We went to see her
with Monique—who had a profound admiration for her work and made
me read her books, which were unknown at the time—in a beautiful villa
on the outskirts of Paris, surrounded by a large park full of yellowing, almost
leafless horse-chestnut trees. Violette—whose terrible physical appearance
Maurice Sachs drew so unforgettably—cried over her loneliness and isola-

tion: she suffered or pretended to suffer from a persecution complex, but at times she would calm down and her vulgar face broadened into a cunning grin. She was a "play-actress and martyr," according to the expression coined by Sartre, and waxed ecstatic at the "happy couple" of Monique and myself. She wanted me to pass on to her an old pair of trousers, "with a drop of se-men on the fly," she said plaintively, since she lived alone, without a man, and that souvenir of me would warm her up a bit. In the absence of any available jeans, she got a few photos of us in Spain: with those she would sleep better, would feel less lonely, and could create the illusion of participating in our happiness from a distance. A few days later she telephoned Monique, still from the clinic: while she walked round the garden, someone had slipped into her room and torn all our photos to shreds. "Tell Juan there's obviously someone with a grudge against him."

Outside the lesbian relationships so beautifully described in her books, Violette had had two passions in her life: Maurice Sachs and Genet. Loves that were impossible, if it can be said, because of the difference of sex; she would later relate in masterly fashion their failure, sadness, and humiliations in *La Bâtarde*. Years earlier, as Genet confided to us one day, she had invited him to supper with his friend Java in her small flat near the Faubourg Saint-Antoine. Violette had prepared a dish with a sauce, which she insisted on serving up although Genet was not hungry. As he refused, she adopted a rather whining tone: "I see now how you despise the poor" or something similar. Genet was furious and upset the table and everything that was on it: the sauce fell on her low-cut dress and ran between her breasts. He left with his friend, slamming the door behind them, and the next day he had found her sobbing in front of her door still covered in sauce. From then on he im-placably resisted her admiring approaches, and I am not sure why he low-ered his guard and dined with us and her on the day indicated in Monique's diary.

At that time Genet kept intact his desire to be a provocateur: as minstrel of crime, thievery, homosexuality, he continually exacted payment for the debt that society had contracted with him ever since his conception in his mother's womb; now that he was respected and famous, he made up for the

unhappiness and injustice suffered as a child and youth. He responded
rudely to admiration from the establishment, displayed a crude frankness to
hypocrites, unscrupulously extracted money from the rich to give to those
who like himself had not enjoyed good fortune and upbringing from the
start. His anger was sudden and violent: his first publisher, the North American translator of his work, Jean Cau—who came to justify being fired by
Sartre—were all at one time or another on the receiving end of his caning
attacks.

When invited to attend an official dinner organized by the world of culture in homage to a minister, he replied by asking whether he had been invited in his capacity as ex-jailbird, pickpocket, or queer. Once, on the terrace
at the Flore, he was furtively greeted from another table by a shamefaced homosexual and assailed him with the cry: "Hey, did your fancyman stick it
right up the other night?" In a restaurant where we were having lunch, an
overpainted lady was talking and slobbering over her lapdog at the table next
to us; Genet gave a look of disgust and the woman asked him: "Don't you
like animals?"

"Madame, I don't like people who like animals."

I can equally remember the time when, a number of years later, Monique
and I accompanied him to see a fervent admirer of his, the wife of an important state personage, whom he wanted to have intervene on behalf of a
friend. To please him, the woman quoted from memory a sentence of his
that had for some reason been aired in the newspapers some time ago. "You
know," she said, "when I read or hear something intelligent, I always retain
it." "And when you hear something stupid, you always let it out," responded
Genet. She took the jibe without flinching and, showing real magnanimity
and self-control, noted down all he asked for and interceded favorably on his
behalf.

The performance of his plays was beginning to pay dividends, and for the
first time he was living fairly comfortably. After the worldwide success of *Le
Balcon*, he distributed his royalties among his protégés and kept for himself
only what was strictly necessary.

Until then, his strategies for getting loot could have filled an anthology of tricks and wiles, worthy of a hero of the Spanish picaresque novel: loans, sponging, hotels abandoned without bills being paid . . . Genet acted on these occasions without remorse; his morality worked at a different level. Once at this level, his behavior would be, on the contrary, a model of scrupulous rigor. But the level varied—and I noticed this only later. His absolute surrender to friendship did not exclude the seed of possible, unexpected betrayal.

His usual recourse when he had no money was to sell publishers the titles of books that did not exist: *Le Bagne*, *La Fée*, *Elle*, *Splendid's (La Rafale)*, *Les Fous* . . . When Gallimard acquired the publishing rights to his "complete works," Genet swindled money out of Gaston by promising wonderful things: *Jean la folle*, *Les Hommes*, *Football* . . . The founder of NRF, who had a literary scent as keen as a real hunting dog's, had moreover a weak spot for Genet: while he was always able coldly to refuse help to an aged or hard-up author, he always fell into Genet's continuous traps with ill-concealed excitement. He derived intense satisfaction from the certainty he was being deceived. Old Gaston was a "law unto himself," under whom Gallimard would never be a mere book-producing factory: his personality, whims, and imagination then exercised a healthy influence, and the poet, with his carefree insolence, enjoyed untrammeled his protection and approval.

Genet now called me *l'hidalgo* and seemed to feel at ease in my company when he turned up on the rue Poissonnière. Monique was his mailbox and helped to solve the small but annoying problems of daily life: arranging meetings, avoiding troublesome encounters, and obtaining the sedatives Nembutal or Supponéryl.

He lived alone in modest hotels nearly always situated next to a train station, as if thus to underline his light-footed mobility. His belongings fitted into a small or average-sized suitcase: a change of clothes, a few books and notebooks, sleeping pills and medicine, and his manuscripts. At that time he was still writing: months earlier he had published *Le Balcon*; *Les Nègres* and *Les Paravents* would soon follow. He read the newspapers and commented on political events: the Algerian war, the last stings in the tail of French imperialism . . .

His monastic austerity and seclusion suggest the idea of sanctity: a real detachment from property and possessions. He ate frugally, hardly drank, and the only luxury he allowed himself was the small Dutch cigars in metal tins, which he smoked continuously. Apart from satisfying his modest personal needs, money burned his fingers: he always kept it in small bundles in his trouser pocket, ready to give it out to his protégés, someone he just got on with, or the lad or tough he had just picked up.

We talked above all about politics. Although I was physically in Paris, I continued to live mentally in Spain. My brother Luis and a large number of my Barcelona friends had joined the clandestine CP, and I was a fellow traveler on the fringe, but a useful coordinator from outside the country of press campaigns and cultural activities against the Franco régime. I was beginning to get to know the work of writers like Céline, Artaud, Beckett, and I knew in my inner self that their literary expression, like that of Genet himself, was much more beautiful, rich, and daring than the one my colleagues and I had as our goal, but at the same time I was convinced that it was a luxury we could not afford. The situation in Spain, I then thought, demanded that we be clear and practical (read "facile and Manichaean") as in the realist documentary novel (*Karl Marx, l'éternel voleur d'énergies!* as Rimbaud would have said). Thus, I steeled myself for years against Genet's *dangerous* political influence (which would not, however, prevent it later from seeping through to me in a slower, more lasting fashion).

Genet sympathized with our political options and liked to discuss them with Luis and his friend Octavio Pellissa, when they came to Paris to inform or get instructions from the leadership. As I discerned later, he was attracted and fascinated by the discipline, impenetrability, and secrecy inherent in the hierarchies of the Communist parties and their perennial "besieged fortress" mentality. He felt above all instinctive hatred for the social system within which he lived and the ethnic, cultural, and economic inequalities engendered by its power. However, our exclusive support for Spain equally shocked him and was the target of his irony. Genet knew the Peninsula well and found Spaniards resigned to their fate, sentimental and bland, in a word, incapable of repeating the revolutionary deeds of 1936.

Machado was then our bible and I lent Genet a translation of his poetry and *Juan de Mairena*. He returned the books to me after a few days and rattled off a string of criticisms: he thought the writer's human and literary horizons narrow and limited; his obsession with Castile was a way of narcissistically contemplating his navel and resurrecting the retrograde values of the countryside. Machado not only wrote in Spanish—as Genet wrote in French—but wanted *to be Spanish*, a cultural identification that Genet could not understand and labeled as chauvinist. He was left totally indifferent by the moral landscape of France: neither the gardens of Versailles nor the cathedral of Rheims stirred any emotions in him. So why, then, that love of Soria, Castile, the trees on the riverbank, the slow procession of poplars? The fatherland, he would say much later, could be an ideal only for those who didn't have one, like the Palestinian fedayeen.

"And when they get one?" I asked him.

He was silent for a few seconds.

"Then they will have won the right to throw it down the lavatory pan and pull the chain, just like me."

After one of his frequent absences, Genet reappeared one day on the rue Poissonnière with a youth in his twenties. Abdallah was the son of an Algerian man and a German woman, had worked in a circus from childhood, and could perform as an acrobat. His very seductive face revealed a harmonious blend of female and manly features. He had a gentle voice, a gracious and elegant manner, and always spoke with great delicacy and self-restraint.

Their relationship was as father to son. Genet had decided to turn him into a great artist and invented tightrope-walking tricks for him that required patient, disciplined training. An admirable poetic text, *Pour un fun-*

ambule would be the result of the coming together of their wills. Abdallah enthusiastically surrendered himself to the task, Genet seemed very pleased with his progress, and their friendship radiated a wonderful moral beauty.

When Genet was traveling, Abdallah came to see us, and both Monique and I were very happy in his company. After a few months, Genet told us that his friend had received his draft notice and, faced with the prospect of being sent to "pacify" Algeria, they had both agreed he must desert. Abdallah did not respond to the notice and came to say farewell to us with a glowing smile: he was excited by the adventure and knew it stimulated the vitality and energy of Genet, for whom desertion was an absolute value. Rootless from birth, a child of the foundling home, he preached the virtues of exile by example. Living near him implied getting rid of one's own parameters, throwing off the habits of upbringing, breaking with past feelings and attachments, living like a foreigner in a perpetual state of moving on. To match the image Genet wanted of him, Abdallah took on his nomadic ways, constructed his own life around a risk-filled enterprise, and would walk the threadbare tightrope without any harness or safety net. But he was young and strong; Genet's will sustained him, and he cheerfully trusted that fortune would smile upon him.

When we accompanied him to the Gare de Lyon, where he took the train to Bordighera with his acrobat's gear, I did not realize that the situation would be repeated with Ahmed and Jacky. Monique and I kissed him on both cheeks and he waved smaller and smaller goodbyes from the window as the train moved away.

Genet traveled for several months: he followed Abdallah through Italy, Belgium, and Germany and closely supervised his training. L'Arbalète had just published *Les Nègres*, soon to be staged by Roger Blin. His good-humored messages and telephone calls showed he was going through a creative phase: his only complaint was about the difficulty of getting sleeping pills. Monique mailed him some from time to time, but it was a dangerous operation. When he settled down in Amsterdam with Abdallah we decided to go and see them and left Paris by road along with Octavio. Monique's friend, Odette, would follow on by train the next day.

Genet showed us the city, joked about De Gaulle and his *folies de grandeur*, saying that "France is drooling over his big fat cock." I have never seen him so happy to exist as then, and I would never see the like again. He ate with an excellent appetite, clowned around when Monique was taking photos, took an interest in the situation in Spain and Octavio's recent exile. Then he led us to the hall where Abdallah rehearsed his dance number every day.

The lad was wearing a garment designed by Genet himself and emphasizing the slender grace of his body. He climbed up to the wire stretched between the two posts and began to sway with an unreal agility and lightness. His feet hardly seemed to touch the rope while he shook to a calypso rhythm about two meters above the ground. When he reached the moment for the lethal jump, we all held our breath, contemplating his incredible defying of the law of gravity: his acrobatics was a form of levitation. *Sévère et pâle, danse, et si tu le pouvais, les yeux fermés*, wrote his friend. The tightrope walker kept his eyes open: when he finished and jumped down on the carpet beneath the stuccoed ceiling of the dance hall where he practiced, I suddenly noticed his tense concentration, the sweat bathing his forehead, and the fragility of his beautiful smile. Genet hid his Pygmalion's pride and said that Abdallah had improved his technique, but that the act was not ready; he must forget the spectators, concentrate entirely on the dance, lighten his movements even more. Abdallah listened to him, tired but satisfied, and we waited for him to change his clothes before going out for dinner.

I shall follow the coherent disorder of memory rather than a strictly chronological account of events.

We—that is, Monique and myself—went to the first performance of *Les Nègres* at the Lutèce theater. Although I am not at all fond of theatrical events—they nearly always bore me and I no sooner settle down in my seat than I get an irresistible desire to cough, my legs get pins and needles, or I get a backache—I was fired by the poetic density of the text, the wonderful stage set, and the delivery and mimicry of the actors: the play is even more beautiful and provocative than *Le Balcon*, and I prefer Blin's production to Peter Brook's recent version of the latter at the Gymnase.

One member of the audience got up halfway through and left, obviously displeased: it was Ionesco. The next day Gaston Gallimard's secretary, who had witnessed the incident with us, asked him why. "I felt I was the only white in the theater," the writer replied, "and I was happy to accept the challenge."

Genet continued living in Holland in flight from prying journalists, but when I saw him again he agreed for the first time willingly to discuss literature and the theater. The writers who were then the center of attention, Malraux, Sartre, Camus, were a matter of indifference to him. He said the literature of ideas was not literature: those who cultivated it had got the wrong genre. Their language was flat, conventional, predictable. Their enterprise was no adventure, but just a local bus journey. Why did they waste so much energy?

In fact, he preferred poets: Nerval, Rimbaud, Mallarmé, and, unexpectedly for me, Claudel. His desire to be a writer came to him in prison after reading Ronsard. He had equal respect for Céline, Artaud, Michaux, and Beckett. Years later, when he had withdrawn into total, irrevocable solitude, he would talk to me with real feeling about Dostoevsky and *The Brothers Karamazov*.

We went back to Amsterdam with Florence Malraux and a friend. Genet booked rooms for us in a central hotel, but we were surprised to find that the management would not let us stay: we were not "legitimate" couples. Genet laughed complacently: in contrast, Abdallah and himself had no problem. Blessed Holland, the homosexuals' paradise!

Abdallah was now training with Ahmed, a childhood friend also working in the circus. It was Christmas and we spent the day walking up and down by the canals. The two lads showed us the red-light district, the dance hall frequented by the Guyanese and Curaçaoans, prostitutes on the watch behind their windows like sirens spotlighted in an aquarium.

On New Year's Eve we went to Haarlem and saw the *Regentesses* by Hals. Genet was a passionate admirer of the work and declared that in it the painter discovered *goodness*. He was moved by the paintings of the Dutch masters, was a constant visitor to the Rijksmuseum, and a good many years after writing on the genius from Leyden, he would confide to Monique that, after seeing himself naked in the mirror, his aged body reminded him of Rembrandt's *Bathsheba*.

The rue Poissonnière continued to be his *point de chute*. He would suddenly turn up, between trains, to collect his sleeping pills and correspondence or arrange a meeting with his publishers. He avoided worldly fame and recognition like the plague. One day, on a visit to Gallimard, he saw a stack of books in the room where authors signed books reserved for celebrities, booksellers, and critics: it was a work by Montherlant. After making sure that nobody was watching, he changed the author's set phrase of *With the compliments* into a startling *With the compliments of that twat Montherlant*. The volumes were sent to their destinations and some academics and distinguished minds rang up to protest at the outrage and sent their copies back.

Meanwhile Abdallah had perfected the tightrope dance that he began to perform successfully in Belgium and Germany. We received optimistic news of his tour. "You who are aflame, who lasts a few minutes, you shall be that fiery wonder," Genet had written for him; and the audience, "unaware that you are the incendiary, applauds the blaze." The photographs that we received showed him slender and graceful as he hopped along the tightrope in his tight-fitting, dazzling costume. One day we learned indirectly of his accident: he had taken a fall during his act in Belgium and had broken his leg. A subsequent operation was satisfactory, but he had to embark on a lengthy period of therapy. Genet remained at his side to encourage him. Abdallah wanted to get back to his dance, darkly foreseeing that if he did not, he would cease to delight his friend: he perhaps knew that the enterprise was greater than his strength; nevertheless he insisted on triumphing over destiny. The life he knew and appreciated before meeting Genet had lost all attraction for him. He had deserted not only the army but also everything that usually satisfies the "normal" individual: routine work, hobbies, friends, the family circle. His moral and emotional surrender to Genet was a journey of no return: a burning of bridges, a scorched-earth policy. So he would continue to dance on the tightrope, would accept the total solitude of its challenge, would fuse with that brief, precise image that kept the audience on tenterhooks as he boldly executed his lethal leap.

Genet's territory was discontinuous: it displayed crevices, ups and downs, breaks, sudden disaffections. He patiently constructed sets that he would suddenly abandon, leaving his actors alienated and orphaned. He was unselfish, faithful, generous, on the surface submissive to his lover, but at the same time, voluble, possessive, demanding, capable of harshness and cruelty. That discontinuity nevertheless tended to repeat itself, obeyed subtle cycles of chance and acquired with time a strange coherence.

When Abdallah fell for a second time, the moral fullness of his friendship with Genet was cast down into a gray, inhospitable reality that had no future: the tightrope walker with the pure, delicate gestures, endowed with miraculous precision would never dance again. It was difficult to settle down to an ordinary life: the experience had marked him forever. He was henceforth condemned to be a deadweight in Genet's life, the irritating reminder of a frustrated dream. Neither attempted the futile process of reinsertion into society. By way of consolation, Genet gave him a Giacometti painting, and with the proceeds from the sale of that he could travel for months around the Far East: escaping from himself, exiled from the world, he had begun, probably unawares, his implacable countdown.

Genet was then active in the struggle for Algerian independence. L'Arbalète published *Les Paravents*, which would not be performed for many years because of the burning relevance of the main theme.

He often came to our place with Jacky. The youth was the stepson of Lucien, that *pêcheur de Suquet* to whom he dedicated some of the novels and poems of his early writing. Genet had continued to see Lucien after his marriage, helped him get established, and had known Jacky from childhood.

The latter soon revealed an irresistible passion for cars: at the age of thirteen or fourteen he would break into them whenever he could and drive off at top speed. The police arrested him but released him straightaway as a minor. His spontaneous contempt for legality, his boldness and brazen attitude amused and captivated Genet, who discovered an incipient spiritual affinity with the boy. Some time earlier, Jacky had left home and we gave him shelter for a few days. By the side of the bourgeois, conformist Lucien, his precocious deviations gave him in Genet's eyes the attractive allure of the marginalized.

As I write these notes I am rereading *L'Enfant criminel*. Genet's childhood experience of prison, that *moral region*, which was both cruel and fascinating, of corrective centers for minors would never cease to obsess him. Informed on by the blind musician whose guide he was—Spain with its splendor and rags soon crossed his path—he would be sent to one of them to be reformed because he had spent the small amount of money the blind man entrusted to him on the stalls and sideshows at the fair. Genet once told me that when he realized his "crime," he thought of committing suicide. Instead, he got to know that savage world which sowed his dreams with abjection and glory, created an unbridgeable distance between crime and punishment, and kept intact his stubborn, rebellious pride. The severity of the sentence forced upon him behavior that was its equal: he would strive to live up to it. From then on, the boy trained in the hypocritical mimicry of an acolyte could surrender to the hard tool of his Senegalese lovers, steal, beg, prostitute himself, accept his idealized image as a professional delinquent with arrogant panache.

Once he was invited, as a famous writer, by the director of a Swedish youth institution to speak to the adolescents on the path to rehabilitation. After the visit to this "humanized," open center, Genet's speech so appalled the philanthropist that he broke off his translation: Society wants to castrate you, turn you into gray, harmless people, strip you of all that distinguishes you from it by drowning your rebelliousness, taking away your beauty; do not take the outstretched hand, do not fall in the trap, take advantage of this bloke's stupidity to clear off and leave him to it . . .

As Genet told me when he related the incident, the youths listened without understanding a word, the director was furious, and, forgetting his liberalism and noble sentiments, drove him out with all manner of threat and insult.

The adolescent who broke from his family and headed instinctively to him for help did not belong to that class of rebel who would settle down. Jacky did not aspire to a home of his own, nor a comfortable existence, nor a job, but a difficult and dangerous livelihood where he could spread out and have faith. He was lively, persistent, pleasant, and not without physical charm. When he matured and became a man he would naturally enter Genet's life.

It is not my intention to narrate the events that might frame a biography, but to define and delineate with the help of a number of facts and details the poet's physical and moral space: his vitality, humor, whims, playacting, his anger, simulated and real: the singular grace conferred by knowing him—and also the penalties.

His affinities and fits of pique were immediate and unpredictable. The presence of someone whom he found unpleasant enclosed him in a prickly, repellent silence that would force the blighted individual to leave his field of vision. He liked to contradict commonplaces and so-called truisms, to dismantle cheekily the most solid certainties. He greeted in icy silence taxi drivers' clumsy attempts at conversation or replied to their trivial comments with biting irony. When the porter in a big luxury hotel drew the balcony curtain to reveal to him the sublime panorama that could be contemplated from there, he ordered him to close the curtain again and bring, if he had one, a screen or panel with the photograph of a factory. The peacocks of the literary world brought on immediate nausea: one day he was leafing through one of their novels and exclaimed: "Why the hell don't you copy me and shut your trap when you haven't got anything to say?" But if he felt at ease, among people he appreciated, he was affectionate and responsive to their problems, establishing restrained, respectful relationships. He was upset by aggressive use of the *tu* form: despite our long, deep friendship we always used *vous*.

He sometimes wrote to me from Greece, Morocco, Spain, or some

French provincial city. On the envelope he added under my name, "Monique's friend" or "concubine." On one occasion—now I'm leaping ahead several years—I accompanied him after lunch to the Gare du Nord: in the compartment of the carriage where he sat down was a middle-aged lady who recognized him and started up a conversation. As it was departure time, we said goodbye and I got out. Two days later I received a letter from him:

> Juan, here you have the visiting card of that idiot in the train [. . .] She adores the *End of the Romanovs* and is deeply moved by Anastasia's adventure. She voted no in the referendum. Her hero is Tixier-Vignancourt. "He's the best lawyer in the high court" and "his voice is like bronze." May '68? God forbid that '69 turns out the same [. . .] her husband is a fat pig waiting for her at the station. This pig is the mayor of a tiny seaside town.
>
> But. . . when we arrived at A., where she was getting off, I noticed that there was an enormous suitcase on the luggage rack; it was enormous, most likely very heavy: that's what she was hinting, that she was young but beginning to feel her age and feeling weak, there wasn't a porter on the station at A.
>
> Well, then!!!
>
> I laughed sarcastically and took my two minuscule cases and walking stick in one hand. She had to grapple with her big case and wait for the old pig to come and help her.
>
> And thus, as the Popular Front used to say, we both went *un bout de chemin ensemble*.

When Genet took hold of someone's life he also embraced responsibility for his family: first Lucien's wife and her children; then Abdallah's mother, a stout, semiparalyzed German who lived alone and whom Monique occasionally visited when Abdallah was away: she spoke in difficult, broken French, complained about her isolation, and one day lifted her skirts to reveal an enormous hernia. Soon to follow would be Jacky's very young wife, their son, and Ahmed, Abdallah's childhood friend. As I found out much later, he took equal care of Mohamed's home in Larache and the future of his son.

To sort out his innumerable problems over passports, residence permits, visas, criminal records and reprieves, Genet would unscrupulously use his reputation and the snobbery of the powerful; he had recourse to Pompidou, Defferre, or Edgar Faure and wrote a flowery letter to the Chinese ambassador. When he needed some support, he displayed incredible energy and tenacity, and mobilized the weight of his friendships. He demanded absolute dedication: he wanted everything immediately.

He liked to arrive home at lunchtime, rush into the kitchen, and there help himself, without wasting a moment, to the *petit salé aux lentilles* simmering in the saucepan. Then he gulped it down, sitting anywhere, like a hungry, badly brought-up child, a smile dancing in his eyes.

Jacky would also avoid military service. Genet traveled with him to Italy, where he practiced on the racetrack at Monza, and when the lad had mastered the steering wheel, he bought him the hot rod necessary for a career as a professional driver. For months he accompanied him to trials and competitions in various European countries. On 2 June 1963 Jacky drove at Chimay, close to the French border, and we went with a couple of married friends to see him. Genet was as nervous as a father on the night before his son takes an examination decisive for his future: he ensured that Jacky ate and rested properly, swamped him with advice. He stayed with Jacky on the track until the starting flag was up, and when his Lotus won the race, Genet's face radiated happiness.

In the meantime Abdallah had returned from his trip to Japan and the Near East. Genet had got him a pardon and showed a watchful concern for him, but inevitably their relationship deteriorated: Abdallah would never be the "rare and precious" artist that fired the poet's passion with his bravery. He had withdrawn from all that tied him to life and knew that his place had been filled by a rival.

He attempted suicide in Casablanca, and when his friend went to see him, he would testify how he had returned specterlike from the "compact squadron of shadows."* Abdallah was having a stormy relationship with a hard, humorless Greek girl, Erika, whom Genet could not stand: he acted

*José Ángel Valente, *Poemas a Lázaro.*

aggressively and vengefully toward Genet and made him responsible for his own failure. We often saw him, with him or her—but never with both of them—fragile and vulnerable like a condemned man with a temporary stay of execution. Alone he was still the intelligent, sensitive, delicate, and modest youth—now a man—who captivated us from our first meeting. But he had an anguished, precarious air about him. Genet had the unfortunate idea of making him Jacky's trainer and having him go to his competitions and practices. He made a pathetic attempt, but gave up immediately. There were frequent squabbles, and Abdallah left the phone off the hook the night Genet was to call him at home. That was what he confessed to Monique afterwards, but Genet was probably right when he retorted: "Not so, he was really afraid I would *not* call him." When none of us had news of him, Ahmed slipped away from the barracks to find he was still awaiting execution. He broke with Erika one day and came for some Nembutal saying it was for Genet. On 12 March 1964, forewarned by the latter, the owners of the *chambre de bonne* in an attic on the rue de Bourgogne forced open the door to find a corpse.

After the police inquiry, we met at the morgue with a small group of friends. Abdallah was unrecognizable: the poisoning caused by the sleeping pills had blackened his face: he was a black. Genet said tearfully he had returned to Africa, got rid of all that was alien to his origins, that had deceitfully clung to his skin . . .

It was a gloomy burial in the small Moslem cemetery at Thiais. Genet could hardly stand up and stumbled along after the mufti. Suddenly we spotted among the tombs Ahmed, who had in turn deserted and was hiding from the police. A bitter wind blew and, as befits these melancholy circumstances, the drizzle did not miss its appointment.

I frequently went to see Genet in his hotel on the boulevard Richard Lenoir. He looked calm on the surface, but Abdallah's irrevocable gesture had unleashed within him a series of inner springs previously hidden. His brilliant, original, ever surprising way of arguing suddenly coalesced in a mysticism of surrender, an absolute leap into godless transcendence. With his self-immolation, his friend had won the last, most difficult battle, toward which his singular tightrope-walker's art inexorably led. His physical anni-hilation was the victory that canceled out past failures: Genet read there the symbol of his strength and purification.

It was difficult for me to follow him along those paths: I knew he was waging an intense debate within himself in terms of exultation and guilt. I respected and shared his grief but realized in my powerlessness that I could be of no help to him.

Genet returned to Paris after an absence of several months. On 22 August he asked me to come and see him by myself in the Hotel Lutecia. When I got to his room, he was dressed as if to go out, but told me straightaway to sit down, that we would eat later. I did as he said, surprised by his solemn tone, and lis-tened to his voice—that grave, severe, inimitable voice for great occasions— as he announced his irreversible decision to commit suicide.

To my great dismay, he explained he had destroyed all his manuscripts, his essays, the two plays after *Les Paravents*. Never again would he even touch pen or pencil. He had written, and handed me, the holograph will in which he left his wealth in equal shares to Ahmed and Jacky and designated Monique and myself his executors. When he concluded his brief statement, he seemed calm and cheerful, as if he had removed a great weight from his shoulders. He made me promise not to tell anyone and invited me to lunch.

For some time I saw him regularly and tried to show him the futility of his self-punishment. Genet would not listen: he spoke of Abdallah's gesture in the beautiful language of a Mawlana or San Juan de la Cruz. Although the obsession with death was intense, I nevertheless sensed that his inner re-sistance was just as great. To tell the truth, I knew no one with as much vi-tality or attachment to life: his physical energy was awe inspiring. His use and abuse of sleeping pills would have destroyed anyone else's health, though it hardly made an impression on his. I can remember the time when, stuffed with painkillers and injections to combat his toothache, he jumped like a rabbit out of the dentist's chair when the nurse exhorted him to a little more patience as he proceeded to another interminable extraction: he hit the street like a whirlwind, to everyone's astonishment, and crossed over Paris, charged like an electric battery, until he found another dentist.

Although I had promised him I would keep silent, I told Monique every-thing. Genet's decision was obviously absurd, but we didn't know what to do to reason with him. She then had the idea of talking to Sartre: he alone, she said, was sufficiently intelligent to argue convincingly with Genet. As she told me after seeing him, Sartre was less anxious than we were: he was sure Genet would not kill himself. He told Monique that he did not know what growing old was and that Genet's remorse owed less to his sadness than to a lack of it. If he had burned his manuscripts, he added, that was not to punish himself but simply because he did not judge them to be at the level he re-quired.

His opinion gave us some relief, but Genet was still obsessed by the idea of committing suicide. He did not even read the newspapers, seemed to have lost interest in everything, and his rejection of putting pen to paper went to the extreme of refusing to put his signature to checks and documents. He had obtained a considerable sum from his publishers and gave this out to his protégés and Abdallah's mother. Gradually I was filled with the uneasy impression that he was using me as a sounding board, that my presence acted only to strengthen him in his intentions. It was a difficult situation and I was unsure how to end it. One day, while we were having lunch near home, I abandoned my restraint and tact, sought a way to provoke him and brutally handed him a pen. Genet threw it to the other side of the dining room and shut himself up in a curt silence. It was a breaking-off, and I did not see him again for almost two years.

Monique and I went to live in Saint-Tropez, where we learned of Genet's two suicide attempts, in Domodossola and Brussels, and of the serious car accident that put an end to Jacky's dreams, like Abdallah's years before. From the news we got from various friends, we deduced that Genet was slowly emerging from the tunnel. On a trip to Paris, Monique saw him a cou-ple of times by herself and recounted the change in our relationship: Arab passion had erupted in my life, the most secret part of myself escaped her.

Genet seemed delighted by the occurrence; he was tremendously pleased by my homosexuality and wanted to see me. When we finally met, he was once more friendly, ironic, and incisive, but we were neither the same as before: by mutual agreement we would in the future avoid all mention of Abdallah.

Apart from fleeting bouts of luxury—when he stayed in five-star hotels— the poet's room was small, modest, totally bare of decoration: a bed, a couple of chairs, bedside table, and washbasin. Also: an ashtray with his cigar butts, a few newspapers, his suitcase and walking stick.

He now walked along leaning on it fairly coquettishly and bypassed the areas where people recognized him. He had lunch anywhere, walked, read the Paris press in bed. He had a paradoxically monogamous relationship with French: Genet was completely resistant to other languages: he understood only Italian and the coarsest expressions in Spanish.

At night he hardly ate and went early to bed. He took his dose of Nembutal, and overcome by sleep, it was as if he sank slowly into a well or the grave: his nightly journey to darkness with the rigid face mask of death. Every day, at dawn, he would arise like Lazarus.

Genet had come back to life, but did not write. At times, he seemed indifferent and alien to literature, like a believer who had inexplicably lost his faith and state of grace. His prodigious intelligence still functioned but worked only on barren land: the electric charge, the generating spark of his work would resurge, miraculously, only in the terminal phase of his cancer.

His previous lyrical transports—"I know no other criterion of the beauty of an act, object, or being," he had written, "than the song it rouses in me and that I translate into words in order to communicate it to you: that's lyricism"—were replaced by more humdrum, routine feelings and reactions: like a father, he scrupulously worried over the errant ways of his protégés. Ahmed was preparing a horse-riding act in Spain; Jacky was divorced and would follow in Abdallah's footsteps to Japan. Genet had for many years not been to the cinema or theater or read any literary works: he had always lived on the edge of the fashions and interests of the literary world, but now he did without literature. His inner song—if there was one—was not translated into that beautiful, repellent flame that had flared up and spread like fire ever since the miracle of *Notre-Dame-des-Fleurs*. He also was living on after the mutilation of his transcendent impulse, like Abdallah after his fall from the tightrope or Jacky after the accident that almost cost him his life.

In a strange delight in symmetry, destiny had reduced all three to the same level.

The scandal aroused by the performance of *Les Paravents* at the Odéon briefly rescued him from his state of protective anonymity. However, if he again took up his pen, it would only be to support the revolutionary groups he favored: the Palestinians, the Black Panthers, the Baader-Meinhof gang.

The May '68 events restored his old combativity and energy. Genet went to the Sorbonne, was overcome by the applause of the occupants, and went back into hiding. One day while we were having lunch at home, we heard shouts from a demonstration opposite the nearby *L'Humanité* building. The day before, it had been the leftists hostile to the "prudent, responsible" line adopted by the French CP. As we realized at once, these demonstrators belonged to the far right: they were waving French flags and shouting against "Moscow gold." Unhesitatingly, Genet grabbed hold of the soup tureen and tried to throw it through the window onto the demonstrators reassembled at the foot of our block. Monique snatched it from him: it belongs to a neighbor! He then picked up a plate, which soon smashed against the beret, the skull of a fifty-year-old individual who looked like a member of the Action Française invented by Buñuel. His forehead bled slightly as he looked up at the furious genie who was insulting him. *Grossier personnage!* he spat out.

During my stay in California, Genet bombarded me with telegrams: he wanted me to help him pass illegally over the Canadian frontier in order to meet up with the Black Panthers. Just as I was getting ready to meet him in Toronto, I heard it was unnecessary. The immigration official to whom he had handed a passport that did not belong to him had fought in France during the world war and loved Paris chic and French *esprit*. He could even whistle *la Marseillaise*. Genet smiled and whistled with him. The policeman forgot to look at the photo and date of birth, which were patently false, and twixt smiles and patriotic whistles, Genet slipped into the United States, to the perplexed dismay of the FBI.

He then pursued his wandering life: he stayed for several months in Jordan and Lebanon with the PLO guerrilla fighters, traveled to Pakistan and Morocco. He wrote to me from Tangier, complaining about the heat, "just when I feel like rain," and his recent stay in Barcelona: "Oh, the Mediterranean, that big salt lake—all that makes me want to crap!" Later he would turn up again in Paris with Mohamed, a physically attractive youth, whom he helped to climb out of poverty and settle down in the city of his birth.

Finally, I no longer saw him but received news of him through others: discontinuity repeated its irregular but predictable cycles. I glimpse, as I write these lines, the mysterious coherence that infused everything he touched, that extended beyond his work and wove into the very life of the poet the complex pattern of attractions, rejections, orbits, circles, tensions, ruptures of a kind of solar system with its fixed stars, satellites, dead planets, and shooting stars: a zone at once moral, poetic, and physical, the Genetian universe, whose subtle laws have yet to be deciphered.

To know Genet intimately was an adventure from which no one could emerge unharmed. Depending on the situation, he provoked rebellion, self-awareness, an irresistible desire for sincerity, the break from old feelings and attachments, disarray, an anguished void, even physical death.

If in my youth I imitated more or less consciously some literary models from America or Europe, he has in fact been the only adult influence on the strictly moral plane. Genet taught me to cast off my early vanity, political opportunism, my desire to cut a figure in the life of literary society, to center in on something deeper and more difficult: the conquest of my own literary expression, my subjective authenticity. Without him, without his example, I would perhaps not have had the strength to break from the hierarchy of values accepted on the right and the left by my compatriots, to accept proudly my predictable rejection and isolation, to write all I have written from the time of *Conde Julián*.

In January 1981 I bumped into Jacky by chance in Marrakesh, next to the square of Djemaa el Fna. I had not seen him for years and took some seconds to recognize him: he had grown thin, his features were purer and more expressive, and his thick black beard gave him the severe, almost forbidding appearance of a mountain Moroccan.

As our conversation soon revealed, it was not just a physical change: his intelligence and sensibility had sharpened. He had just accompanied Mohamed to the Sahara and was unhurriedly returning, sometimes on foot, stopping to rest in the villages. He led a solitary and ascetic life. He sometimes painted and wanted to learn Arabic, as he had previously learned Japanese. He had very little money but seemed happy.

As I was writing these pages, a journalist gave me the bad news of Genet's accidental death in one of those anonymous hotels he frequented near a train station or on the road to an airport: in recent years he had exchanged the train for the plane, but his readiness to depart, his permanent transitoriness remained the same. I had lost sight of him since his throat cancer and successive chemotherapy treatments: his group of friends was limited to Jacky, Mohamed, and the Palestinian comrades. Stays in Rabat and Larache alternated with brief visits to Paris, where he went only to get his royalties or a medical examination. He had lost interest in Europe in its entirety and was at ease only among Arabs. He met his end on one of those trips to the France he so hated, when he wanted to correct the proofs of his last book, *Un Captif amoureux*. His wish to be buried in Morocco, to leave no trace of himself in his country apart from his beautiful, repellent, and poisoned prose, apparently complicated the formalities of the funeral. As with Abdallah twenty years before, his body remained several days in the morgue; and as Abdallah blackened by poison had returned to his African origins, Genet would in turn be reintegrated symbolically in his adoptive land: as I later learned from his Palestinian friends, the customs official asked those accompanying the coffin whether it was the body of a migrant Moroccan worker. They proudly proclaimed it was.

The solitude of the dead, he had written in relation to Giacometti, is "our surest triumph": Genet, the honorary Moroccan worker, rests in the old Spanish cemetery in Larache—it is presently abandoned and can be reached only by crossing the town rubbish dump. His tomb looks to the sea significantly from amid the graves of our forgotten compatriots, again and forever that *Gênet d'Espagne* who rose from the pages of the *Journal du voleur* like the glow from a blazing fire.

A Black Cat on
the Rue de Bièvre

AT THE END of April 1982, after a short get-together to launch a book of mine at Ruedo Ibérico's now historic bookshop in Paris, I went out for dinner with a group of friends in one of the many North African restaurants in the area: a cheap eating-house where they served up an excellent couscous, according to José Martínez, the publisher of anti-Francoist books around whom we had gathered twenty years earlier to create the magazine *Cuadernos de Ruedo Ibérico*. We went round the place Maubert-Mutualité, across the boulevard Saint-Germain and, deep in conversation, turned down a narrow side street, on the left of which, some fifty meters from the corner, was the bistro: a square, reasonably sized room whose shape, as I sat down, suddenly reminded me of one I already knew. Only then did I notice that we were on the rue de Bièvre—now famous for being the street where President François Mitterand resides—a small street that years ago was much visited by me over a number of months. In Arabic I asked the waiter looking after us the number of the restaurant: "*Setta u aacharin, yasidi*, twenty-six, sir." While my companions were choosing the menu, I began to reconstruct mentally, behind the Moroccan décor of the moment, the layout of the furniture in the old office of the magazine *Libre*, censored by me to such an extent that I failed to recognize it when chance led me back inside. Nonetheless, those few square meters at 26, rue de Bièvre had played an important part in my life and that of a handful of Spanish writers: the critical quarterly magazine of the Spanish-speaking world that should have welded us together became, in fact, for a series of imponderable reasons, a weapon pitting us against each other, till in the end we were enemies. The personal relationships that united its initiators—almost all of them protagonists of the misnamed Latin American *boom*—went sour and, in some cases, ended there. Feelings of doubt, mistrust, and even outright hostility replaced the old warmth and camaraderie. A black cat had inopportunely passed through the magazine's home: the famous Padilla episode. The consequences of this shattered our original attempts at dialogue and discussion. Hatred, aggression, and attacks would henceforth transform the Spanish cultural community into a world of goodies and baddies worthy of a Wild West film. *Libre* thus meant an end to many friendships and illusions. Ever since its closure, for financial as much as political reasons, after a year and a half of tense, floundering existence, I had not been back to that intersection on the boulevard Saint-Germain where the future president of the French Republic already resided in 1971. I thought it was not only a joke on me but also a sign of fate that eleven years later our premises had undergone a metamorphosis into a humble couscous restaurant. That night, throughout the meal, I couldn't take my mind off the forgotten chapter of the magazine and, still savoring the familiar taste of mint tea, I decided to return there in print when time and opportunity allowed.

In the spring of 1970 a journalist active in the fringe movements that sprang up from May '68 telephoned me that a friend of hers, who closely followed issues in Latin America, was prepared to finance a political-cultural magazine aimed at a Spanish-speaking readership. She gave me her address and phone number, and after a brief telephone conversation I went along with the journalist to see her in her elegant residence on the rue du Bac. Albina de Boisrouvray was then a very young, exceedingly beautiful woman, with a passion for literature and the cinema, whose origins—her maternal grandfather Nicanor Patiño had been the famous Bolivian "king of tin"—explained her familiarity with the real problems in the world. A recent trip to

Latin America—where she would later return to collect eyewitness accounts and material on Che's capture and assassination—had brutally revealed to her the oppression, injustice, and backwardness dominating the
majority of our countries and inspired the idea of creating a medium of
expression for those striving to denounce them in the fields of politics and
literature. By way of a visiting card she modestly referred to her articles in
magazines and weeklies like *Il Manifesto*, *Politique-Hebdo*, or *J'accuse* and
defined the exact limits of her involvement in the enterprise: she agreed to
advance the sum of one hundred thousand francs to set up the magazine and
to respect scrupulously its independence. I filled her in on the broad outlines
of my idea for the future publication, its aims and ambitions, the list of possible collaborators who could advise me. Albina responded affirmatively to
my plans, and we agreed to meet again once I had taken the first steps and
spoken to my friends.

During the weeks after this meeting I explained the project by letter or
word of mouth to a dozen writers, including Cortázar, Fuentes, Franqui,
García Márquez, Semprún, Vargas Llosa, and Sarduy. I can remember Severo Sarduy listening to my panegyric to Albina—"young, beautiful, refined, a millionairess, and moreover, left-wing"—and exclaiming in his inimitable accent: "It's not true! Or else she's got cancer."

As my contacts were so geographically scattered, we decided to postpone
all discussion of the proposal until some timely event brought us together.
This appeared only months later with the première of a play by Carlos
Fuentes at the Avignon festival. We friends of his had promised to be there,
and on the day of the first performance we gathered to discuss the magazine
in Cortázar's summer residence in the nearby locality of Saignon.

I had driven from Paris with two journalists, and as we reached the Proven-
çal village where we had our rendezvous, I spotted straightaway the coach
that had brought Carlos's many friends from Barcelona. Donoso, García
Márquez, Vargas Llosa were waiting for us in the garden to Cortázar's small
chalet: the latter was now separated from Aurora, and his companion at the
time, Ugné Karvelis, acted as hostess. Cortázar had just returned from

Cuba—where he had numerous relationships with writers and bureaucrats from the world of culture—and passed on to Vargas Llosa and myself the best wishes of the already "controversial" Padilla.

When we tackled the subject of the magazine, my colleagues agreed with me that the enterprise was both interesting and opportune: its central goal, I emphasized, should be that demilitarization of culture which Sartre had proposed years before in a gathering of writers in Leningrad. The radicalization of the Cuban revolution and intensification of political and social conflicts in Latin America tended to create a cold-war atmosphere in the field of Hispanic letters and enclose the island's writers in a besieged-fortress mentality damaging to their interests. A magazine like the one we were proposing, determined to lend critical support to the Havana régime from outside, would not only help to avoid the cultural isolation of the latter but would also strengthen the position of intellectuals who from inside were struggling, like Padilla, for freedom of expression and real democracy.

The *Mundo Nuevo* operation—immediately denounced by Cuba as a cover-up for the CIA—had aroused the suspicion of Castro's cultural appointees toward any initiative stemming from Europe. Although the image that was then broadcast of Emir Rodríguez Monegal, dangerous superagent, brought a smile to the lips of those who knew him, the fact is that the past connections of *Encounter*, *Preuves*, and *Cuadernos* with United States secret services had shrouded the magazine that succeeded the one Gorkín edited for many years in a cloud of suspicions difficult to dispel. Rodríguez Monegal declared that the magazine's source of finance was completely private, and, as facts testified, he was telling the truth. However, the links existing between old and new publications—symbolized by their remaining in the offices of *Cuadernos*—maintained an air of ambiguity that we were all fully aware of, no one more so than Emir himself. If authors later associated with the *Libre* project—like Paz, Fuentes, García Márquez, Donoso, Sarduy, or I—had published texts or interviews in *Mundo Nuevo*, others, like Cortázar and in general those collaborating with the Casa de las Américas magazine, kept at a prudent distance. The suspicions of the group in the leadership of Cuban culture increased two years later because of our dismay

at the attacks by the Armed Forces journal on Padilla, whose criticism of
Lisandro Otero and defense of Cabrera Infante's novel caused a furor. The
famous interview with the author of *Tres tristes tigres* in *Primera Plana* in
August 1968 was like a time bomb going off: the idea of a dark conspiracy
against Cuba began to take shape. Coinciding as it did with the then surprising support from Castro for the Soviet invasion of Czechoslovakia, the
cultural policy of the revolutionary government progressively retrenched
and hardened. The disillusion and worries over Cuba, shared by myself and
a nucleus of fellow travelers, echoed an increasingly harsh and sectarian policy from the revolution. Although it was a risky business, the idea of building
a bridge between ourselves and the latter, of favoring dialogue between
Cuba and the non-Communist left in Europe and Latin America, was,
nevertheless, a tempting one. As events soon demonstrated, it was to prove
unviable. Inevitably, during our informal conversation on Cortázar's garden
stairs, the issue of Cabrera Infante's participation in our project provoked the
first revealing confrontation: while Vargas Llosa and I were in favor provided it were strictly literary, our host categorically declared that if Cabrera
Infante came in through one door, he would leave by the other. I can't remember opinions expressed by others present except for Donoso's words in
the bus taking us to Avignon, as shocked and irritated by Cortázar's veto as
I was. However, political arguments that seemed convincing persuaded me
to give in: I see now that our idea of a publication should have been buried
there. The need to keep up contact with the Cuban revolution and to help the
friends who from within, and in more and more difficult conditions, shared
my ideas and views overcame my hatred of proscriptions. *Libre* was born
out of deals and compromises: the future involvement of Cuban writers demanded the sacrifice of Cabrera Infante, and both Cortázar and Vargas
Llosa, our permanent links with the Casa de las Américas, who became our
ideal intermediaries, promised to defend our proposal to their colleagues at
the next annual meeting of the editorial board. As we gathered around Carlos Fuentes, in the splendid papal precinct that was the showcase for his play,
the future promoters of *Libre* innocently drank to the success of the endeavor.

A PRODIGIOUS CONDENSING OF *impressions, images, rhythms, smells, immediately on alighting from the plane in an airport where against all expectation nobody was waiting for you: the island accent sweet to your ear, the instant warmth of the air, dark, smooth-skinned or bearded faces, olive-green uniforms and caps, diffuse aromas of vegetation, the royal palms' slender trunks and lethargic fronds. Irregular flights, clearly an untimely arrival, radiograms aimed at no one. You went through police formalities, got a taxi, hesitated between the address of the Casa de las Américas and the one of the newspaper run by Carlos Franqui. Chose the latter and wound up with suitcase in the entrance hall to* Revolución *guarded by armed militiamen. Franqui came and welcomed you simply, joked about the functioning of the Cuban postal service, and accompanied you to the Free Havana Hotel, where your room had been reserved.*

It seemed as if the plants from all the greenhouses in Europe had suddenly fled to a rendezvous in Havana: frambesia, bougainvillea, aracaurias, species with lobular leaves of rubbery consistency, ficus with enormous knotted trunks, their ophidian roots airborne. Bustle in the street, a wealth of gestures and movements, a mulatto girl walking along in tight trousers, her hips trembling, just like a crème caramel in an old man's clutch, the taxi driver said.

There are cities that take over a traveler from the moment he arrives, and others that require careful treatment, react unpredictably. There are also those where a foreigner will never settle, and their encounter will be like two strangers chatting in a café or train compartment and then going their different ways.

The subtle Havana breeze, bathed in a unique, luminous glow: gusts of wind from the Malecón, Empyrean calm of the Prado, protective wind on the quayside, somnolence of an alley shaken by the slight tremor of a fiesta.

The human tide of the Revolution invading the streets of the Vedado. A demonstration against the murder of an infant brigadier; an endless procession of volunteers, array of angry, patriotic placards, hymns spluttered out over the loudspeakers, satirical ditties, slogans, and messages.

You and Franqui made your way through the mass of people present at the event, all there to hear the words of their Leader. Suddenly, an ice-cream seller in an understandable rush entrusted his cart to your companion; to your wonderment, the director of Revolución *gleefully took over the business and dispatched ice creams to his customers with the speed, enthusiasm, and efficiency of someone who had been doing it for a lifetime.*

Your letters to Monique communicate your feelings of blissful joy, soaked in an atmosphere of solidarity favoring lyrical transport: the people had regained their dignity, which they proclaimed; happiness was within the reach of everyone; despite the boycott and threats, nobody was prepared to give in. How could one live, after so many frustrated dreams, without Cuba's warmth and fervor? What better token of love than to invite her to share the Island with you?

Curious sensation of experiencing a prismatic acceleration of time. The spontaneous popular reaction to the Punta del Este conference and exclusion from the Organization of American States: swaying syncopated movements, circles of raised hands, thousands of throats clamoring against unacceptable foreign interference. Third anniversary of the fall of Batista: high-pitched speeches, phrases chorused to a pachanga rhythm, a determination to die defending the conquests of the Revolution. Your trip to Santiago and the Oriente province: a sumptuous splendor of vegetation, white sandy beaches, militia troops dancing under the coconut trees, the harvest freed from the slavery of centuries, peasants happily cutting sugarcane, political discussions and conversations with a Caribbean musical lilt.

The literary experience of Pueblo en marcha, *your contradictions and ancestral guilt exorcised, the application of moral deconstruction to a past that fascinated, captivated you: the appropriation of a mulatto universe into whose sweet charm you sank in innocent ritual beatitude.*

In your besotted, confused state of mind, impossible to distinguish the complex superimposition of layers: Spanish, African, the truly insular, created and imposed by the Revolution; the simultaneous presence of a residual past condemned to extinction and a future transmuted into present with hasty, jubilant fervor.

Fruitful discovery of the lucumí *and* abakuá *brotherhoods: litanies of the ñáñigos tiny dancing devils, mysteries of the* fambá *room, religious syncretism, ritual sacrifices, ceremonies and altars from the* santería *shop. Instinctively you homed in, headed for promiscuous areas with knife-edged existences; salty nights on the quayside, supper at the San Román tavern, musical soirées with irredeemable, leathery sirens, infinite cuba libres on the curbs of Jesús María, fertile, porous commingling in the working-class districts. Capillary action, osmosis of the two levels: the militiamen of the defense committees are simultaneously ñáñigos, prostitutes become literate and join in the re-education programs.*

The itinerary for your wandering, paralleling those of a deceased infante, communed with his premonitory vision of Bulwer: meticulous trawl through a seductive, worn-out world before the Pompeiian torrent of lava, the purifying fire, swept it away before your eyes.

Medullar belief in a shared destiny, free from all notions of social class, economic power, racism, exploitation, surplus value. Evening chats in the Central Park, captivating incursions into Regla and Guanabacoa, exchanges oiled by rum and jukebox music, a leveling familiarity, an immediate tú. *Personal gravitation toward fresh magnetic fields, tacit subterranean affinities, burning ideals still uncorroded. The siege the island suffered instigated the closing of ranks, erased and abolished the frontier between public and private. Leaning on your balcony on the eighteenth floor, you contemplated the panorama of the city transfigured by the dusk in apprehensive excitement: captive horizon, cowardly, wan light, gently iridescent breeze, evanescent labors of a* tortillon, *slow, gentle palpitating of a gigantic wounded panting animal.*

In your watchtower, your lame devil's vantage point, you were lost in your solitary thoughts: the intermittent flickering of aerials on some skyscraper, crouching shadows, confused silhouettes, an all-embracing blackness, the muffled whelp of an animal about to be swallowed by the whirlpool, to disappear with you into the night, into the vortex of the abyss.

Like that innocent wisp of white cloud that naively appears in a smooth, gleaming sky and gradually gathers around nebulas with brilliant, expansive, voracious contours, dull and threatening in their presence, the arrival of the first symptoms of decay would pass you by, be cast aside as meaningless and uncertain, despite the cautious forecasts of the meteorologists.

Through different channels and avenues, your friends carefully communicated their message: Lunes *had been closed down, Party functionaries were taking up leading positions, culture had lost its autonomy and little by little bowed before the directives of obtuse new commissars. An embarrassed silence at your questions, conversations broken off at the arrival of strangers, worries regularly silenced by your wish to counterbalance possible defects against the enormous benefits brought by the Revolution.*

Walterio Carbonell, Padilla, and Cabrera Infante came to say goodbye in Rancho Boyeros on 21 February, and the prophetic photo of you and them, preserved in your archive at Boston University, appeared the day after on the pages of Carlos Franqui's daily newspaper.

D URING MY LAST fleeting visit to Cuba—invited along with fifty-odd writers and artists to the anniversary celebrations of the assault on Moncada, in July 1967—I found myself in a very different situation than the one I had experienced on previous stays. The difficulties created by the comprehensive United States blockade and by the mistakes of the Cuban leadership itself were compounded by a climate of reserve, if not fear, which those of us who had been brought up in a dictatorship scented more easily than people accustomed to the rights and freedoms of democratic society. It is not my aim to delineate here the transformations suffered by the Cuban revolutionary project from its inception to the historic failure of the giant sugar harvest of 1970: I have referred to them in another context and I won't cover that ground again.* I shall point out only that the popular enthusiasm that I had known had been replaced by a sloganizing enthusiasm, which was hard pressed to hide its forced, purely official character. The warmth of our welcome, Franqui's bustle of activity to ease our path and give a touch of spontaneity to the festivities were not enough to hide the presence of a ubiquitous, all-powerful bureaucracy that was discreetly tracking our movements from behind the scenes. I can remember how during a happening organized by Franqui opposite the old Caballero funeral parlor I was interviewed live on television, and while we were preparing the outline of the eventual interview, the journalist in charge asked me not to mention the name of Cabrera Infante when referring to Cuban narrative, although he had not as yet broken with the revolution: I

*See my essay "Cuba, Twenty Years of Revolution," *The New York Review of Books*, 26 April 1979, 17–24; "Neither God Nor Master," an interview with Ernesto Parra, *Black Rose*, Spring 1979.

obeyed his advice on the surface and refrained from naming him, but I did remark that the most important Cuban novels in recent years were *Paradiso*, *Tres tristes tigres*, and *El siglo de las luces*. The next day, I had a telephone call in my room at the Hotel Nacional: it was Lezama Lima. He thanked me for having referred to his novel and added: "Do you know that it is the first time in my country someone has spoken about it on television?" But for the majority of the guests, especially those who were visiting Cuba for the first time and had no knowledge of our language, it was a successful trip. My friends—Marguerite Duras, Nadeau, Guyotat, Schuster—were delighted by the predominant atmosphere of freedom that, in the eyes of Dionys Mascolo, dwarfed the freedom they enjoyed in Paris. Castro's honeymoon with European intellectuals—described by him in a famous speech as Cuba's only real friends—had reached its high point. In 1967 the Supreme Leader willingly allowed their observations and criticisms. K. S. Karol, who was then writing his book on the revolution, was the object of Castro's individual attention; he accompanied him by jeep and helicopter in his journeys around the island. Surrealists like Leiris and Schuster thought they had discovered the libertarian revolution they dreamed of: when they bumped into a hardened Stalinist like Siqueiros at the opening ceremony of the May Art Exhibition, the poet Joyce Mansour gave him a tremendous kick up the backside "on behalf of André Breton."

For someone who knew Cuba well and had many friends among its writers and intellectuals, the outlook was quite different. During my stay in Havana I managed extensive conversations with Franqui, Padilla, and other companions whom I will not list since they still live in the country: as a result I found out about problems and obstacles they met with, the continual police presence and the ravages of self-censorship. I was also visited at the Hotel Nacional by Virgilio Piñera: his worsening physical state, the signs of a life of panic and distress were quite visible. Frightened like someone on the run, he wanted us to go out to the garden to converse freely. He related in detail the persecution suffered by homosexuals, the way they were being spied on and rounded up, the existence of the camps run by the UMAP (Military Units Supporting Production). Despite repeated moving evidence of attachment to the revolution, Virgilio lived in constant fear of betrayal and blackmail: his voice trembled and even when walking within the beautiful, well-kept hotel grounds, he could speak only in whispers. When we bid farewell, I found the impression of moral solitude and misery emanating from his person quite unbearable.

My feelings and opinions on the Cuban revolution were perceptibly modified in the course of that rapid and exhausting trip. The ideal of a more just, egalitarian society that was also free and democratic originally proclaimed by the 26 July movement had been replaced by a schema I was well acquainted with from my visits to Soviet-bloc countries: that "real socialism" where, as the Berlin student leader Rudi Dutschke once said, "all is real except for the socialism." From then on, my external support for the revolution lacked enthusiasm and conviction. With Franqui's discreet exit just before Castro's speech in the Chaplin Theater in August 1968, my rather vague hope for some modification in the sectarian *caudillo* approach diminished even further: in the space of two or three years, Cuba had ceased to be my model.

While I ate my share of couscous at the Moroccan restaurant in the old *Libre* office, I began to review internally my gradual alienation from the Castro régime: the descent from that "lyric effusion" I detected in my fellow travelers in 1967—like the "revolutionary tourists" in Hans Magnus Enzensberger's masterly description—to the more prosaic, lucid attitude of someone who has ceased to see the world through the blinders of ideology and has shed a number of scales on his eventful journey.

On 8 November 1968, just after 2 P.M., I went down the boulevard Bonne Nouvelle to stretch my legs and buy *Le Monde*, when a report from the paper's Cuban correspondent suddenly caught my attention: "The organ of the Armed Forces denounces the counterrevolutionary maneuvers of the poet Padilla." The article, signed with Saverio Tutino's initials—also the special envoy of *Paese Sera*—reproduced some passages from the *Verde Olivo* diatribe against the poet, whom it accused not just of a catalogue of literary-political provocations, but also—and this was much more seri-

ous—of having "happily squandered" public moneys during his time as the
director of Cubartimpex. According to the author of the editorial, Padilla
led a group of Cuban writers who allowed themselves to be swept along by
sensationalism and foreign fashions "by creating works whose effeminacy
was mixed up with pornography and counterrevolution."

Padilla's polemic with Lisandro Otero, the vice-president of the National
Arts Council and the old and new editorial boards of *El Caimán Barbudo*, in
the summer and autumn of 1967 over the relative merits of *Tres tristes tigres*
and a now rightly forgotten novel by Otero had split the Cuban intellectual
coterie into two irreconcilable factions: with a rashness verging on blindness—the casual attitude that would lead him to play a game much beyond
his strength and for which he was clearly unfit both morally and physically—Padilla had set the literary talent of the emigré against the mediocrity
of the official writer, dubbed the Writers' Union "a pathetic puppet show"
and railed against "the false hierarchies established by the degree of give in
a writer's backbone, his age, and posts in the government"; in Cuba, the poet
concluded, "it is a fact that a humble writer cannot criticize a novelist–vice-
president without being attacked by the short-story-telling director and the
poet-editors entrenched behind that generic title, *the editorial board*."

His sarcasm at the expense of the docility and conformism of his colleagues brought a series of reactions from the "young revolutionary authors"
grouped around *El Caimán Barbudo* and Otero himself. When the echoes
of the polemic had still not faded, Cabrera Infante's break with the revolution and the prize obtained by *Fuera de juego* in UNEAC's annual compe-
tition put the spotlight back on Padilla. Placed in an uncomfortable position
by the violence of the attack from the man he was defending, Padilla reacted
with characteristic ambiguity: if on the one hand he disassociated himself
from Cabrera Infante in a letter sent to *Primera Plana*, on the other—from
an official perspective—he kept on with his "provocations." Whatever the
state of play, he was obviously vulnerable and his friends were extremely
anxious when they read Tutino's note in *Le Monde*.

On Franqui's advice, I got into contact with Cortázar, Fuentes, Vargas
Llosa, Semprún, and García Márquez and tried to talk by telephone with

Padilla from Ugné Karvelis's Gallimard office. Given the futility of the telephone calls—his number never answered—we resolved to send a telegram signed by us all to Haydée Santamaría in which, after declaring "our consternation at the slanderous accusations" against the poet, we manifested our support for "every action undertaken by the Casa de las Américas in defense of intellectual freedom." Haydée's telegrammed response—received two days later—filled us with amazement:

> Inexplicable how you can know from so far away whether accusation against Padilla slanderous or not. The cultural line of the Casa de las Américas is the line of our revolution, and the directorate of the Casa de las Américas will always be as Che wished: guns at the ready, firing on all fronts.

After that I heard little or very little of Padilla and a group of friends who, like Virgilio, Rodríguez Feo, Lezama, Arrufat, Walterio Carbonell, or Pablo Armando Fernández, seemed under direct attack from the *Verde Olivo*, UNEAC, and the appropriation of cultural power by that group of unashamed opportunists who had distinguished themselves three years earlier with their ridiculous, pitiful invectives against Neruda. The number of trustworthy visitors had been considerably reduced since Franqui's demise, and the coded messages or letters I sometimes received already pointed to the almost paranoid atmosphere of mistrust so eloquently described by Jorge Edwards in his controversial account:* Marx's justice-bearing fraternal project had undoubtedly been replaced by the tangible reality of Orwell's universe.

*Jorge Edwards, *Persona non grata*, 1973.

THE UNFORGETTABLE ATMOSPHERE *of expectation during the missile crisis: general uncertainty, diffuse apprehension, unusually authentic human relationships, hazy reading of signs leading to the cataclysm. But calm and good humor prevailed: the last drop of life was squeezed out. Scarcity of products, liquidation of small street-traders, egalitarian austerity imposed by decree, accepted with resignation or heroic glee.*

You were preparing a filmscript for ICAIC and surveyed possible locations with Gutiérrez Alea and Sarita Gómez. The saltpeter wind of the Caribbean not only corrodes the fronts of buildings and battered wooden houses, car bodies, and metal railings: it also eats into the faces and looks of those dwelling in poor districts, devotees of Ochún, Yemayá, and Changó: wrinkles transformed into crevices, sudden old age, sickly smiles, sidelong glances, opaque, glazed eyes, rusted tone of voice.

One Sunday in November 1962 Franqui took you to an agricultural development near Havana frequently visited by Fidel. After a time spent looking around the plots, a procession of official cars warned you of his arrival: el Comandante *was there surrounded by other* comandantes *smoking cigars like him, chorusing his every word. Franqui went to greet him and introduced you: here's a Spaniard, he said, with a smile, he's had the bright idea of paying us a visit rather than rushing off like other writers you know. Fidel joked with you and while he explained his plans for cheese and milk products with a passion that would have delighted your father, you gave him a good looking-over. He had a bright, cunning, roaming expression: out of the corner of his eye he spied the effect his words were having, and at times you caught a mistrusting, evasive expression of instinctive suspicion.*

Unfortunately for you, he decided on the spur of the moment to show off his shiny vinegar tanks: although you went in cheerfully prepared to follow his guided tour to the bitter end, your innate allergy to acetic acid was more powerful than your own strength of mind and forced you to leave the cellars sick, at the point of suffocation. He seemed upset by the violence of your reaction, and after a lordly tour of the estate left without saying goodbye.

From then on, you saw him only from a distance and in public, on his impromptu visits to Franqui's paper, jumping out of a jeep or perched on his orator's podium, speechifying with a magisterial sweep of the forearm, wagging a hypnotic index finger, in his extremely didactic style.

A scheduled meeting with the volunteer coffee-planting brigades in Havana's future green belt. The collective enthusiasm seemed real and people signed up to sow before or after their normal work hours in factories or offices. Some of your writer friends joined in the campaign with great energy and gusto. The scene impressed you favorably, but Franqui took it upon himself to turn on the cold shower. Coffee would never grow there because the land was not suited to coffee bushes.* He was of peasant stock and saw the gap between reality and slogan. You were surprised and asked why they were wasting so much time, effort, and persistence in an activity doomed to failure.

It had been Fidel's personal decision. Who would bell the cat?

In the entrance hall to the ICAIC, where you had gone to pick up your check, you bumped into its director, Alfredo Guevara, and took the opportunity to talk to him. You were alarmed by the attacks on him from the leading group in the old Cuban CP because of his so-called softness for decadent bourgeois art. Blas Roca, Vicentina Antuña, Edith García Buchaca criticized him for allowing the screening of Accatone *and* La dolce vita: *their sour confrontation with the ICAIC perhaps augured the arrival of difficult times, of a period of narrow-minded, puritanical sectarianism. Guevara listened, his smile never fading, modulating his s's with sybaritic delight: they can shout as much as they like, he said, what Blas and these people don't realize is that before passing a script or buying a European film, I tell the plots to Fidel, and if he likes them, that's the end of the matter.*

*It never did grow. Years later not another word was heard of Havana's wonderful green belt.

Your first interview with Che, organized by the Casa de las Américas, came to nothing: the person allotted the task of accompanying you got lost, and you reached the Ministry of Industry out of breath only to be informed by the orderly that Che was busy with other people; he used your regrettably late arrival to justify leaving you in the lurch.

For the moment you were happy enough to survey him from the guests' stand during the great revolutionary celebrations. Fidel had the power; he was in temporary attendance. Unlike Fidel, Che distanced himself ironically from any attempt at servile flattery. His subordinates admired and feared him: he wore a halo of obvious charisma and seemed to defend himself from it by digging himself in behind a barrage of taunts and barbed comments.

When you finally met him it would not be in Cuba, but Algiers, where you had been invited with a group of French sympathizers to the ceremonies commemorating the first anniversary of independence. Che Guevara was there, en route from a long trip to the USSR, and Jean Daniel had an idea for a magnificent scoop: interview him for L'Express *on the recent, undoubtedly instructive, experience. You phoned the ambassador "Papito" Serguera and got an appointment at the embassy for that same night. Having learned your lesson, you showed up on time, but he in turn kept you waiting in a modestly furnished room where, on a low table in the middle flanked by a sofa and two armchairs, stood out in all its glory the cheap edition of a book: a volume of Virgilio Piñera's plays. Che and Serguera had hardly arrived when, before saying hello and settling down on the sofa, Che imitated you, took the book, and immediately poor Virgilio's work went hurtling through the air to the other end of the room, as he aimed a peremptory bewildered question to all gathered there: Who the fuck's reading that pansy?*

Did you foresee then what would happen, what was going to happen, what was happening to your brothers in nefarious vice, the reviled crimine pessimo, *and along with them,* santeros, *poets,* ñáñigos, *lumpens, idlers, and scroungers, unadapted or incapable of adaptation to a monochrome reading of reality, to the implacable, disciplined, icy glare of ideology?*

Rescue the scene from oblivion, resurrect the brief, dazzling transfiguration.

The raw morning light of the tropics, a halt on the road, time to put gas in the car that was taking you or bringing you back from somewhere, a small kiosk with little cups of coffee and fresh fruit juice, a quiet spot, early morning or late-night customers, and the eruption, his unreal, titivated, tiny, ageless, baggy-eyed eruption, all atremble, my boyfriend, where is my boyfriend, soft, tremulous tones, but piercing, almost challenging, a leaf blown down by a gust of wind, swept along by panic, where is he, what'll become of me, questions fired at no one, only at his own terror, amid the embarrassed silence of the sleepless café, of the customers silenced by the spectacle, frantically tidying his scant hair, combing without a comb, no face powder, no lipstick, only winks, nervous tics, Saint Vitus's dance, a ravaged smile, feverish contortions, uncoordinated, uncontrolled gestures.

An impression of the black district of Jesús María, leaving your favorite spot early in the morning: small bars and shops shut up, deserted pavements, tumbledown houses, as if emptied of all substance, drunks arguing crossly in a dark alleyway, old propaganda posters torn down by the wind. Cuba is not the Congo, is not the Congo, the Congo, but no clue or indication as to what Cuba is.

Before, afterwards, some day or other when your friend the poet Navarro Luna fetched you from your hotel to take you to the closing session of a political education course for hundreds of young girl volunteers, to what promised to be—yet would not be, as you later realized with the lucidity of hindsight—a routine, anodyne soirée.*

See Forbidden Territory, pages 115–17.

I MADE THE FIRST steps toward eventual publication of the magazine on my return to Paris in December 1970 after a three-month stay in Boston. The quest for a suitable person to be editor-in-chief led to some friction. Apparently, Ugné Karvelis had a candidate for the post, but Franqui deeply mistrusted her: sunk in a Kafkaesque nightmare in which reality and neurosis came together to the point of total fusion, Padilla had sent us various messages to put us on our guard against her "double game." Julio Cortázar's former partner had gradually woven a net of privileged relationships between the literary coterie on the Rive Gauche and the leaders of the Cuban revolution, and although I was not then aware of her uncontrolled aggression, limitless thirst for power, and incredible, almost Florentine capacity for intrigue—characteristics I would experience at my own cost years later—our differences of opinion on the evolution of Castro's régime and the future role the magazine should play encouraged me to keep her at a distance. The candidates I toyed with had the drawback of being Spaniards or Latin Americans long resident in Europe and consequently out of touch with the real day-to-day problems in their countries. While we drew up a short list of writers suitable for the job with Severo and Albina, García Márquez suggested the name of a close friend of his, whose ideas, political and cultural perspectives, he pointed out, were very close to my own. Days afterwards, Plinio Apuleyo Mendoza came to see me, and after an open, informal conversation we agreed on the focus and options for *Libre*: support for Allende's socialist experiment and liberation movements in Latin America; critical backing to the Cuban revolution; struggle against the Francoist régime and all other military dictatorships; the defense of freedom of expression wherever it was threatened; the denunciation of Amer-

ican imperialism in Vietnam and Soviet imperialism in Czechoslovakia. Plinio was, moreover, on very friendly terms with the leaders of the Venezuelan
MAS—at the time the liveliest, most dynamic political group in Latin
America—whose involvement in the project I judged to be indispensable.
This detail, and the interest shown by García Márquez, persuaded me he
was the person I was looking for. I introduced him to Albina, and after
agreeing on the material basis for his work with her, he immediately began
to carry out the duties of chief editor.

The selection of a secretary was less onerous: Cortázar put forward the
name of Grecia de la Sobera, at the time married to his friend Rubén Bareiro
Saguier. The office where the magazine was to be based was supplied by Albina: small premises situated in the basement of 26, rue de Bièvre, belonging
to one of her former employees. The room looked straight out onto the street
and had a washbasin and back room. After furnishing it with bargain-
priced office equipment—tables, armchairs, filing cabinets—we discovered
it was useless for receiving visitors and even for just walking round: the
pompously titled *Libre* news office in France was really a pleasant cubbyhole. When describing the minute area of the future couscous restaurant,
and perhaps alluding humorously to the stormy personal relations of its former occupants, García Márquez would quip years later: "That small space
was only fit for fucking in."

As we had agreed in Saignon, Cortázar and Vargas Llosa took advantage of
their trip to Havana in January 1971, on the occasion of the annual meeting
of the committee of the Casa de las Américas, to explain the idea of *Libre*
and try to enlist the support of Cuban writers. The independent nature of
our enterprise and impossibility of controlling it from afar aroused the latter's suspicions, despite the fact that the statement of intent and list of collaborators constituted the best possible guarantee of our favorable attitude toward the revolution. As both informed me on their return, the Cubans had
listened politely to their arguments and made no promises of active participation.

During the following weeks—packed with gossip hostile to *Libre* and alarming news filtering through from Havana—Plinio and I wrote a note that, with the backing of Cortázar and friends resident in Barcelona, later appeared in the first issue of the magazine:

> Present circumstances in Latin America and Spain urgently demand the creation of a means of expression open to all those intellectuals who critically face up to the requirements of revolution. *Libre*, a quarterly publication with totally independent sources of finance, will offer its columns to writers struggling for the real emancipation of our peoples, not just political and economic but also artistic, moral, religious, sexual emancipation [. . .] *Libre* will engage in revolutionary tasks at all levels fundamentally available to the printed word: "to change the world" according to Marx's program, and "to change life" following Rimbaud's desire.

Albina's social life and family background—that "dirty Patiño money" soon to be thrown in our faces—had surfaced right from the inception of the magazine: those who tried to tar our friend with the original sin of her ancestors seemed to be unaware, on the other hand, that a revolutionary bourgeois like Marx had lived almost all his life on the appropriation of the surplus value of Engels's workers. Such accusations, however grotesque and unjust they were, nevertheless succeeded in their objective: namely to put us on the defensive from the start and force us to justify a modest economic contribution that really required no justification whatsoever.

As we were assembling the contents of the first issue, which carried contributions from Vargas Llosa, Cortázar, Paz, Donoso, Fuentes, and my brother Luis, together with some of Che Guevara's unpublished writing with a prologue by Franqui and a study from Teodoro Petkoff, the small office on the rue de Bièvre buzzed with life and activity. Plinio had a flow of Latin American visitors interested in the project, while Grecia held court with her retinue of admirers. The worries I had felt on my return from Boston concerning the risks inherent in the venture—worries that brought me to the point of throwing the project overboard after a most painful attack of shingles—gradually dissipated as the magazine took shape. For the first and only time in my life I experienced the joy and problems of collaborative work—work that, I should make clear, was carried out in a totally disinterested way. Through Marvel Moreno, Plinio's wife at the time, Plinio himself, and Rubén Bareiro's wife, we corresponded with our future collaborators, laid the basis for *Libre*'s distribution in Europe—entrusted via Sarduy to Editions du Seuil—and discussed its possible impact on Spanish America. The storm gathering over our heads caught us completely unawares. One day I was woken up by the ring of the telephone to be told very excitedly by Plinio that Padilla had been arrested.

On that gray March day in 1971, the *Libre* office telephone rang continually. Heberto's friends called from Spain, England, Italy, asking us what they should do. The naked brutality of what had happened came as confirmation of the fears we had been harboring for months and suddenly confronted us with our own irremediable impotence.

At Franqui's insistence, I contacted Cortázar in order to draw up a letter of protest to the Supreme Leader and request he intervene. The author of *Rayuela* set a time for me to see him in his home on the place du Général Beuret, and we composed together what would later be known as the "first letter to Fidel Castro," a letter that won the approval of Franqui, to whom we had spoken while drawing it up. We then decided it should be a private letter, so the recipient could consider our case without the inevitably damaging impact of a blaze of publicity. Our only proviso was that if we had no reply after a given period we reserved the right to send a copy to the newspapers.

In respectful, measured tones the statement proclaimed the signatories' solidarity with the aims and principles of the revolution, expressed our worries over the use of repressive methods against intellectuals exercising their right to criticize from within, and sounded the alarm as to the negative repercussions of such actions on writers and artists throughout the world "for whom the Cuban revolution is both symbol and banner." Once we had collected some fifty signatures, including those of Sartre, Beauvoir, Claudín, Calvino, Fuentes, Moravia, Nono, Paz, Anne Philippe, Susan Sontag, Semprún, and Vargas Llosa, we sent the letter to the Cuban embassy, pointing out we would at some time in the future publish the letter. Plinio had tried in vain to track down García Márquez in Barranquilla and, in the mistaken belief that we had his approval, included his name on the list. This detail would be disowned later by the author of *Cien años de soledad*. With his consummate skill in wriggling out of tight corners, Gabo would carefully distance himself from his friends' critical position while avoiding confrontation with them: the new García Márquez, genial strategist of his own enormous talent, victim of fame, devotee of the great and good in this world, and promoter at the planetary level of real or would-be "advanced" causes, was about to be born.

A few days later, Vargas Llosa called from Barcelona to announce the visit of Jorge Edwards, whose diplomatic mission in Cuba had come to an end and who was now to take up his position in Allende's embassy in Paris. Edwards wished to see me and Cortázar, and his startling account of recent months, later brought together in the pages of *Persona non grata*, convinced me that Heberto's arrest might be much more serious than we had thought at first. The Padilla case was not simply an unfortunate episode in a struggle of internal tendencies, but the fruit of a political decision taken personally by Castro. For reasons that he alone knew, the Supreme Leader had decided to put an end to any form of dissidence and establish the intangibility of his "ideological monolith."

When our letter appeared in the newspapers, I was traveling around the Sahara, Algeria, and Morocco. I read the summary of Padilla's retractions at the UNEAC shortly before my return to Europe in one of those collective taxis that ply between Tetuan and Tangier. I had bought the *Herald Tribune* and the contents of the brief news item from the United States agency made me fume in angry indignation. After telephoning Plinio, I decided to stop off in Barcelona, where Vargas Llosa now had the complete text of the "confession" and wanted to discuss the matter with me.

It is an unreal, grotesque exercise to review with hindsight the *Prensa Latina* transcript of Padilla's statement at the UNEAC. The extravagant staging of the act, Dostoevskian revelations of the accused, the palinode of his supposed accomplices, the cultural commissars' references to the "beautiful night" ruined by Norberto Fuentes's obstinacy are not only a parodying remake of the Stalinist trials but a really Ubuesque setup that would have sent Jarry himself into fits of ecstasy.

Beating his breast, Padilla confessed he had been "unjust and ungrateful toward Fidel, for which he would be eternally repentant." He admitted that the revolution could not "continue to tolerate that poisonous situation with all those disaffected little groups from intellectual and artistic areas of life." Against the mistaken, embittered posturing of his friends, he counterposed the "humility, simplicity, sensitivity" of the very "intelligent" State security police, a "group of most valiant comrades working day and night to ensure moments like this" through "long, intelligent, and extraordinarily brilliant forms of persuasion" that had made him see "clearly every single one of my errors." After revealing he had written a "clever little novel" that would fortunately never be published, "because I have torn up and will tear up each little bit I might come across some day," he declared he felt "so fed up, so sick, so pathetically sad, so damagingly counterrevolutionary that he could not bring himself to write." In that bankrupt state, he had experienced his detention within his heart like a "just, moral imprisonment" where he had written "pretty pieces, new poems"—on Spring, for example—"in a kind of desperate catharsis."

For those of us who knew Padilla and were aware of his literary and political interests, that distressing caricature of a confession seemed sown with snares and traps for his guardians and coded messages aimed at his friends. The poet knew by heart the official discourse imposed on Trotskyists and Bukharinites during the great Stalinist purges and had taken over its formulas and clichés, exaggerating them to the point of absurdity. The abject mea culpas, the typically Vishinskyan references to "the French Pole Karol" or "the old counterrevolutionary agronomist René Dumont," his boundless licking-up to the system that oppressed him might deceive the state functionaries who had organized the act, but not the readers of Swift or Brecht. Apparently giving in to force and using their language, Padilla had recourse to the cunning of a Mark Antony in his harangue on the assassination of

Caesar. If, as one of Valle-Inclán's heroes says, "Spain is a grotesque reflection of European civilization," the theatrical staging of Padilla's surreal confessions of guilt at the UNEAC was a grotesque Caribbean reflection of the infamous Moscow purges.

I have often wondered how the leaders of Cuba's cultural life could have fallen into such a clumsy trap. The whole proceedings constituted a bloody mockery of the principles of freedom, dignity, and justice that the revolution was trying to defend and no doubt had defended at the beginning. That its protégés could not see this has always filled me with incredulous amazement. When Padilla says, "You have to live this experience" and adds, after correcting himself and mercifully hoping that the present company "does not have to," that "you have to live it, to really feel it, to be able to understand what I am saying," the message he was transmitting to us could not have been clearer.

That having been said, with the greater objectivity brought by retrospective vision of the facts, if the Poet's extravagant palinode lay bare the mechanisms of oppression within Castro's "Leninist-caudillista" régime, it also betrayed a series of idiosyncrasies and traits in the accused that fostered the farce he had to perform. When Padilla spoke of his character defects and grave psychological problems, his words introduced a brief note of sincerity into the oneiric context of the ceremony. Together with the warmth, generosity, wit, and humor that so seduced and seduces his friends, Padilla would sometimes surprise us with his frivolous, narcissistic behavior: he loved to adopt the airs of an enfant terrible, throwing himself into irritating or pathetic histrionic attitudes. Incomprehensible carelessness and thoughtlessness pushed him into a game from which he would necesssarily emerge the loser. His intelligence was often cynical and corroding: irresistible vertigo seemed to drive him to the abyss, to that "moral and physical self-destruction" he had mentioned in the course of his speech.

On his return from the USSR, where he had lived for a year working as a proofreader on the weekly *Novedades* in Moscow, he had a perfect knowledge of the mechanisms of "real socialism" as practiced in Soviet-bloc countries. He had been traumatized by his internal analyses of that society of zombies. I remember how when he stopped off in Paris he accompanied me to a literary cocktail party in the gardens at Gallimard and, while contemplating the cheerful, complacent writers and intellectuals prancing on the well-kept lawn, glass of whiskey or champagne in hand, he had exclaimed with a sarcastic roar of laughter, "Oh, if only they knew!" He had come back from the society of the future *and he knew*. However, he had continued his journey to Havana, into the lions' den, without taking the elementary precaution of donning the protective mask of conformity. Just like my friend Martha Frayde, he had continued to express his ideas at the top of his voice; like her, he had reaped the punishment his rashness deserved.

The shocking, ridiculous ritual of the famous soirée at the UNEAC is, of course, one of the greatest blunders of the Cuban revolution: all those involved, whether as judges, accused, or mere witnesses, were inevitably marked, and the blight similarly reached those who felt obliged to react after reading the transcription of the official Castroite news agency.

In spite of my great repugnance at the idea of setting foot in the Spain of the time, I made a short stopover in Barcelona. Vargas Llosa lived in an apartment on the Vía Augusta, not far from the Bonanova district where I was born, and when I reached his house, I found him in discussion with a group of friends who, at one time or another, had traveled to Cuba and proclaimed their solidarity with the revolution: Castellet, Barral, my brother Luis, Hans Magnus Enzensberger . . . It was there, together with the complete text of the UNEAC session of self-criticism, that I learned the recent breathtaking news from the island. The Supreme Leader's violent speech against the "libelous, bourgeois, intellectual, CIA agent gentlemen [. . .] the brazen pseudoleftists who want to win their laurels in Paris, London, Rome [. . .] rather than in the front-line trenches" and his declaration at the National Congress for Education and Culture, held at the end of April in Havana, where, in his desire to preserve the "ideological monolith" of the revolution, he launched the hunt for all forms of deviationism and heterogeneity, indicated that Castro's régime had decided to weed out its hesitant or lukewarm supporters. These were dubbed as "rubbish," "intellectual rats," "minor agents of colonialism," etc. In the great clear-out of "foreign fashions, customs, and extravagances," homosexuality in all "its forms and manifestations" was to be eliminated, African religions were dubbed "seedbeds of delinquency," and rebellious youths were to be condemned to forced labor in the pursuit of norms of moral hygiene that astonishingly recalled those dictated by Fascist régimes.

Our measured, respectful letter to Castro thus earned the signatories a terrible diatribe in which the most worn-out clichés and stupidest accusations came together. Such a disproportionate reaction—on top of the tragicomic masquerade performed by Padilla—forced us to take the bull by the horns and reply to the flood of insults. Our second letter to commander Fidel Castro, written on that 4 May afternoon in Vargas Llosa's flat, was not a response that matched up to the challenge: rather than analyzing point by point the accumulation of regressive decisions that over recent years had transformed the Cuban revolution into a totalitarian system, it concentrated its reply on the UNEAC spectacle, although toward the end we partially made up for our mistake by adding, following Enzensberger's advice, a paragraph that should have really been at the center of our thinking:

> We are not alarmed by the contempt for human dignity shown in forcing a man to accuse himself ridiculously of the worst betrayals and vilest acts because he happens to be a writer, but because any Cuban comrade, peasant, worker, engineer, or intellectual might also be the victim of similar violence and humiliation.

Although none of us had the slightest illusion as to the impact of our protest, we decided to gather the greatest possible number of signatures at the foot of our letter before sending it, this time to *Le Monde*. The following day, with the text of the letter in my pocket—while Vargas Llosa wrote his resignation from the Casa de las Américas committee—I returned hotfoot to Paris.

When I reached the *Libre* office, it looked as if it had been hit by a hurricane. Latin American writers and press correspondents wanted to know our po-

sition on the incident, and the telephone would not stop ringing. Although
the varied points of view of its collaborators prevented the magazine from
taking a stand, with Plinio's agreement the office became our center for co-
ordinating the collection of signatures for the second letter. With a delightful, inexcusable lack of awareness, we telephoned the four corners of the
earth, forgetting that our publication's limited budget did not cover such ex-
penditure. But our moral indignation at the time and solidarity with our Cuban friends on whom the trapdoor had just closed meant more than any
arithmetic calculation. A year later, as a result of Rubén Bareiro's momentary arrest by the Paraguayan police, the passionate Grecia would equally
move heaven and earth to get help, in one of her frequent attacks of remorse
inspired by her real or imaginary infidelities. Among other reasons, *Libre*
died from its telephone bill. The political vicissitudes of the day and the defense of writer friends led us to take on a humanitarian role that we were not
equipped for. If the magazine closed after four issues, it was due not only to
the crisis within its staff but also to our generosity, lack of foresight, and
light-headedness.

The great majority of those who subscribed to the first letter and others
who, like Resnais, Pasolini, or Rulfo, had not had the opportunity to do so
approved the contents. Yet there were defections as well, including some important ones. Cortázar, who when we wrote the first protest letter had told
me to include Ugné's name, had called hours later to ask me to withdraw
it—after taking a quick look at the text, he said that he could not back it. Her
friends similarly decided to withdraw, and the day we were preparing to
send it to *Le Monde*, Barral telephoned me from Barcelona to get his signature removed. Although he was a close friend of Padilla, with whom he had
transacted some good publishing deals when the latter was in charge of Cubartimpex, I was not at all surprised by his decision: by that time I knew only
too well the strength of his convictions and his noble idea of friendship.

The letter, with sixty-two signatories, appeared when I was in Syria,
where I participated with other European intellectuals in a broadcast on the
Palestinian struggle. On my return to Paris, on 27 May, the statement had
caused an enormous stir in the Hispanic world. Letters from writers op-

posed to our position, bristling with accusations and invective, had been published or were circulating in Cuba, Chile, Mexico, Peru, Uruguay, Argentina, and Spain. Luigi Nono, who had visited the rue de Bièvre weeks earlier with a message from Franqui, was to reveal signs of an uncouth *qualitative leap* in the direction of stolidity and ideological lunacy by way of a mouth-watering telegram sent from Chile that invited me to "suspend publication *Libre* magazine financed by Patiño real mortal insult to Bolivian miners and all Latin American comrades in struggle."

Predictably, the prodigious, irrepressible lie-machine went into action at once. The presence among the signatories of some of the most outstanding, respected writers from Europe and Latin America had unleashed a groundswell of frustrations, envy, and rancor, which, under the varnish of revolutionary inflexibility, concealed the crudest possible settling of accounts. The Supreme Leader's decision to pillory us gave the green light to attacks on all fronts, in which every weapon and method was legitimate: the history of the last fifty years is littered with similar cases whose victims have been symbolically or actually hurled into the Great Dustbin of History.

"Accusations rain down on the imprudent who dare to violate taboos," writes Maxime Rodinson, the veteran third-world militant, summing up his own experience. "Analysis becomes insinuation; description, slander; criticism, attack. Your past, background, private life, anything that will bring discredit without requiring a great effort—that necessary to understand and impugn your ideas—will be dragged out. Doubt will be cast on your sources. Who wrote the book you are quoting? Is it a Trotskyite, Bukharinite, a bourgeois? Who's the publisher? Where does the money come from? Why now? What's their tactic?"

I remember how some journalists—"with good intentions" or simply after a sensationalist story—turned up on the rue de Bièvre to photograph the *hôtel particulier* or mansion where *Libre* was produced. Their amazement and annoyance when they discovered the magazine's microscopic fief were truly comical. Did the dangerous imperialist publication financed by Patiño come from that little hole with its secondhand furniture?

Parallel to opportunist proclamations of loyalty and enforced collection of signatures, the would-be orthodox revolutionaries had launched a ridiculous campaign—a tissue of lies—against us: on my stop in Algiers weeks earlier I had happened to come across Régis Debray in the street; Debray had just been on a quick visit to Cuba, after pressure from left-wing intellectuals in the West got him released from a Bolivian jail. When I asked him what he knew of Padilla, who had quoted him as his "fine example" of a revolutionary intellectual in his polemic with *El Caimán Barbudo*, Debray replied that Padilla was but a CIA agent getting his just desserts. Later on, when I was back in Paris, Simone de Beauvoir indignantly related to me how she and Sartre had bumped into Alejo Carpentier on the boulevard Raspail and how he had brusquely turned his back on them and stuck his nose up against a shop window, worried and afraid he might compromise himself just by saying hello to them. Friends had told them that the Cubans were spreading the rumor that Sartre was also a CIA agent. Even before *Libre* saw the light of day, the magazine was enveloped in an atmosphere of suspicion and espionage. However, as we were able to confirm over the following weeks, that atmosphere was not entirely without foundation. One day a North American "professor" appeared on the rue de Bièvre, speaking in perfect Spanish and expressing great interest in *Libre*; after interrogating Plinio on our political position and cultural orientation, he said he could give us material help, if we had any problems, through a private foundation whose funds he controlled. But in the course of conversation the would-be professor revealed an astonishing ignorance in matters literary. His insistence in getting Franqui's address and the wonderful philanthropy he exhibited convinced Plinio that he really was a United States secret agent. He too must have scented the reticence, since, despite his promises, he failed to show up again.

About the same time K. S. Karol, whose book on the Cuban revolution had enraged Fidel Castro, told me of an incident that befell him a year earlier and that related to the Leader. The wife of an important official personage, whom he had seen a lot during his stay in Cuba, had just separated from her husband, and after establishing herself in Paris, had come to ask him to help her find some work connected with Latin America. Karol was not at all suspicious of her and entrusted her with the typescript of his manuscript *Les Guérilleros au pouvoir*, in which he set out a series of criticisms of regressive decisions in the areas of police repression and censorship alongside analyses and commentaries that were very favorable to the revolution. On the occasion of the annual reception offered by the Cuban embassy every 26 July, Karol turned up at the banquet rooms, not worrying that he had not been sent an invitation that year. As soon as the ambassador saw Karol, he told him he had no reason to be there, since he had written an anti-Cuban, counterrevolutionary work. When Karol expressed surprise that he could know the contents of an as yet unpublished book, the ambassador maintained an embarrassed silence. On the basis of this episode, the writer reached the conclusion that the friend who had requested the pleasure of typing it had secretly passed a copy on to the embassy.

Days after Karol related this anecdote, Plinio told me that while dining with friends, he had met a very interesting woman, the ex-wife of a Cuban dignitary, who seemed very close to our perspective on the magazine and was offering to work gratis for us. I was alarmed and asked what her name was: it was the same person.

"I hope you didn't agree!" I exclaimed.

"No. Why?"

"She's a spy!"

When I brought him up to date with what had happened to Karol, we broke into wild fits of laughter. Our beautiful conception of a revolutionary vanguard cultural magazine had imperceptibly been transformed into a mediocre, well-worn plot for some pulp novel.

The first issue of *Libre* was ready for the printers just as the Padilla case burst upon us. The burning topicality of the affair and the role that the magazine's main collaborators played in it persuaded us to postpone publication until autumn in order to include a dossier of documents, eyewitness accounts, and other background articles indispensable to a correct appreciation of the problem. With Cortázar's agreement, we added a short introduction in which we declared:

Many of *Libre*'s collaborators believed it incumbent on them to state their position on this question. The opinions expressed show to what extent there exist shades and differences of opinion in the evaluation of the same event among those on the left. A critical magazine, *Libre* considers it helpful to discuss the Padilla case because of the ideological implications it has for problems in our time, such as the way forward for socialism, artistic creation within the new kinds of society created, and the position and commitment of intellectuals in relation to the revolutionary process within our own countries.*

The dossier reproduced in its entirety the UNEAC session in self-criticism, fragments of the declaration from the Cuban National Council for Education and Culture, Castro's speech at the closing ceremony there, the text of the two letters that we had sent to the Supreme Leader, the correspondence between Vargas Llosa and Haydée Santamaría, as well as a number of disquisitions, open letters, and comments from European and Latin American writers. After all these years the latter offer some meaty lessons: by the side of the dignified ludicity of writers like Paz, Fuentes, Revueltas, Ponce, Valente, or Enrique Lihn, the reactions of others evoke the twittering of those "well-trained budgerigars" that Bataille once ridiculed. Julio Roca's interview with García Márquez is a remarkable feat of juggling, whose virtuosity earns admiration rather than respect. But now, as then, the first prize for grotesque slipperiness goes to the famous "Polycriticism in the hour of the jackals."

When Cortázar submitted his text, our immediate reaction was one of rank incredulity. Could the subtle author of *Bestiario* and *Las armas secretas* have written those lines of crude doggerel, which deserved a place on their own merits in a Ukrainian or Uzbeki anthology from the glorious days of Zhdanov?

As Marvel Moreno said, after reading the "poem" in the *Libre* office, it seemed like "a tango to words by Vyshinsky." But worse than the accumulation of insults and clichés against "the pinko liberals [. . .] signatories to self-righteous statements," who until then had been the author's friends, were the lyrical outpourings and bombast to that well-known Shining Future that awaits us.

*My apologies to the long-suffering reader for the part I played in the composition of this stodgy paragraph.

It was only later, when we read the *Libro de Manuel* and other works that followed, that we were disappointed to find that their author was really the *cronopio* we had read and been dazzled by fifteen years earlier.

To give our endeavor an appearance of unity in diversity, we strove to keep associated with it people, like Cortázar and his friends, who had adopted a position opposed to the one we defended. This wish to preserve our pluralistic team of *Libre* collaborators brought in its wake, however, a number of concessions that I would soon find unacceptable. I can remember the distinguished English Hispanist J. M. Cohen—who had been a member of the UNEAC jury the year it awarded its poetry prize to Padilla's book— sending on to us Lisandro Otero's letter, a response to another one from him protesting against the humiliation inflicted on the poet. This epistle—an incredible hodgepodge of eschatological references, insults, and obscenities— faithfully reflected the hysteria then dominating the official Cuban media and, consequently, in my view was worthy of publication. Cortázar disagreed. For my part, I had written a parody comparing Padilla's ordeal to that experienced centuries before by an Andalusian poet, Abu Bakr Ben Alhach: he was guilty of writing satirical verse about the eminent judge Ibn Tawba, who condemned him to a liberal flogging and to being put on show in the marketplaces, a public abasement, "with town criers in front and the rod behind." Such an act of justice inspired the favorite court poet, Abú Ishaq de Elvira—a favored precursor of the official bards of our day—to write a magnificent work translated into Spanish by García Gómez, which includes these lines:

> A whip is more eloquent than any telling-off,
> or the deceits churned out by some lout . . .
> It makes a man dance a dance without music,
> although its hide is heavier and harder than an elephant's.

> This conceited fellow has had a good taste of it,
> tearing off strips of skin like broadbean pods . . .
> Tell him, if a satirical verse crosses his mind again:
> "Remember when you were walking around with your breeches undone.
> Recall the punishment meted out for your stupid slanders

of our glorious leaders and exalted chiefs,
people upon whom the Merciful One
bestowed great prerogatives,
allowing them to be honored with great veneration.
They are the finest flour among all people
and everybody else is in truth just leftovers in the sieve."

My congratulations to the new Caudillo and Sublime Chief did not reach
the pages of our second issue: foreseeing Cortázar's reaction, Plinio persuaded me to withdraw it. Gradually my physical move away from Paris and
the rue de Bièvre—my university lectures in New York, my stays in Morocco—was compounded by a moral distancing from *Libre*, whose hesitat-
ing direction and defensive attitude were less and less in keeping with the
original ambition behind the idea. The four issues that came out—coordi-
nated after mine by Semprún, Petkoff and Adriano González León, and, finally, Vargas Llosa—undoubtedly contain worthwhile creations and essays,
exemplary interviews and surveys, but, at the same time, texts and articles
that were obviously the fruit of compromise and which I am ashamed to
read today. In the end these accommodations turned out to be futile: when
the final issue went on sale, the likes of Cortázar and his ilk no longer figured
on the list of collaborators.

The growing difficulties caused by production costs and postage ex-
penses to Latin America, the ban on sales in Spain and other dictatorial régimes, the Cuban boycott, internal dissension, and our amateur, rather last-
minute approach to organization intensified throughout 1972 until they
killed off the magazine. The offers of economic help we received meant giving up our independence, and Vargas Llosa, Plinio, and I agreed that it was
better to close the magazine down.

After almost two years of effort, tensions, fleeting successes and abundant
reverses, we gloomily had to admit that our ambitious venture had been a
failure.

The history of *Libre* as it passed through my mind during that dinner in the
couscous restaurant on the rue de Bièvre is much more than a mere anec-

dote: to the extent that it repeats, with a minimum of variants, a combination
of situations experienced by Western left-wing intellectuals over the last fifty
years, it belongs to a historical trend of which examples abound. Many of the
supporters of the Cuban revolution, who thought they saw there the model
for the society of the future, were familiar with the sad path trodden by Bar-
busse, Romain Rolland, Éluard, Aragon, Alberti, or Neruda—all eyewit-
nesses to the brutal truth about the Soviet system and the deportation, murder, or gagging of their writer-colleagues but who kept silent when they did
not applaud the parody of the trials, who carried on with their journeys as
revolutionary tourists enjoying privileges that ordinary people lacked, having perfected that "habit of lying knowing that you are lying" denounced by
Enzensberger in one of his essays. But the idea that something similar could
happen again seemed impossible. When we visited Cuba at the beginning
of the sixties, we had more or less come to know Lezama Lima, Virgilio Piñera, Padilla, Reinaldo Arenas, César López, Walterio Carbonell, Arrufat,
Luis Agüero, and other authors who years later would suffer UMAP sentences or be reduced to silence. And the adoption of Soviet-style repression
by the leadership of the Cuban revolution filled us with bitterness and anxiety for the fate awaiting our colleagues; we were amazed to see how the
brand-new rivals to the processional oxen, indifferent to the destiny of the
Bielys, Pasternaks, or Akhmatovas—not to mention now those who per-
ished—refused to admit the reality of the new persecutions and the physical
or moral suffering of the victims, as if both were the price to be paid for the
construction of their utopia. The rationalizations for their pitiful deaf-and-
dumb game—we mustn't discourage comrades in struggle, supply the enemy with weapons, etc.—were the same as before. Sitting comfortably in
their bourgeois democracies, the standard-bearers of their so-called revolutionary causes, entertained by the unmovable leaders of the latter on their
periodic visits to get an "overview," celebrated or covered up with their complicity every one of their oppressive measures, even the most distasteful.
Their outright defense of "real socialism" and the adoption of postures that
were militant in word alone also ploughed along the same furrow as their
European predecessors. As Vargas Llosa rightly says, exposing the terrible
consequences of their Manichaean attitude, "Latin American intellectuals

have been the main instruments of Latin American underdevelopment."
The bloody, reactionary dictatorships in the Southern Cone and in Central
America would justify their unreserved support for Cuban autocracy. The
frightening "essential" distinction established by one of them in a memo-
rable interview between "the mistakes and even crimes that can occur within
a socialist context and the equivalent mistakes and crimes that may occur
within an imperialist or capitalist context" would logically lead to the equally
"essential" difference between the corpses of the Vietnamese, Guatemalans,
Salvadorans, and Afghans: the absence of the three Latin American members on the Russell Tribunal when it met in Stockholm to judge Soviet
crimes in Afghanistan—after condemning in previous years North American crimes in Southeast Asia and Central America—an absence publicly
criticized by its president, Vladimir Dedidjir, would be the inevitable consequence of that peculiar Thomist or Zoroastrian sally into metaphysics.

As we would see later, to our surprise, the followers of the official Cuban
line, who stigmatized the inconsequentiality and frivolity of pinko liberals,
would keep well clear of any analysis, in line with Marxist doctrine or basic
honesty, of their own relationships and social practice, their own actual style
of everyday life: the fact that they preferred, for example, United States
scholarships or professorial years in California to a prolonged sojourn without any kind of privilege in that political laboratory where their dreams of
harvests without slaves or imperialist powers, nourished at the cost of other
people's suffering, would run the risk of fading into nothingness. My experience in those months at *Libre* thus showed me that the high level of artistic
awareness of some of my colleagues did not necessarily match their level of
moral and intellectual rigor.

"On the morning of April 16, Doctor Rieux left his office and stumbled
over a dead rat in the middle of the stairwell," writes Camus in the first chapter of *La Peste*. From those now-distant days in which I too spotted my first
rat, a lot of water had flowed beneath the bridges of the Seine, one bank of
which passes by the street where the magazine had its home. The expulsion
of my friends from the CP, my trips to the USSR and Czechoslovakia, my
brief visits to Cuba with writers and artists in the May Art Exhibition, the

frustrated *Libre* venture, and incidents in the Padilla case would gradually swell the invading ranks of rodents till it too became an epidemic. Reality is sometimes strangely symbolic: I remember how as I left the Moroccan eating-house where I had dined with my friends, I suddenly spotted the mementolike corpse of a genuine little mouse opposite 26, rue de Bièvre.

CHAPTER V

Monique

WHILE I WAS going through my sergeant's routines in the Mataró infantry regiment, we promised each other in our letters to live as an open, mobile, undomesticated couple whose relationship would not be affected by my frequent absences nor by our mutual carefree "infidelities," but our somewhat illusory aspiration not to fall into the trap of humdrum bourgeois existence, to love each other without living together every day, and to respect our individual freedom of movement immediately clashed with the insidious inertia of habit. Once I was settled in the pleasant, modern, comfortable flat on the rue Poissonnière, I ceased to be tempted by the idea of the occasional return to my small hotel on the rue de Verneuil. Home comforts and work rituals, the desire to be near Monique, our daily renewed complicity were stronger than my theories of independence and apprehensions as to the hermetic knot of a couple. The trial period that we set ourselves for a few months was imperceptibly transformed into life together, and when our time ran out neither of us made any reference to the fact. The precautionary measures dictated by the failure of Monique's marriage and my Gidean rejection of the notion of family succumbed to the quiet persistence of daily reality, to the complex, subtle web of emotions created by that physical nearness. When I went to Spain months later, I did so knowing that it was a fleeting visit at the end of which I would return to Paris: it was disconcertingly easy—in light of my youthful aversion to the bourgeois couple—the rue Poissonnière had become my home.

I remained inflexible on only one issue: my firm decision not to have children, not to extend under any circumstance our family tree. The origin of this obsession is obscure and deeply rooted in my childhood: a desire to leave behind me only my books, not to submit to paternity's hazardous fatalism. Of all the arguments I have mulled over when analyzing this question, not one satisfies me entirely nor totally clarifies the instinctive source of the feeling. Was it a wish to prolong the giddy irresponsibility of adolescence, not to mortgage forever the precious gift of freedom? A desire to ensure my eventual progeny should avoid the experience I had to endure as a child? Was it an anxiety of existential or even metaphysical proportions? Was it an exaggerated, sickly fear of passing on the fragility and psychological disequilibrium from my mother's side, as revealed in the lives of my grandmother and Aunt Consuelo? Whatever it was, the anguish certainly existed and pursued me for years. I can remember one day as we were leaving a cinema on the Champs-Élysées, Monique suddenly felt queasy and wanted to throw up, and the friend with us began to joke and was quick to offer his ironic congratulations: although we were taking every step to avoid such an outcome, the possibility of an error and a subsequent abortion filled me with horror. A few months after we met, Monique had endured this experience in order to terminate a pregnancy by someone with whom she could not and did not wish to live, and the detailed description in a letter sent to Mataró moved me to tears. From that point, I knew what it meant to place oneself at the mercy of a stranger, the moral and physical torture of brutal, clandestine, rudimentary operations often carried out without anesthetic; however, my gut rejection of paternity was even stronger: I would not have hesitated to force abortion on her at the risk of irrevocably endangering our real, if fragile, relationship. Fortunately, it was only a false alarm and I was not compelled to push the privileges of my egoism to the extreme of cruelty. As time passed and the danger diminished, my neurosis associated with the fear of having children gradually faded until it vanished entirely at the time I began frequenting Arab haunts and we moved to Saint-Tropez.

The abrasive harshness of the destiny imposed on women, the unflinching calm and courage with which they often face up to it, will make you always doubt that the terms *weak* and *strong sex* have even a margin of precision. As you could later verify in the texture of patriarchal societies, as much in the Spain of thirty years ago as in Latin America and the Islamic world, the surface strength of the male usually masks thoughtless, even childish attitudes, insecurity concealed by arrogance, a pitifully real feebleness in the trials of existence, while as a natural reaction of self-defense, the female's inferior status endows her, in contrast, with a capacity for thought, magnanimity, and fortitude wrongly attributed to the other sex: when tried by pain, old age, and the other burdens and setbacks of life, her resistance is usually more lucid, spirited, and less complaining than the male's. To be truthful, your fear and even repulsion at the idea of becoming a father cannot be imputed only to masculine feelings of weakness and egoism: they also reveal a healthy mixture of skepticism and detachment, shared by a growing number of women and men, from the servitude of the species. By choosing writing and the gestation of books as a substitute, you saved yourself from the contingencies of the chance law of genetics, you willingly broke the chain of cause and effect. The debt and respect owed to parents came to an end with you: you were not and would not be responsible for the existence of anybody else. This decision not to propagate the species on a planet with limited resources and armed to the teeth with destructive weapons earns your unconditional approval more than two decades later. Shoddy creation is not prolonged through any fault of yours: the surprise of beauty will come to you as an extra. When life presents you in your fifties with the sparkling gift of a young girl, your attachment to her will be free and light: an almost divine offering or manna, the gracious enjoyment of which will be intoxicating.

These first months of life together stand out in my memory with diaphanous precision because of their exhilarating, fertile novelty. The move from Pablo Alcover to the rue Poissonnière, from the dull life of a son at home to a radiant conjugal state, and subsequent changes in scenery, characters, and action confronted me with a combination of novel, unexpected situations and responsibilities. When I arrived, Carole was four years old: her parents' early divorce had spared her the tensions and traumas usual in children from broken marriages, but I had to work tentatively and carefully to integrate myself in her life without disturbing or upsetting the paternal image. On the rare occasions that she called me daddy—absentmindedly and no doubt unconsciously—I immediately corrected her, insisting she call me Juan, pronounced Spanish-style. We related well together from the start, perhaps because of the imprecise nature of the family bond. When she entered puberty she went through a stormy phase, and circumstances forced me to act repressively, yet she bore no grudge against me. Even at the toughest moments in her youthful straining at the traces, she always kept up normal communication with me.

After a few weeks of this life, our process of three-cornered adaptation received outside help from an unexpected quarter. Hélène, our home-help who went out dancing every night in the hope of catching a boyfriend unblemished by the stigma of Arab or African origins and got telephone calls from suitors named Tony, Dédé, Jojo, and others of identical exemplary stock, began to feel vaginal pains and suffer hemorrhages—frequently described, *hélas*, as she brought us coffee in bed—until one day her condition worsened and we had to call an ambulance at midnight to take her to hospital. Freed of her presence—her chattiness had the knack of riling Genet—we decided to search out a Spanish woman whom a friend had recommended. Vicenta was waiting for us in a café on the rue de Buci: small, gentle, dressed in black, around forty, she had just arrived from her village of Beniarjó, where she had left behind her husband and a large collection of brothers and sisters, in-laws, nieces and nephews, and cousins. We were pleased by our first impressions of her, and she came back home with all her bits and pieces.

She was overjoyed at the idea of looking after a girl: she didn't have any children and her later solitary pregnancy, a few months after Antonio's arrival, ended sadly in a clinic from which she wrote us a moving letter, which I still have among my papers. Although she knew not a word of French, she immediately enveloped Carole in her noisy country affection: carrying her in her arms, covering her in kisses, humming carols and lullabies. At the beginning, the little girl was overwhelmed and irritated. *Tais-toi!* she would say to her. Tetuan and Melilla, Vicenta unflinchingly replied. While we had wrongly imagined that she would soon learn the language of the country, we soon realized that communication was operating in the opposite direction: Carole was starting to speak Spanish, at times interpolated with turns of speech and swearwords from Valencia. Within months, they understood each other perfectly. Vicenta took her on Sundays to the Piles bar on the rue Tiquetone or to someplace off the rue de la Pompe where she used to meet her friends from Valencia, and Carole amazed them all with her childish charms and surprising linguistic know-how. Vicenta's role in her upbringing was central and in any case softened the inevitable problems created by her parents' separation and my eruption, however discreet, into her world. The practical intelligence and instinctive wisdom of that simple woman, whose horizon remained within the bounds of her native district, were a constant source of wonderment to me. I remember the day when Carole came back upset from the Champ de Mars gardens, where she had gone to play with some other girls, to tell us of an individual who, we deduced, had masturbated in front of them; before Monique and I could embark on our futile, embarrassed commentary on the incident, Vicenta swept her up in her arms, exclaiming joyfully: "That's right, it must have been fiesta-time in his village!"—an unexpected explanation that had the virtue of calming Carole down while making her immediately forget the episode.

The quiet, pleasing warmth of Vicenta's presence on the rue Poisson-nière did not benefit only the little girl: it was a blessing for all three of us. Like Eulalia, she was a woman of strong personality; but, as I realized at once, Vicenta did not suffer from Eulalia's whims or coquettish ways, nor from her apprehensive, insistent melancholy in relation to her own or the family's destiny. In contrast to the tenderness impregnated with anguish that suffused my relations with Eulalia from the day I left Pablo Alcover, my affection for Vicenta was cheerful and straightforward, based only on pleasant cordiality. Apart from us, her world verged entirely on Beniarjó and surrounding districts. When we went for a drive in the car, Monique had attempted to show her the beautiful spots of Paris and "la Francia." A waste of

time: Vicenta looked and saw nothing, making immediate comparisons
with scenery or places near her village from which the French points of reference always came off badly: the place de la Concorde had an illuminated
fountain like the one in Beniarjó, but the latter was always changing color;
the Loire reminded her of the half-dry but better-shaded river that flowed
next to her neighborhood; people in Paris went out dressed anyhow, whereas
in her village they really smartened up on Sundays. In the field of morality
she was similarly strictly bound by the standards of her own world and remained alien to all she observed in France: over the years she spent with us,
she saw pass through our house couples coming together and falling apart,
women changing husbands, homosexuals (solitary or paired-off), and she
showed the greatest possible ease and lack of concern—easy come, easy go,
she would comment imperturbably on learning of some divorce or breakup—but such jovial condescension came to an abrupt halt at the approach
to the Beniarjó area. There, the most rigid, austere tradition reigned supreme: any transgression brought down on the heads of the guilty the ful-
minating sanctions of society. I remember her once referring to a girl whom
we had placed with some friends, hinting she would never find a husband—
that is, she added, unless she hooks a Frenchman—and when we tried to
find out why the girl was being ostracized, she explained how the young
girl's uncle had interfered with her as a child and that the whole village knew
about it. Wasn't it ridiculous to reproach her for something so far back in
time for which she was not at all to blame? In France, it would be, replied the
unruffled Vicenta, but not in Beniarjó.

Some weeks later her husband arrived and I went with her to meet him
at the Gare d'Austerlitz: dry, reserved, rather rough and ready, he had been
a goatherd in Extremadura up to the day he arrived in Valencia, where he
devoted himself to the orange harvest and was soon to meet his bride-to-be.
The three of us caught the métro, and after settling him at home, I suggested
to Antonio that he should go for a walk with me to get to know his way
around the city. "No, don't worry, señor Juan, I've seen enough," he calmly
replied. As I realized at once, his only worry was about finding work as soon
as possible: after several frustrated attempts in various factories, he managed

to get a job as a porter with a fruit-importing firm in Les Halles. Despite the fact that Monique's flat at the time comprised just three rooms, a kitchen, and two bathrooms, we adapted as best we could to the new situation. I wrote in a tiny cubbyhole that was once the kitchen, and Carole slept alongside us in the dining room. When Monique was coming back from work, Antonio would leave to load and unload trucks, returning home only at daybreak. This promiscuity didn't bother us, and Vicenta's cheerful, irrepressible character was a perfect match for our irregular, disorderly existence. Whatever time we turned up, she would quickly get our supper without losing her cool or good spirits: we've got meat, eggs, anything. She cooked as she had been taught at home, not at all impressed by the refinements of French cooking. One weekend when we went to the Mont Saint-Michel and came back determined to savor an exquisite foie gras given as a present to Monique, we discovered to our dismay that the delicacy of our dreams was not in the refrigerator. We asked Vicenta what had happened to it. "It's there," she said, pointing to the trash bin. "We were stupid enough to open the tin, and threw it away after a mouthful. It's not a bit like our rabbit *fuagrá* back home! Now *that's* really tasty."

Antonio and Vicenta's setting up home in our flat soon drew to the rue Poissonnière a good number of relatives, friends, and neighbors from their area; the responsibility for that soon becoming a veritable Sunday invasion was not truly exclusively theirs. In the neighboring compartment in the train that brought us from Spain to Paris, there was a group of emigrants eating, drinking, singing, clapping—the dust of their country still clinging to the soles of their shoes—who remained supremely indifferent to the reproving looks of the natives, visibly upset by a din and hullabaloo outside their notion of civilized behavior. One of the emigrants had gone to the lavatory before me; when I went in after him, I discovered he had left his passport next to the automatic washbasin tap. I glanced at his name (José), place of birth (Lora del Río), and home (a village in the Valencia region) and popped into his compartment to give it back. José chatted with us for a bit (it was the first time he had left Spain), asked for our address, and some while later, after Monique and I had forgotten the incident, he turned up with a group of Valen-

cians. Apparently they had found work on a building site in Rueil-
Malmaison: the following Sunday, they were going to cook a paella and
wanted us to come and eat it with them. At the back of my mind I had the
idea I was preparing a novel or documentary on the emigration that was de-
populating whole regions of Spain, and we accepted their invitation. That
autumn I went several times with Monique and her daughter to eat in the
wooden shacks where they lived, shacks that were very similar to those I
would visit alone years later at the invitation of North African friends. The
meals were noisy but pleasant: surrounded by compatriots exiled for economic reasons, I felt more in Spain than I did when in Spain itself, enveloped
in an atmosphere of warmth, spontaneity, and stimulating straightforward-
ness. Monique would later confide that she was fascinated by my attitude in
that exclusively masculine world of manual laborers: as she would then discover, my intellect and emotions were always seduced by men not belonging
to my own social class—never by men or women from our own social milieu. Although I am sure she was correct in her observation, my instinctive
affinity with men who earn a living by the strength of their arms and who
lack those "bourgeois" stigmas that, like the sacraments of the Church, make
their mark, did not include at that time a sexual component except in a sublimated form. This innate attraction, which confers on social inequality a
very similar role in the interplay of the complementary and opposites to that
normally played by difference of sex, would later deepen, become sexual, as
it reached out and went beyond the limits of my language and culture into
the incandescent brilliance of Sir Richard Burton's Sotadic Zone. But at that
stage it represented only a strange trait perceived by some third person as a
whim or eccentricity. Monique was passionately drawn to the world of masculine friendships: to the extent that she did not feel rejected, she was attracted by my ambiguity. On the beach at Peñíscola she had once seen me tip-
sily caress or let myself be caressed by one of our fisherman-friends who had
stretched out next to me by the side of the boats, and the spectacle really
stirred her up: it didn't go any further and I made love to her in the hotel—
still smelling of him, she said—while my friends drank and dived in darkness, drunk and naked. The Sunday meals in Rueil-Malmaison went on for

some months: once or twice, in response to our friends' invitations, we invited them to the rue Poissonnière. Monique's diary for 2 December 1956 pinpoints a detail: seventeen Spaniards in the house! Vicenta and Antonio prepared paella for everybody, and the banquet went on till very late, much to the excitement and happiness of Carole, spoiled and entertained by those nostalgic expatriates separated from wives and children.

Along with this chance invasion by José's worker-friends began another, slower, more furtive, and interstitial: Vicenta's brothers, sisters, and relatives gradually disembarked in Paris, appearing at our flat with their bags and big old suitcases. We had to help find them jobs and accommodations and, through Jadraque and Monique's friends, we managed to salvage some of them. The fresh migrants from Beniarjó trundled leisurely along from the rue Poissonnière to the Piles bar and from there to the vast pavements of the rue de la Pompe. Sometimes, Vicenta extended the sphere of her recommendations to other villages in the region: the girl dressed in mourning who came to our flat asking after her, she's from Benifla, Vicenta said, but she's a good soul. After a time, we had combed the entire field of our friends and acquaintances, and closed down our free employment agency with a feeling of relief. The untimely appearances and visits became less frequent. We had been drained by those months of intense Spanification and, as we admitted to each other, laughing at the end of a particularly hectic, rowdy day, we'd about had enough of it.

Your immense vitality allowed you to ride roughshod over the needs of sleep, take on the boreal rhythm of arctic nights: writing a novel or following the timetable at the publishers, reading for pleasure or out of duty, chatting at length after supper, drinking calvados in your favorite bars, going to transvestite haunts, getting drunk and making love. While you devoted the weekends to visiting Rueil-Malmaison or towns on the Normandy coast with Carole, you finished off your respective days with a tour of the cabarets on the rue de Lappe, next to the hotel where Genet was then staying, or with dinner in one of those modest Vietnamese eating-houses in the environs of the Gare de Lyon. Then night seemed young and somnambular, and you did not notice the first signs of aging and wrinkles till the early morning. Your body obeyed every caprice and decision without rejecting any, as if it were a mere appendage or instrument of your will. There was no such thing as tiredness, and you bravely fought off the impact of alcohol with Alka-Seltzer in the course of the long evenings. At that time Monique professed a real worship of queens. Guided by her cousin Frédéric, you began to explore their lairs and hiding places: you sometimes went to dine at Narcisse, a restaurant where you joined in an extravagant *réveillon* with streamers, confetti, and hysterical shouts from a group of Spanish males decked out in mantillas and combs, as if on the lookout for the hero of *Sangre y arena* or some remote, improbable Escamillo; at other times, you dropped in on the dance at the Montagne de Sainte-Geneviève, where a huge, brazen queer, also from your country, performed a number of acts with a profusion of obscene gestures, propelling, whirring his tongue round as fast as an electric fan. Genet later told you that the most audacious, provocative queens he came across in his wanderings and stays in the prisons and red-light districts of Europe were always Spanish. Whether beautiful or repellent, pathetic or derisory, their rejection of any notion of decency, their defiance of all norms and good manners, the waggles and grimaces of their laboriously re-created bodies endowed them with an exemplary moral hue. The fact that Spain forged and exported the most outrageous specimens was no product of chance: it revealed the great power of the taboo, the social stigma that marked them. Their excessive response was directly related to that excessive rejection. Unlike the Sotadic Zone, where an extended, diffuse bisexuality erases and removes the frontiers of what is illicit and becomes secretly and implicitly integrated in the marrow of society, the gravitational pull of the Hispanic canon determines the existence of centrifugal, extreme, disproportionate reactions. The plentiful numbers and aggression of the queens, Genet explained to you, were in response to the oppressive atmosphere that shaped them: it was the reverse of constrained official machismo, its lower, lunar, cleft face, its other visage.

In the company of Frédéric and Violette Leduc, who had been recently discharged from the sanatorium where she had been held, you made for the rather sordid haunts by the Gare de Lyon or Montmartre in preference to the more bourgeoisified, elegant dives on the Champs-Élysées. When Monique discovered Michou, the basement on the rue des Martyrs became her favorite port of call. You often went there with other couples or married friends: there was a promiscuous atmosphere, and one night Monique was invited to dance by an individual who, deceived by her short hair and black trousers, was hoping for a good time with someone of his own sex. "I was taken for a transvestite," went the triumphal entry in her diary. A trip to Hamburg, at the invitation of Rowohlt, the publisher, stepped up your interest in the leafy glades, shady arbors, and exuberant foliage of this nocturnal jungle. From the sixteenth to the twenty-second of April, you inspected with him the notorious establishments on the Reeperbahn and St. Pauli: the Rattenkeller, Katakombe, Rote Kotze, Mustafa. The German and Spanish transvestites were more insolent, exaggerated, and bare-arsed than the Parisian variety: you were set alight by a women's wrestling match on a hard-earth pitch, surrounded by customers drinking whiskey or champagne with bibs to keep off the splashes. After a few weeks, Rowohlt paid a return visit and wanted you to take him to a spot for masochists; but none of your friends knew of the existence of such dens, even through hearsay. In this predicament, Monique had the fortunate idea of posing the problem to Gaston Gallimard: it seemed he had dealings with an inspector from the vice squad who quite obviously ought to have been well informed on the matter. Old Gaston was greatly excited by anything that broke the monotony of his publishing kingdom and hurried to meet the request: days later, he gave Monique the address of a restaurant on the rue Guisarde where, according to his friend, his colleague-publisher would find the atmosphere he sought. Monique gave the details to Rowohlt and we headed there with him, after taking the precaution of reserving a table.

The delectable, troubling Sadian emotions that besieged you on the way there vanished as soon as you arrived: the entrance to the joint, a tiny doorway, forced the customer to stoop down to get in, and while he clambered in, head lowered and back bent, someone on the other side hung a cowbell around his neck like a scapular to the hoots of laughter of those who with similar ringing chimes observed in delight the newcomer's humiliation. Inside, the childish, rowdy, rough atmosphere would have horrified the author of *Justine*. The waiters were arrogant and insolent, decided the order without taking into account the customer's wishes, and if the opportunity presented itself, regaled the latter with an elbow in the ribs and a string of insults. The sepulchral silence and seriousness of a torture chamber had been replaced, to your friend's consternation, by the festive shouting match of some paunchy, bald-headed schoolboys. Although Rowohlt hid his disappointment, you realized that what Paris had to offer in the genre was false rather than mediocre, no more than a pretense. Accustomed to greater rigor and depth, he went back to Germany convinced that the French still had a long way to go to reach the level of his fellow countrymen in matters of self-knowledge.

If Genet avoided nightlife and took himself off early to bed, Violette Leduc longed to accompany you and break, if only fleetingly, the oppressive solitude that enclosed her. Monique's diary recalls a few evenings with her in the course of 1957: her extraordinary ugliness and playactress manner had the virtue of disarming the usual misogyny of the queens, delighted to exhibit themselves to that ingenuous, cunning woman who was amusing, eccentric, and above all incapable of overshadowing them or arousing feelings of jealousy. When Violette, with the success of *La Bâtarde*, suddenly met fame and fortune, she surrounded herself with the flamboyant retinue of homosexuals of her dreams: a queen in dazzling Carita wigs and suits made by the best designers, whose apparitions at Laurent's or other elegant places would be welcomed with murmurs of derision, curiosity, or wonder.

Divided among politics, writing, social contact, and nocturnal habits, your life was none the worse for the wear and tear. Your physical relations with Monique would never reach a more satisfactory level, and you had cast aside one by one the old hankerings after independence, carefree mutual "deceptions." Monogamous, a possessive, subtly jealous husband, you gradually adapted to the classical, conventional partner's role: holidays in the Midi, plans for trips to unknown countries. For a time you would consider your latent homosexuality as something belonging to a distant past: but love for Monique was not accompanied by physical or emotional interest in other women. At a sexual level these were still the object of an indifference that you would strive to hide. Your amorous life was restricted to Monique and the tiny bubble encapsulating you. You were worried by the precarious, fragile nature of your happiness. What would happen if the bubble burst, if she or you suddenly stopped loving the other? Entrenched in your tepid but pure heterosexuality, you discarded the idea of repeating your second-rate experiences in the Barrio Chino and began to avoid situations that could refresh your magnetic attraction to those the Party dubbed "our exploited comrades." But your distance and withdrawal from the female world gathered apace. The exception you triumphantly lived confirmed the rule learned in adolescence. If to the outside world you were the same as everybody else, you were and continued to be so for some time, in a unique, unusual style.

My trips to Spain opened more or less extensive parentheses in our life together. While the "concubinage" was consolidated and displayed the characteristics of a stable matrimonial bond, the brief visits back to Barcelona and incursions into the Almería region momentarily reestablished my elemental condition. Monique and her entourage soon got used to my disappearances: although I was not yet that "ever absent" husband she would describe later, my political involvement and the bedazzling scenery of my adoptive province often transformed me into a fugitive from domesticity. Customary French ignorance of Hispanic realities, which reached the point of confusing the tattered screen of the Pyrenees with the cement wall or curtain of Stalin's vice-regencies, wrapped these trips in an aura of anxious expectation. With her innate love of melodrama, Marguerite Duras never missed an opportunity to ask Monique if I would come back, if the Francoist authorities would allow me out again, if this eclipse from Paris and her life was or would be final, period. Another friend at the publishers, equally worried by my absences, had summed up her repeated, almost morbid curiosity in very Parisian fashion: "I don't want him to leave you, you know. But if he were to, I'd like to be the first to find out!" All in all, the gaps as we planned them never went beyond that halfway house between fleeting pleasure at my recovered freedom and incipient nostalgia or melancholy. Just as when I had been on military service, we wrote or telephoned each other daily: but, unlike then, my letters mentioned only in passing my odd coitus with a whore and assumed a joking voyeuristic tone in respect to my nocturnal sorties with Luis, María Antonia, Jaime Gil, or some other friend to homosexual bars or areas. Implicit censorship excluded my solitary adventures in those dens in the Barceloneta or Barrio Chino where, as on Raimundo's floating shipyard, I took a dip in that warm camaraderie between men while highlighting and piling up anecdotes and details of my folkloric fondness for queens. Even more significant: the letters no longer refer to possible mutual "infidelities," the happy *calafells* we allowed ourselves. Unsure of myself, conscious of the fragility of our links, my attitude had perceptibly changed. I am jealous of her, and my lack of interest in women of her background, whose attractiveness, culture, and intelligence could compete with hers or foment potential rivalries condemned me to a position of inferiority. The freedom that we theoretically granted each other when we parted was in my case a dead letter: keeping as I did a careful watch on my latent homosexuality, my so-called unfaithfulness was limited to encounters with whores, generally under the influence of alcohol. But it was not the same in her case, and there was that risk it might firm up, as in the months of my stay in Mataró. In spite of my protestations of permissive liberalism, the idea disturbed me: insidiously, my inner responses had become, without my noticing at first, those of a traditional Spanish husband. I discovered I was extremely vulnerable and in turn that intensified my dependence on Monique and the suspicious cunning and close-mindedness of one who felt the legal owner of a body. Although I fought to hide my anxiety and repress symptoms of my possessiveness, the submerged tension influenced our relations. If my ambiguity seduced Monique and created that opaque, secret area that had impelled her from youth into the world of homosexuals, my unsure but exclusive heterosexuality, the anguish of which began to overwhelm me from autumn 1958 on, symmetrically altered her bonds with me. I knew that her adventures and infatuations did not endanger the link between us: however, my inability to make a practical response—by arousing in turn a feeling of jealousy toward another woman of her type—introduced an element of imbalance that would worsen over time. I feel now that her acceptance of bisexuality could have diverted the course of events: our relationship could have recovered its lost harmony, its dimension of strangeness and mystery. My oppressive espousal of the criteria and prejudices predominant in the Spanish world around which I gravitated frustrated any such possible outcome. The more uncertain and cloudier my impulse toward women became, the greater would be my external parade of starkly heterosexual behavior. Trapped in that mire by my own mistakes, I clutched with all my strength to the safety of a branch, a would-be erotic normality, at the very moment it was beginning to fail me and the branch was giving way. Determined to hide the source of my anxiety from Monique and everybody else, I erected obstacles and barriers against the desirable solution. On our now-routine visits to homosexual bars I showed no signs of sympathy or affinity: my condescending, mocking attitude was that of an uptight Spaniard, like the political militants I went about with. I adopted as my own the jokes and reproving opinions toward the queens that I heard daily around me: I dropped in on the sordid misery of the ghetto, but I belonged to the planned, clean city outside.

Monique could not correctly interpret the symptoms she perceived: I had painfully swallowed the key. Our life would continue to be the same on the surface; however, she was increasingly weighed down by my deficiencies and excesses, the scenes of jealousy when she took an interest in other men, and the inevitable recourse to alcohol on our daily *calafells*. She wrote to herself in her diary, "I still love Juan." Holidays in Spain and Italy, a change of scene and friends for a while restored to our bond its former luxuriant freshness. But the degeneration and weakening I so feared continued to filter through. One day I read F. Scott Fitzgerald's *The Crack-Up*, and I felt cast down by cosmic pessimism: it was impossible to return to Spain, I had no future, I did not even know whether I would be able to maintain my heterosexual front. I had set up camp on precarious ground, rife with uncertainties, and, or so I believed, perhaps I could only be rescued by the flame of Revolution.

In an interview granted some time ago, Jaime Gil de Biedma perceptively observed that from a particular moment in time a stable amorous relationship usually brings us the bad tidings about ourselves: that we aren't really as we thought we were or, to put it more sharply, as we imagined we were. The shock ought to have a dampening effect, but it does not or will not, except retrospectively. The discovery that we are worse, much worse than we supposed—subject to jealousy, pettiness, incongruous attitudes, passionate outbursts, emotional ambivalence, sickly self-pitying, bad faith, irrationality—is not usually accompanied by feelings of shame or by good resolutions. The visitor who lives within us and acts in this way enjoys absolute impunity. His real name is Mr. Hyde.

The process favoring his installation in our inner being is not fortuitous and, as I know from experience, follows a path that any honest, competent cartographer could trace out, whatever its sharp bends and diversions. The leafy proliferations that, from the initial buried seed, conceal the reasons for our behavior from others, do not prevent us from reaching the root of the evil, if we so wish. If I had confessed earlier to my repressed homosexuality and been completely sincere with Monique, I could have been spared the state of tension and crisis in which I lived with her for four years, the concealed anguish I communicated to her, the consequences of my frequently aggressive, incoherent behavior. Lacking both the necessary lucidity and courage, I did not follow the only path that might have led me to resolve the problem, and I was gradually snared by a trap of my own setting. Although I could add in my defense that at the time I had still not yet gotten to know any of those immigrants whom I passed daily in the street and whose violent, imperious figures matched the one that with periodic belligerence stalked my dreams, the fact was that, fearful of their power over me and the danger they evoked in relation to Monique, I tried to avert my gaze from them, although my heart, piniomed in their grasp, beat quickly at every chance moment of those fleeting, brutal, unsettling encounters. The deliberate rejection of openness, at the behest of a combination of social, political, and moral pressures heaped up from childhood, pulled me into an untenable, painful

situation where, sucked down by my own contradictions, I saw neurotic ir-
responsibility as a possible refuge and value. My family's propensity to allow
ourselves to be trapped by circumstances in moral prisons or swamps from
which escape verges on the heroic; to fabricate with total sincerity compensatory fantasies providing momentary relief, however much they remain
unrealized; to set ourselves deadlines to ensure they become fact and a pos-
teriori justify our failure to meet them; to run away from the naked truth and
shirk the Gordian knot by projecting our own frustrations or dissatisfaction
onto other persons or places—the whole pathetic inheritance of subterfuge,
weakness, resignation, evasions, and spinelessness that ruined our maternal
grandparents' life or mental health—has at different times hung over my
destiny and that of my brothers but has never exonerated, if I keep to my
own example, an incomprehensibly tardy reaction. Disturbed by my frequent moods of equally exaggerated euphoria and depression, Monique put
me in touch, through Dr. Frankel, with my compatriot Ajuriaguerra—at
the time the director of a psychiatric center in Geneva who also held private
consultations in Paris; my obstinate hiding of the truth, of the central cause
of my lack of equilibrium, made our conversation a tissue of deceit: lying to
him as I did, he could not help me, and he must have understood that, for
when I did not keep the next appointment he did not even bother to call
me to find out what had happened. The plethora of events I have already
referred to—absorbing political militancy, Luis's arrest, the Milan affair,
etc.—distracted me from the tension and anguish that oppressed me without, however, erasing them entirely. When I was at my most active and involved, relations with Monique improved: I felt close to her once more, we
recovered our lost complicity, and my passionate surrender to the cause of
revolution, first the Spanish and then the Cuban, brought us together again,
allowed a cautious exchange of warmth. Our joint trips to Spain, full of sus-
pense and novelty, and the sorties to Italy, to the beaches where she always felt
happy, gave breathing spaces in which the perceptible worsening of things
was halted. On the sand dunes of Guardamar or in Garrucha we experienced unbridled enjoyment of scenery swathed by the sea mist, the quiet, luminous sea, the warm, penetrating protection of the sun: reptilian lethargy,
sips of iced wine, fertile, enclosed, succulent siestas. But our return to Paris,

social life, contact with friends who held a passing interest or attraction for her, brought me back to the reality of the blind alley in which I was trapped, the dilemma I dared not confront. My reading at the time betrays a morbid delight in works soaked in pessimism and authors imprisoned by the gentle music of impotence, the dawn melody of suicide: Pavese, F. Scott Fitzgerald, Larra, Ganivet. My despondency and inability to drag myself up succeeded, as was my intention, in making Monique feel guilty. When I came back after going out I sometimes found on my desk messages from her, like bottles hesitantly cast into the sea. Aware that my neurosis was progressing, she lamented the fact that her vitality, energies, and love were of no use to me and that, despite her efforts, she could not communicate them to me. Her sadness was searing, but it filled me with secret satisfaction. The help she could have given me depended on cooperation that I withheld. In such conditions and states of mind, the small hell to which couples often descend hovered threateningly on the horizon. The bad tidings about myself would leave me indifferent rather than surprise me: the patient clinging to his sickness finally found no other consolation than to scatter the seeds of his illness.

Seen from the vantage point of time, my behavior in those years now seems unreal. The duality of my relationship with Monique inevitably affected relations with everybody else, tinged my whole life with a diffuse irrationality. Taciturn and powerless, I acted like a spectator at my own jealous outbursts, absurd accusations, shocking eclipses of moral sense. If my travels and absences at first brought me relief, they soon became a fresh source of friction. Deprived of my sullen, menacing, hypochondriac presence, Monique would feel relieved of a deadweight, pleased to feel free to move around. Consciousness of my own weakness spurred on my wily, tortuous imagination: the unconscious desire to snare the woman responsible for my distress in a web of ominous culpability. A comparison of the letters written on my first visit to Cuba with the ones I sent on my second reveals a sharp growth in my self-pitying recriminatory attitude, in my desire to prevent her from being happy, from breathing far from me. The discovery of her mother's throat cancer in January 1962, during my impassioned, elated stay in Havana, had frustrated any possibility of a trip, of her following my suggestion that she share the feelings of intoxication and enthusiasm the island aroused in me. On my return to Paris, I found Lucienne with a tube down her throat, voiceless and shriveled up, forced to endure a torture that worsened daily, the sterile contemplation of which was overwhelming her daughter. As she adjusted to the certainty of her mother's death, Monique seemed prey to a compensatory agitation that intensified my neurosis and ate into our already corroded ties. Although she had different reasons, with a base in reality, she swung, like me, from periods of illusory hope and forced happiness to others of gloom and despondency. My behavior toward her did not help matters: our parallel, superimposed unhappiness was a cruel repeat of the old situations in my own family. Rather than help her withstand the painful trial she was experiencing, I criticized her for her moments of forgetfulness, her emotional generosity, indomitable vitality, and, unable to take reality by the horns, I sought refuge in militancy as if in a protective religious order: but neither Marx nor Lenin nor the working class had anything to do with my real worries. In truth, my case was quite similar to those middle-class youths who, as Octavio Paz would later write, "transformed their personal dreams and obsessions into ideological fantasies in which the end of the world takes on the paradoxical form of a proletarian revolution without a proletariat." During my second stay in Cuba, while her letters told me extensively of her mother's daily torment and her fortunate discovery of Jorge Semprún's book, I threw in her face "the irreversible distance between us," the "dialogue of the deaf" that we sustained, my lack of attachment and indifference to the world around me: I drank a lot, I fucked two women, and "I don't know where we fit in, nor what's left to us." The letter's bitter tone was sincere, but my factual account purposely leaves out the little "matter" that, apart from the two women, there was the owner of a small bar in the Jesús María district, a cheerful, festive mulatto whom I twice went to bed with in a drunken state. Although that relationship was of no importance to me and did not meet my expectations, its omission from the letter shows my attempt at the time to make it difficult for Monique to diagnose the causes of my neurosis. As she was writing in her diary *cafard atroce*,* I was consciously covering my tracks.

*January 1963.

The latent disquiet dictating my behavior—not mentioned here in any kind of self-justification—was the certainty that I must irrevocably enter turbulent waters full of dangerous currents where I would have to swim alone: like someone deceived by the weakness of the current who loses his footing and disappears under a high wave, I was afraid of leaving behind all that made up life till then, afraid of getting lost on the open sea. Mine was not the pleasant, jocular, likeable, carefree homosexuality of the queers Monique had dealings with. The ambiguity that attracted her was no doubt the result of a female ideal of man that is much more widespread than is generally believed, which is both insensitive and hostile to the features, traits, and attributes of extreme combative virility; more or less explicit effeminacy was at the antipodes of my own desire. At different stages in my life I have had occasional or sporadic sexual relations with women, but never, absolutely never, with queers or heterosexuals from my own cultural and social background, those who are classically attired, well brought-up, elegantly mannered; later, I would extend this rigorous demarcation line to my own ethnic group: from 1963 my passion and longings would be aroused only by the rough, sunburned sons of the Sotadic Zone. Nevertheless, even before my initiatory meeting with Mohamed, I could mentally delineate, with the detail and precision of a miniaturist, the masculine image that had attracted me ever since it had magically erupted into my childhood; intermittently and unconsciously it had crept into my dreams until it finally harassed me with hustling determination. As Ibn Hazm beautifully said, I was exchanging a green and pleasant land "for one hedged in thorn." Monique could not follow me there; I knew that only too well. My persistent lying was thus a last futile attempt not to leave her before facing up to that forbidden territory where "by implacable decree" and absolute rule of love "from which no one can steal himself," I would soon enter.

The most unhappy period for you both undoubtedly came after your second trip to Cuba. Lucienne died just after you had returned under no illusions as to your future as a couple. When her suffering came to an end, you accompanied Monique and a group of friends to the sinister cremation ceremony.

The urn containing her ashes, which the undertakers handed you after a tense hour's wait, bore a symbolic value in your eyes: they summed up seven years of life together; Lucienne's scattered atoms epitomized the history of your relationship. Nine days later you were in Venice, where Monique decided to go in search of distraction and alleviation for her distress. On your previous visit in 1957 you had walked along the canals, explored the labyrinth of side streets and *cuppo di sacchi*, zigzagging in a *vaporetto* from jetty to jetty, in an ecstatic feeling of aesthetic delight and mutual fulfillment. In March 1963 your walks along the Via Garibaldi, against a luminous backdrop of stagnant water and ruined mansions, testified to the change in the interval—your solitary, icy lack of communication. The room in the Hotel Montecarlo, near San Marcos, would be the scene of disputes and recriminations. Prickly, unapproachable, you carried things to the breaking point while ensuring it never materialized. Like those people who destroy domestic property in apparently uncontrolled fits of anger but let loose on objects of little value, making certain not to touch anything valuable—clearly revealing some vigilant inner mechanism at work—your double behaved with a selective irrationality that tempered, but did not destroy, your exercise of will. This attitude, which you would later see painfully repeated in relatives and friends, now exemplifies for you those very ambiguous notions, madness and reason: that vast intermediate area in which the neurotic sets traps and tripwires for everyone else only really to run away from himself and rush headfirst into the sea, all the time wearing his life jacket. But the retrospective lucidity with which you now judge yourself did not then come to your aid: for a hateful length of time you would live irremediably in the shadow of your Mr. Hyde.

Suppositions, nightmares, a split existence: the impression that you were a powerless witness to the wiles and maneuvers of a character who looks like you, acts in your name, carries your documents, writes your signature, wears your clothes and shoes, is identified with you by the neighbors, the tenant in your flat, that you embody his crimes and betrayals in a fading dreamlike unreality. You evoke his oneiric, spectral exploits, are his judge and memory, grapple with the upset of his fleeting reappearance: your desire to wash your dirty linen, pillory him, separate yourself out from him. You peer into the hidden corners of a distant schizophrenia and observe with relief that he has gone for good. The morbid product of passing mystification or a real being, swept away in a healthy, vigorous cleanup? Faced with the threatening dislocation, you are unsure of your ground, don't know what to reply.

On my return to Paris, I found the tensions in our life together unbearable and went on one of my habitual flying visits to Spain, but with characteristic ambivalence, I persuaded Monique to meet up with me and, two weeks later, we were swimming together on the beach at Torremolinos in a state of deceptive contentment. It was there I would learn by phone both of Benign Cordero's death and the sudden worsening of the "Grimau affair."

On 17 April I was back in France. It is not my intention to recount here the futile activity of that period: collection of signatures, acts of protest, hopes that Franco would suspend the execution of the death sentence against Julián Grimau at the last moment, would not go through with his iniquitous act of vengeance. Our failure intensified my feelings of indifference and distance from my public persona, my grating awareness of its absurdity. Monique was to leave for Corfu with the Gallimard delegation to be present at the meeting of the jury that would days later award the Formentor prize to Jorge's book. The night of her departure, I went for a walk around Barbès. Ever since Algerian independence, the police had slackened their siege of the area, and it was possible to wander around without coming across their somber hostile patrols. I can remember how, as on other occasions, I examined the Arab cafés from the outside, their customers leaning on the counter or sitting at tables, absorbed in a game of dominoes or a Spanish hand of cards: a compact, homogeneous world, but also one that was attractive and lively, from which I felt painfully excluded. No European ever set foot there, as if an invisible frontier forbade entry and, despite my attempts to overcome my timidity, I finally resigned myself to walking by. Weren't any possible awkward approaches doomed from the outset by my total ignorance of their language, culture, patterns of behavior, and idiosyncrasies? Given their bitter experience of persecution and the discrimination of which they were victims, how would they look upon a *nesrani* who nervously peered into their ghetto? The strange, captivating music of their record players invited me to hover around their territory. What were those intense, tormented voices that they listened to with such fervor and nostalgia trying to express? After tramping, like an intruder, around the rue de la Goutte-d'Or, rue de Chartres, rue de la Charbonnière, I walked down to the boulevard de la Chapelle, thronged by indigenous promenaders, and sat at the bar of a café on the corner of boulevard Barbès, which vibrated regularly as the overhead métro rushed by. To my left, with his back to me, a young man was talking to a friend in Arabic and, suddenly, when his friend went off, he turned to me. Thin, sinewy, of average height, dark-eyed, a big black mustache, his face radiated a lively sense of strength and warmth. He asked for a light, and noticing that my hands were trembling as I handed him a match, he gently calmed them in his own. He said, *Merci, khuya*, in a mixture of French and Arabic. I don't know what we talked about or have the slightest idea what we drank: perhaps two or three rounds of beer, quickly replenished by the waiter when I caught his eye, with the aim of prolonging this chance conversation that promised so much. I was afraid to break off the thread, that we would each go our own way; but, belying my apprehension, my new acquaintance waited for the waiter to give my change and left with me. "I don't know where I'm going to sleep," he said. "Do you know anywhere we can spend the night together?" Trying to conceal the fact that my heart was pounding furiously, I just replied that there were many hotels in the area, that we would find a room in one of them. We went up the boulevard de Rochechouart and immediately hit upon one, at the top of the rue de Clignancourt. It was a poor, shabby room, with one double bed covered over with a long bolster. While I undressed, Mohamed slipped, eagle-eyed, between the sheets, his fleshy lips smiling beneath his wild mustache. My slow descent into pleasure was accompanied, in the disturbed slumber of the night, by the lucid regaining of serenity.

Mohamed had to get up early and, as we woke up late, I took him by taxi to porte de la Chappelle, where he and a gang of immigrant miners were digging out an underground gallery for a public works firm on the first stage

of the future motorway to the north. As we got up, he had told me simply
that he wanted to be my friend, and we agreed to meet at six o'clock that
afternoon, when he left work. For a few days, while Monique was away, I
carried on, going with him to work in the early morning and picking him up
hours later in a large café on the rue Ney, opposite the entrance to the métro.
We drank, dined, fucked in some down-at-the-heels old hotel in the shadow
of the Sacré-Coeur, in a mood of frank, happy complicity. The terrain I was
penetrating was deceptively easy: in spite of Mohamed's naturalness and
warmth, expressed in hoarse, jumbled French—the bodily immediacy
uniting us, our nightly colluding connection, rested on precarious foundations. Our reciprocal lack of knowledge about each other did not seem to
bother him very much; but the recondite strangeness of his world, sheathed
in the magnetism radiating outwards, forced upon me the challenge of clarifying and determining the reasons for my captivation. My later desire to get
to know, explore step by step the universe where his life unfolded, to intoxi-
cate myself with his language and culture, to delimit the imprecise boundaries of the exotic were then given life. My tardy vocation as linguist and eth-
nologist, which has made me devote an apparently absurd amount of time
in recent years first to the study of North African Arabic and then of Turk-
ish, was the result of my resolution to draw nearer to a physical and cultural
bodily ideal, the white heat and refulgence of which guided me like a bea-
con. The act of transforming the stigma inherent in my deviation into a fertile curiosity for what was alien would thus open the way to a state of grace
beyond the reach of the bourgeois trapped in the conventional rigidity of his
petty world. By suddenly conjugating sexuality and writing, I could in contrast forge a new language, decanted and purified in the harsh, combative
expression of my desire, a long, seminal process originating in that initial
chance encounter: Mohamed, and his box of Gitanes, drinking at the bar in
the café on the boulevard de la Chapelle, a bar I had entered before I had even
seen him.

My lack of experience of his world, reactions, and character required the
choice of an emotional strategy: rather than spelling out the questions
crowding in upon me, I allowed him to answer them himself as I gained his

confidence. Was he married? Did he have any children? Why did he live
hand-to-mouth with no fixed abode? Who looked after his suitcases of
clothes, and where did he go to get changed? Gradually, he explained to me
that his wife and children lived in a mountain village near Oujda; in recent
months he had shacked up with a *kaḥba* whom he had rowed with the day
before we met; although his idea when emigrating to France had been to im-
prove his family's lot, it was all a miserable waste of his time: not only had he
squandered his family's money on that evil whore but also, through her, he
had got himself into some tight corners. What were they? Mohamed related
the confused story of a pistol sold by a *pied-noir* police inspector who had infiltrated the Arab ghetto; apparently, he had slightly wounded a rival with it
in an act of legitimate self-defense. As a result he spent a few days in prison
and was still waiting for the trial, perhaps a summons from the police. If they
imposed a fine, he would find ways of paying it; but if he were deported to
his own country, what would happen to his wife and children?

Converted by circumstance into a good samaritan, I helped him find a
chambre de bonne, renew his labor permits, answer the worried letters from
his family. My naïveté at the time was limitless; however, although Mohamed, with his peasant mixture of innocence and cunning, often lied to me
as one lies to a wife, he never took advantage of the situation. When, on Monique's return from Corfu, I went back to sleeping on the rue Poissonnière
and waited for him at dusk in a café or inside his poky garret, I spotted un-
ambiguous traces of the visit of an unknown woman. Mohamed allowed
himself to be loved by me and then used my conjugal state to disappear in
turn on lengthy tours of the Barbès bars, where he met up with fellow countrymen. On some occasions, he took me with him and would lead me by the
hand into those dense, compact, exclusively masculine preserves, possessed
by a sudden, voracious hunger for knowledge. I was slowly learning the gestures and movements, greetings, polite formulas, guttural words haloed in
subtle magic, which I furtively scribbled down or tried to commit to memory. The only European in the place, I shared the privilege with several Algerian prostitutes. Mohamed's introduction allowed me the quiet corner for
observation that I sought: once the first moment of curiosity had passed, my

presence went unnoticed. Nevertheless, my cultural superiority, centered on my knowledge of French, would soon turn me into a kind of public scribe, to whom Mohamed and his companions would give their Social Security forms to fill in or would dictate messages to their families. In order to keep Monique away from my new friendships, I had invented for myself the plausible profession of a printer obliged to go on frequent visits to the provinces: but no one, apart from Mohamed, ever asked me about my private life, work, or home. For the regulars in the half dozen cafés on the rue de la Goutte-d'Or I frequented while our relationship lasted, I was only an anonymous Spaniard with a smattering of their dialect who wrote their letters for free.

Monique mentions in *Les Cabines de bain* the "margin of perversity" arising from the fact that, though a writer, I have loved or had an interest throughout my life only in illiterate men or in men with only a rough elementary education. It is an accurate observation inasmuch as sexuality feeds on emotions, fantasies, and "perverse" ideas. But, without dismissing their incidence in my case, the primordial factor in my friendships with hillsmen, peasants, or Moroccan infantry soldiers whose features corresponded to darkly ancestral tastes was my need to compensate for the mental refinement required in the act of writing with their exhilarating, pervasive rawness: possessed by them and their rough pleasure, I instinctively looked for a way to counterbalance my physical submission with an intellectual domination capable of establishing an equilibrium between both scales. The enjoyment this indemnification provided me—the sly secretive sensation of taking control of their lives and destiny while they entrusted to my pen the messages to their families—would be as great as that reached through communion with their virility: the act of writing and taking on their voice with the same fullness with which hours or minutes before they had disposed of my body would frequently intertwine the apparent benevolence of writing with the secret delights of erection. This and other discoveries during that brief period of my life had lasting consequences: the framework, backdrop, situations, places in which other more or less ephemeral adventures would arise were then fixed once and forever. Not only the powerful call of faces and features hinted at or dreamed of from adolescence, but also a combination of elements the repetition of which would belie their supposedly circumstantial character. Those who sat beside me clumsily dictating their letters would change over time; but the immutable pleasure-seeker disguised as public scribe would patiently extend his mastery of conventional, more or less accurate French to the wanton, jubilant appropriation of Arabic script.

My friendship with Mohamed was threatened from the start. The wheels of the administrative machine set in motion by his earlier conviction turned ominously on the horizon, despite my efforts to stave it off by getting the sentence suspended. With a fatalism that often irritated me, Mohamed placed his destiny in my hands; but if that relieved him of all responsibility for his future, it burdened me with the duties of an irksome moral guardian. The battle with the administration, marked by defeats and victories, was to last several years; forced to abandon French territory during my stay in Saint-Tropez, Mohamed would obtain, thanks to the good offices of my lawyer, a trial period that was abruptly ended in 1969, a long time after our intimate bonding had ceased, by a second and definitive deportation order. By that date, my experience and knowledge of the Islamic world had broadened and deepened. My choice of comrades with whom to maintain more or less lasting ties no longer obeyed as before the whim of the chance encounter; it was also a response to obsessive and stricter criteria that were as much physical as emotional.

The entry of North African society into my life favorably influenced my turbulent relationship with Monique. Placated, lucid, conscious, I gradually gained in self-confidence and assurance what I lost in relation to her in sickly dependence and aggression. Although my decision to hide what had happened and keep my precious secret was condemned to failure, our life as a couple calmed down. For the first time in years, our holidays in Venice and on the Dalmatian coast were peaceful and happy. My uncontrolled dark reactions gradually disappeared. The silence I kept momentarily conferred an exceptional lightness on my existence. The accursedness associated with the nefarious crime was suddenly transformed into grace. Like a slithering serpent, I was sliding toward new wells and fountains in search of the propitious time and place for that delayed change of skin.

Our relationship reached a plateau in the spotless wintry frame of Saint-Tropez. We rented a small house on the rue de la Citadelle, but weeks later Monique found a more pleasant duplex, with views over the port, that belonged or had belonged to Dominique Éluard. So as not to miss my tiny study-kitchen on the rue Poissonnière, I chose for my office a cubbyhole where you could hardly fit a table, with a small window from which I could contemplate the reddish roofs of the town and where I felt isolated and afloat, like at the top of a dovecote. I worked there regularly in the mornings while Monique read on the beach or put some order into the notes she had taken during her mother's cancer, notes she would later include in *Une Drôle de voix*.

Her decision to move out, to abandon her publishing job, to run away from the literary scene that had been her life till then corresponded to what I had secretly been hoping from her for months. The eruption of virile pleasure into my world demanded body-and-soul surrender to the abyss of writing; it was not only mutual convergence or adaptation but something more complex and far-reaching: the introduction of a personal universe and experience of the world, areas as yet hidden away, into the text of the work that was emerging, until they and I were integrated into it as just extra ingredients. The change my life was undergoing would thus be articulated within a globally generative process; my existence would lose its autonomous character and merely exercise a dynamic function in a world conceived as a space for writing, in the omnivorous textual whole. My daily struggle with successive versions of *Señas de identidad* would stand out qualitatively from my previous skirmishes with literature; it was to be a text marking a break and leap into the void; initiatory, genesic, foundational. As I noticed later, when rereading the novel in print, I only half attained my goal. Both a compendium and a transcending of past narrative, *Señas* turned out to be a hybrid of my newly acquired subjectivity and a formal structure that I did not manage to escape entirely.

Rapidly acclimated to a place that suited us for a variety of reasons, Monique and I lived in apparent serenity. The tensions brought on by my sexual insecurity, periods of depression, ravages of schizophrenia had dissolved in a tranquil working atmosphere favoring an intimate coming together. There, the physical anguish and suicidal fits that had tortured me disappeared forever. When I finished writing, good weather permitting, I would stretch out by her side on the beach; at dusk we would walk down to the town and sit in a small bar, frequented by fishermen and sailors, with whose owners we had struck up a friendship. In winter the port sheltered several cruisers: the guards or supervisors of the odd one were Spanish sailors who, on discovering we were fellow countrymen, came and had a drink with me in our favorite bar or visited me up at the house when they saw the dining room lights were on. The Saint-Tropez rhythm of life with its small-scale rituals intensified, on the other hand, our tiredness and coolness toward Paris. For months we trawled the region in the company of real estate agents: with a neophyte's enthusiasm, Monique forged plans to sell her flat, settle down for good in the Midi, and buy a small house or plot of land there. Her mother's horrendous death agony, which she still had not assimilated, was impelling her toward a break, which she believed to be definitive, with her haven on the rue Poissonière. Carole was pursuing her studies in a school in Saint-Maxime and also seemed entirely happy with the change.

Just as everything was apparently getting on course and our fragile, unstable life together was experiencing a blissful interlude, an untimely, though predictable, factor sent my plans awry and overturned that precarious happiness. By sacrificing my links with Mohamed to the project of provincial life dedicated to work and Monique, I had omitted one essential detail: while the anonymous confusion of Paris allowed for clandestine sexual activity that attracted no one's attention, the social transparency of Saint-Tropez, where the nucleus of North African immigrants lived in their ghetto, visible and marginalized by the rest of the population, doomed from the outset any attempt at a discreet approach. The locals' crude racism, as instinctive and deep-seated as their professed attitude to the guild of *enfoirés* or *sales tantes* to which I secretly belonged, not only distorted my relations with other people but also imposed on me the yokelike torment of homosexual chastity. As at other times in my life, but in a more abrupt, tyrannical fashion, a blind force drove me to meet up with men shaped in the tangible, effulgent image

I had mysteriously formed as a child. In the small bar where we got together with our neighbors, I noticed one day a sailor who was "tall, broad-shouldered, of storm-tanned complexion, whose pure Arab features, energetic chin and mouth" were in retrospect extraordinarily similar to those I would later find in the iconography of Richard Burton and the detailed description of his wife Isabel. Although from North Africa, the customer was a *nesrani*, married with a large family. Hardly had we been introduced than we felt a shock wave of sympathy: he liked his drink and willingly accepted my invitations and, seated round a barrel-shaped table, we soon got into the habit of downing two or three bottles of wine a day. My friend was sensitive to the interest I displayed toward him but, brought up in a *pied-noir* environment hostile to that kind of affection, he allowed himself to be courted in muffled tones in view of everyone, yet he avoided any opportunity to be compromised. The other regulars were in on our libations and chats but harbored not the least suspicion: we were both married and our masculine behavior and ways saved us from any malicious gossip. Alcohol favored our coming together but reduced it to a mere shadow. The Tavel rosé—which Hemingway abused so much—acted as a substitute and had a discouraging effect on me. I was drinking now like I did before I met Mohamed, and the Saint-Tropezians were astonished at my staying power. Monique had obviously noticed the ambiguity of a situation that reminded her of my past bouts of drinking in the Varadero or with the Valencian workers from Vicenta's village, in the course of their Sunday paellas in Rueil-Malmaison. That aspect of my personality attracted her, and sometimes she would venture to mention it and question me. Months later, she would harshly reproach me for not having taken advantage of those opportunities to speak out clearly, the unforgivable cowardice that beset me when facing up to the truth.

I was often possessed, in a glaring limpid trance, by a feeling of alienation and strangeness toward all around me, as I engaged in anodyne conversation with friends, or in the family arena: the certainty I was different from everyone else, with an inner life a million miles away from them, a symbolic statuesque presence at their alien, absurd ceremonies, assumed at times almost physically tangible dimensions. A traitor ambushed in a world of smiling appearance, I was suddenly invaded by a savage desire to act profanely: desires to slash with a knife the tranquil canvas of my life, to declare my violent inner repulsion toward it. My subsequent self-absorption, the mental deafness that preceded by fifteen years the onset of physical atony, developed from that moment; my ability to withdraw into myself when surrounded by people, to be present at the social comedy while inwardly laughing, to elaborate in situ compensatory fantasies at the antipodes of such a universe would thus become fixed traits of my character. Becoming taciturn and furtive, my distance and reserve would soon earn me my solid, deserved reputation as a prickly customer. But rather than these traits, which were suffered or perceived by an immediate circle, I was worried by the frequent ruptures or short circuits produced in me by the most unforeseen circumstances. I can recall how Roger Vailland had told us the story of a regular caller at a brothel who once a week chose the same prostitute and how, once alone with her, he undid a small packet of sauerkraut and handed the varied contents to her for her in turn to put into her vagina. The client watched this to-ing and fro-ing without masturbating, returned the cooked dish to its packet and said goodbye to the woman after giving her a generous reward. As he in the end revealed to her, he then headed home with the sauerkraut, handed it to his wife and with an ineffable smile shared in the family feast. The anecdote, or rather the protagonist's attitude, reflected accurately the sudden blackouts in my social self and the mocking duality with which I intervened—and sometimes still intervene—in supposedly intimate or serious public or domestic scenes: an evening with helpful neighbors, a visit from a relative, an official reception with under secretaries and ministers, a jolly birthday tea. A thought or nomad fantasy detector would have led or would lead in such cases to my immediate expulsion from the place where my visible ventriloquist self acted out of a mental furtiveness similar to the refined client's in the story.

The concentration required by work no doubt contributed to my isolation and the emergence of that touchy ego trapped like a genie in its box. Perhaps the phenomenon is consubstantial with a vocation that is lived like a permanent voracious devouring; however that may be, its effects would still live on even once the genitive cause disappeared: a pleasing indifference to everything outside my personal affections, likes, and obsessions; a pressing awareness that only amorous emotion, sex, and writing are real, that the bourgeois, ordered social world disturbs and interrupts that subjective authenticity which, with the absorbing power of a whirlwind, would henceforth suck me into the privileged substrata of literary creation, personal communication, or complaisant bodily submission. In the face of these patiently conquered dominions, everything else—social ties, involvement in literary and cultural life, vanity, reputation—lacked importance, did not justify any burning of energy. My moral outlook underwent a change and became more pragmatic: the quest for intensity in the triple area just mentioned would then become my basic aim in life.

But I anticipate events: in those first months in Saint-Tropez, dual awareness of the impossibility of avoiding the law of the body and establishing my life with Monique on lies and deceit came painfully to the surface till it swept aside the mediocre array of defenses. The sublimatory arguments behind my refusal to act openly seemed false and even monstrous: a shameful tribute to the iniquitous ethics of Catholicism, like the one Grandfather paid. What tormented me was not the act of revealing the truth to everyone else— convinced as I was that by removing the ambiguities behind which I sheltered myself, I would be freed of a burden whose weight grew daily—but the risk that the situation thus created might ruin and put an end to my close relationship with Monique. The renewal of her happiness with me, after the stormy tensions of Paris and Havana, moved and paralyzed me. Never since our get-togethers in Spain had I seen her so radiant and diaphanous, involved in her work, generous and warm toward friends new and old. Several times throughout the spring, as the climate got milder and we stretched out in the sun in one of the bays near the town, I had tried to be frank with her and reveal what had happened with Mohamed. But for one reason or another, the words stuck in my throat, my heart beat violently, and after an exhausting struggle with myself, I pitifully abandoned the attempt. In my mind's eye, I had written various scripts in circumstances and settings favorable to a clarifying conversation: a walk through La Garde Freinet woods; dinner alone in some restaurant in the port; the relaxed togetherness of post-coital calm. However, when the moment of truth came, things happened differently: not even alcohol succeeded in unleashing my tongue or sparing me the rage and humiliation of failure. Monique's trusting smile, the vulnerability of that smile, her sweet love for life after the trials of her mother's illness made my position cruel, merciless: the idea of dealing her such a blow was unbearable and forced me to waver. I knew from that moment that a man is capable of the worst deceptions or extremes out of mere cowardice.

I now view that indecision and diffidence with a feeling of shame. No woman was in a better position than Monique to understand the problem and dilemma facing me: a devotee of Genet's world and author of *Les Poissons-chats*, she harbored authentic sympathy of feeling for homosexuals, and her reaction would have in no way been cutting or small-minded. She often aired the question with me, as if unconsciously she guessed my anxieties and wanted discreetly to give me a helping hand. As she would later say, it would have been very easy for her to grasp the opportunity to discuss our future calmly. An insistent, ridiculous, inexplicable fear frustrated time and time again favorable opportunities and, full of self-hate, I kept leaving the decision for later. During the months of May and June, I solemnly fixed half a dozen definitive dates, only later to acknowledge my impotence and accumulate new, more wounding fiascos. Was that stubborn resistance caused by my distant upbringing in Spain or was it a response to some concealed ambivalence, a selfish desire to have my cake and eat it? Whatever the truth was, the waiting dragged me down: of all the difficult decisions I have taken in my life, this would certainly be the one that would cost most.

While I was struggling with my contradictions and fears, I received an official invitation to visit the Soviet Union with my family. We were all three won over by the idea of traveling in the summer during Carole's holidays. I was to go to Paris at the end of June to get the visas and sort out the tickets and, to save Monique and her daughter the predictable trying professional commitments on arrival in Moscow, we decided I would see those out of the way by catching a plane a few days earlier. The idea of explaining myself by letter, carefully debated after the failure of various other attempts, seemed suddenly a blessing from heaven. Among the numerous discarded scenarios was the one with an envelope left in an obvious place on her desk as I went on a fishing trip in the bay with one of my fellow countrymen; but diverse reasons—Carole's presence, the lack of a period for reflection before she could discuss the issue with me—persuaded me finally to discard it. If, however, I was to write the letter in Paris, on the day before my flight to the USSR, the inconvenience of a sudden passionate or depressed reaction disappeared. Separated from me for a week by thousands of miles—and the Iron Curtain!—Monique would have time to think and develop a defensive strategy. Certain knowledge of the brutal quarantine I was imposing on her did not dissuade me from that course. I thought that the temporary distancing would allow her to decant her emotions, accept the challenge of this new chapter in our life with greater calm and equanimity.

In a state of anxious confusion, I took a whole day to write the letter in my study-kitchen on the rue Poissonière. I was afraid of being both too clear and not clear enough: I was distressed by the idea of hurting her without really needing to. To make matters worse, a last-minute change of plans was to complicate life even more: my plane left on 3 July—twenty-four hours before Monique's arrival by car from Saint-Tropez—but in her impatience to see her Parisian friends after such a long time away, she moved up her return by three or four days. Her unexpected rush back upset the scenario I had fashioned so laboriously and forced me into a final regrettable pirouette: I would also deceptively advance my departure so that when she arrived, she would think I was in Moscow. The new scheme meant I had to leave home immediately and settle down for two days with all my luggage in a small hotel on the rue Lafayette near the Gare du Nord. I read and corrected the letter several times before I thought it acceptable, and after a gloomy stroll through that district where anonymity hid me like some miscreant, I grasped my inglorious *alea jacta est* and threw it in the mailbox.

I HAD FOR SOME *time been intending to write and to confide to you something that touches me to the quick, but the impression I was heading down a path leading nowhere and a mixture of fear and shame had postponed my decision day by day. I similarly feared that in conversation I would get nervous, not express myself fairly and exactly, lack the necessary sangfroid, communicate poorly. Nevertheless, I have decided to make the attempt, although I know—and I am now sure of this—the real affection you feel for me, the strong and lasting ties binding us together. I know what your feelings are and in a way I also love you much more than I did: with an intensity that I had not experienced and will not experience again; and when I say "in a way," I mean moral love, feeling for your person and your truly unique qualities, all you have represented to me over the last nine years and which you represent beautifully today in your need for love: generosity, tenderness, unlimited friendship for those around you. I would like to have added "physically," in the way I loved you for years—although I loved you less then than I do now—but I cannot lie at the very moment I am trying to see clearly and am trying to bring my behavior toward you and others in line with reality. I know this letter will not surprise you; you yourself touched on the issue, especially over the last few weeks, in relation to ————.** Your instinct did not deceive you as to the deep interest I have felt for some time in a particular kind of man—an interest, I suppose, that was obvious, in spite of my embarrassed evasion. The certainty of my love and desire to preserve it prevented me from talking to you as I would have preferred. Over the last three months I had determined to do so but never found the opportunity. Don't throw it back at me*

---

*The dashes and bracketed ellipses correspond to people's names and paragraphs that have been cut to avoid unnecessary repetition. The original letter is in French.

that I haven't done so before. I was full of hesitation before taking this step, and I needed to gather together all my strength. I repeatedly weigh in my mind the thought of the pain I shall inflict on you. It will be hard for you, but it is even harder for me. I feel totally bound to you, and my letter is the confession of profound defeat and unhappiness. I would prefer never to have written it, but I cannot continue without writing it. I must explain to you why and how I came to realize beyond any shadow of doubt my liking for men and the reason that I had not revealed it to you before.

In reality, I have always been attracted by a particular type of man that you yourself are now familiar with, and I do not think my falling in love with you or your reciprocity were purely chance occurrences. I found in you what I needed but could not find in other women: "masculinity" and an independence that allowed us to live together. My previous homosexual experiences were negative, and from the time we started to live together up to a year ago, I had no relationships with men, nor did I even contemplate one except fleetingly. Your love had inspired me with a self-confidence that I lacked, and for a long time I thought my homosexuality was a thing of the past. You attracted me physically and I felt secure in myself. Things began turning sour when ——— came by, when my cycles of depression and impotence started as a result of my jealousy and loss of that previous certainty—in spite of the ephemeral nature of your adventures and my conviction that you preferred me to everybody else. Consequently, I lived through some difficult years and, on the rebound, I made you suffer them too. Don't think I attribute to you the least responsibility for what then happened: circumstances, as I see now, only contributed to showing the precariousness of my physical relationship with women. You should think rather that without you I would probably never have known a female love that was requited. There were many ups and downs, periods of calm and relapses. The jealousy got worse in my case because after the first cycle of depression I again fucked women but with difficulty, and two out of three times I was impotent. For months, as you know, I went to bed with whores from Saint-Denis until repeated failures made me bring the experiment to an end. In those circumstances, the feeling you were in love, even only transitorily, with other men was unbearable for me. I seriously contemplated suicide and loathed

*myself for not having the courage to go through with it. Afterwards there was
Cuba, the need to hold on to something, to find another door. With* ———*, I
reached a point of intense jealousy, depression, desire to throw everything overboard. I had no release with women and lost control of my actions: the only things
I am ashamed of in my life are a product of this phase; I was not responsible for
myself yet was nevertheless aware of the moral degradation. Then, gradually, I
had the impression I had touched rock bottom, realizing that henceforth I could
not be jealous of you. The day I saw Luis, I explained the situation to him and told
him the only possible way out was some kind of homosexual life. It was then that
he spoke to you, and you mentioned the conversation to me, but I was still probing
and was unable to respond with any certainty.*

*It must be about a year ago that I started to go out with Arabs and I needed a
few weeks to recognize the evidence: I did recover my equilibrium and coalesced
with you once again; but I also discovered that I was totally, definitively, irrevocably homosexual. From then on, as you must have realized, our relationship improved; although differently, I began to love you more than before and reached a
kind of happiness that I had not attained in the past. I felt at peace, pleased to share
life with you, to have you and Carole at my side. As you can imagine, I wanted to
tell you what had happened; but our well-being seemed so fragile that I was afraid
of undermining it. Then there was your need to leave Gallimard, to write about
your mother: I wanted to support you on both fronts, not to wreck a decision that
was central to your future. Despite my secret, life in 1964 was happy, the year
when our relations firmed up and I recovered my lost peace of mind. I then decided
to keep my silence, to help you cut loose from Paris and the publishers, to support
you as you support me. I went to Saint-Tropez prepared to renounce the new life
I had discovered, content to dedicate myself to the novel, you, and Carole. The
months we have spent together have shown me how far I feel morally and emo-
tionally united to both of you [. . .] But they have also shown me that I cannot
do without real homosexual life. The [ambiguous] friendships I have woven are
not enough and, although I am happy in your company, I am choked by this chastity toward my own sex. In Paris I could have kept my secret without arousing suspicion; in Saint-Tropez it is impossible, and if at times I wanted to go to bed with*

————, *I put the idea to one side because of you, your status in the town, the possible scandal that could flare up, the gossip. The reality of life there has rendered impossible the dual sexual life I was leading and confronted me with the need to confess the truth to you [. . .]*

I could not care less about what others think. Since I have been sure of my homosexuality, the only problem worrying me is in relation to you and Carole—the damaging impact that its discovery would now have on her. I am the opposite of an exhibitionist, and my sense of shame and attachment to secrecy are deeply rooted; but I am not afraid of the truth, and the few people I can rely on are you, Carole, and Luis. I told him all about this on my last trip. It remained only to tell you.

This letter explains my anxiety. I know too well what effect it will have on you, and yet I am forced to write it even with the risk [. . .] I am thirty-four, I love you, and I love Carole, I cannot live without you, I feel a boundless affection for you. What should I do? The void that life alone would be terrifies me, but I will accept it if that is what you decide. I would have wished from deep down that things could have been different, that my deviation had not happened [. . .] but what I know of myself now is eating me away and, surrounded by our Saint-Tropez friends, I am suddenly aware that I am a usurper, that our friendliness is fictitious and based on deceit, that I must cast off the esteem of those who would be disgusted if they knew the truth. How often I have wanted to walk out slamming the door behind me when they were talking about me as if I were one of them, to clear off and live friendless in a country where no one understands me, in total isolation. I am obsessed by the destiny of Jean [Genet]. Sometimes when I wake up at night I want to shout out. I then say to myself that this is my truth, that all the rest is fabrication, facile deceit. That if I am to do anything morally valid, I should make a clean break with everything.

I am now on a knife-edge. I can suggest nothing, promise nothing, nothing at all. Your reaction fills me with anguish, but secretly I want to know. I realize I am destroying my happiness close to you, yours when you are close to me, which I feel to be so strong. I have begun the letter time and again with a timid heart. I pray you do not see it as a breakup although I am powerless if you do. I am afraid of life without you: your face, your capacity for love, your eyes, your affection. I have never been closer to anyone than I have to you. You are the farthest I have gone in love.

Although I have written this letter exclusively to you, you can show it to people who love us and want things to go well between us [. . .] I know that the involvement of others would not help you and would be a futile complication.

It only remains for me to add my desire that you find the happiness, friendship, and esteem that you deserve and that I would like to be able to give you forever.

I shall be waiting for you on the tenth in Moscow with all my love and I shall also be waiting for Carole. With tenderest love . . .

T HE REPLY, so impatiently awaited, finally arrived. A
telegram addressed to the Sovietskaya Hotel relayed a
succinct message: AN INHUMAN WEEK I STILL LOVE YOU.
Three or four days later, after meeting her at the airport with Irina, our interpreter, and Agustín Manso, Monique handed me a text, written in fits and
starts during her cruel quarantine, which included a long postscript written
and dated in mid-flight. Her reflections, questioning, reproaches, formulated in difficult, anxious solitude, revealed at once her strength and vulnerability, nobility, love, openness, generosity, doubts, torment.

The basics had been stated: henceforth the success or failure of our relationship—her adaptation to everything she had just discovered—depended on our wish to continue together. The idea of becoming a normal
couple had sunk without a trace, and we were posed with the challenge of
creating something new. But were the love, understanding, and mutual respect that we could count on enough to preserve the strength of ties that we
saw as essential? Was there not the risk that the precipitous, difficult area I
was penetrating, and to which she would have no access, would spread and
reduce our joint life to a kind of pretense? The danger existed and we were
both fully aware of the fact. The decision to hide nothing from each other
clashed in practice with mighty obstacles: the desire not to hurt each other,
not to make ourselves suffer gratuitously. Gradually, we would establish the
rules of a game in which rigor in relation to what was considered important
would be tempered by a sense of restraint informed by affection. Although
we would carry on a physical relationship for a number of years, the center
of gravity in our union moved to the sphere of shared values and feelings.
Monique knew that my Arab friendships were not testing out my love for

her: the sex and characteristics of my companions excluded all potential rivalry. My existence was unfolding on two parallel planes that did not cross or
interfere with each other: without Monique I would have been reduced to
half of my personality. Liberation from the shackles that tied me down in
this way modified the nature of our links. I ceased to be the insecure or grim
lover of the early days and became quite different, and, in the end, more tolerable: a man resolved to integrate writing into his life and his life in writing,
whose circle of interests and affections would gradually be bound only by essentials. Our agreement to preserve what bound us together from passing
storms and disturbances would have a triumphant outcome. Darkly, but accurately, I guessed that the act of not yielding to social pressures and of
bringing my behavior into the open implied progress in relation to the customs of the time, thanks to which my bonds with Monique and the world
were purified and acquired greater integrity. In opposition to the frustration,
hypocrisy, and sordidness of a great many marriages, what we were proposing was that we should both forge a modest victory against destiny. Monique's prophetic fascination for the universe of Genet, her swiftness in tear-
ing me from the dilemma with which I was struggling would be crucial to
the conquest of that new moral territory.

On 17 August 1978, fourteen years after the date reached in my narrative,
I contracted civil marriage with Monique Lange in the mayor's office in the
second arrondissement in Paris.

CHAPTER VI

The Time Machine

IT WOULD BE difficult for me to express exactly my state of mind on that 3 July 1965, when I embarked for the USSR from the old, down-at-the-heels airport at Le Bourget. A sensation of exceptional weightlessness, as if in a sudden change of cabin pressure, wrapped the red tape and formalities of the flight in a hazy cloud of unreality. Freed from the burden that had been depressing me, I felt I was acting under the subtle influence of marijuana. The anguish of the last few days, given over to the painful writing of the letter and preparations for the journey, had waned little by little from the moment I had irrevocably entrusted my fate to the mailbox. My roaming around Barbès, la Chapelle, the Gare du Nord, very close to the place where Monique, on her return from Saint-Tropez, was going to find the bulky envelope and read and reread pages that would shake the foundations of our precarious life, bathed me in a daydreaming haze, almost a state of levitation. I calculated the time of her arrival with Carole on the rue Poissonnière—cheerful, at ease, sunburned, the usual load of bags and suitcases; apprehensively, I imagined her surprise at the letter, her unpredictable reactions to reading its contents, her shock or panic at the setting out of a problem that, although surmised by her, was suddenly going to blind her vision and abruptly stand between us. My disturbed slumbers in the hotel on the rue Lafayette, knowing she was near to me and yet distant and unapproachable—I could not communicate with her, since she thought me already in Moscow—drained me of all life. Reduced to a pale shadow of the traveler who had embarked supposedly two days before, I killed time as best I could, walking around familiar areas in whose anonymity I found shelter, waiting for the moment to merge with the other on the sunny runway at Le Bourget. Once seated in the Aeroflot plane, I let myself be taken over by a kind of fatalism: aware I had burned my bridges, cut myself loose, gone to war against my false image, was moving into a difficult future full of incentive and novelty. My rebirth at the age of thirty-four with an imprecise identity, determined only to end my previous opportunism and lies, was leading me to a chain reaction of ruptures that would gradually contract my circle of friends; the predictable solitude awaiting me would be bearable, I knew, only with Monique's support and understanding. Mixed feelings and emotions, relief at terminating the ambiguity and fear of inconceivable rejection, accompanied me while I moved away from her, flying to where we had agreed to meet two days later, the new, exotic world of the country of the future: that bastion of scientific socialism, cradle of the glorious October Revolution, hope and Mecca of the exploited—the feared, admired, hated USSR, object of ephemeral youthful nightmares and no less fleeting adult adherence, to that Moscow whose very name would send my father into a rage and which, with the freedom granted by my flamboyant change of skin, I was finally about to tour and examine without blinders of any kind.

Unlike my journeys to Cuba a few years earlier, I was heading for the Soviet Union determined to be receptive and open, aloof from both the primeval anticommunism inculcated in my adolescence and the credulous innocence of past Castroite enthusiasms. The rumors that had filtered through from Havana and my bitter political experience in 1964 helped to make me more wary and cautious: under attack simultaneously from the right and the left, from the Communist Party and the régime of Franco, I had lost my previous political innocence and moved firmly forward in a kind of no-man's-land. Reality, as exemplified by my expelled companions, was much more complex and trickier than I had previously thought. I was amazed by the parallels and symmetries between the methods of ruining opponents employed by friends and enemies alike. Accustomed for years to looking at the world from a single angle and dividing humanity into two perfectly delineated camps, I experienced moments of confusion and helplessness before health-ily reacting with resolutions to change my ways: to stop keeping my head in the clouds, to act in the future with greater discernment and lucidity.

I was to go to the USSR without forebodings or preconceptions, endowed only with the curiosity and interest of a voyeur wishing to adopt if not a neu-tral position, at least one that was cold and balanced. To become a movie camera and tape recorder for all I saw and heard, punctually to note down facts, incidents, conversations. To write for the first time in my life a kind of diary.

Although I did not fulfull that last resolution, Monique did so on my be-half. In her notebook, day by day, in minute, almost undecipherable writing, she summed up each day of our visit, and her notes, even in their bare tele-graphic density, allow me today to evoke without anachronism or error the scenes of our fêted bourgeois life in the world fatherland of the proletariat.

The excitement of my first days in Moscow suffered the consequences of corrosive anguish: Monique's delay in answering the telegram carrying my address and the growing, stifling anxiety of my wait. Contrary to expecta-tions, police and customs formalities were completed surprisingly quickly. Being, as I was, a guest of the USSR Writers' Union, the airport function-aries showed no interest in the contents of my suitcase. At the passenger ter-minal I was greeted by Agustín Manso, a Soviet citizen of Spanish origins, a member of the group of Asturian refugee children in Russia during the civil war, whom I had met in Paris months earlier, and Irina, a welcoming, at-tractive comrade acting on behalf of the Union. I went with them to the Ho-tel Sovietskaya, which was reserved, as I discovered later, for select guests.

While Agustín got me acclimated with his circle of fellow countrymen and friends, Irina was busy guiding me through the labyrinths of official-dom and bureaucracy: protocol visits to her colleagues and chiefs at the Writers' Union, interviews with writers and editors of cultural magazines, collection of my substantial royalties, decisions about the itinerary and stages on our journey. To avoid the bother of organized tours of model farms and factories, I emphasized our particular interest in churches and historical monuments, with the paradoxical result that I have never seen as many religious images, churches, and chapels as during my stay in that supposedly atheist world. Knowing how keen Monique was on beaches, I managed to add to the list of planned excursions a few days' rest in the Crimea. Following the rule of countries with "real socialism," a *pirivocho* was to take charge of us and escort our every step. I had suggested Agustín's name to Irina but, as he had predicted, someone else was chosen: a small, lively, bespectacled Lithuanian lad, rather Disney-like in appearance, by the name of Vidas Silunas, whom Agustín had known from university and whose later companionship was as pleasant as it was unburdensome. Vidas, Agustín, and Irina took me to the offices of the editors of the *Foreign Literature Review*, which had published my works; the publishing houses specializing in the translation of Western novelists and writers; the editorial board of *Novy Mir*, where Alexander Tvardovsky welcomed me with open arms, introduced me to his collaborators, and startled me with the frank honesty of his questions. The first and only publisher of Solzhenitsyn in the brief period of Khrushchevian thaw, although previously awarded a prize by Stalin and a distinguished member of the nomenklatura, the poet stood out from his peers because of his greater spirit of independence and praiseworthy openness of mind. I can remember how he immediately wanted to have my opinion of Neruda. The poet or the man? Both, he replied. I told him that 20 percent of his work seemed splendid, 60 percent rather average, and the rest was detestable; as for his personality, I added that objectivity was impossible since he embodied in my eyes everything I hated in other people and in myself: opportunism, self-worship, a cheerful, fatalistic acceptance of a linear concept of history. Tvardovsky's reaction was unexpected: he got out of his seat, embraced me, warmly patted me on the back. While he remained editor of *Novy Mir*, he would never publish a line of Neruda's poetry. He forcefully explained to me how in the era of the purges and Zhdanov's pedantry, Neruda had been the dictator's international custodian, the willing guardian of his ideology. Then, he gave the word to his advisers, and questions and answers turned to issues in contemporary literature in Spain, Paris, Cuba, and countries in

Latin America. But Tvardovsky was a rara avis in Soviet officialdom. In the other cultural centers that I had occasion to penetrate, the dialogue with those in charge inevitably went along different paths. Outside the field of the universal classics, my hosts' literary tastes revealed an amalgam of incredible ignorance, obtuse dogmatism, complacent, desperate mediocrity. They hardly advocated a single modern writer whom I admired: neither Proust, Joyce, Kafka, Svevo, nor Borges were circulating in Russian, nor were they then in the course of being translated. The advisers for the Spanish section were making known the work of Celaya and Marcos Ana, but not Cernuda; that of Dolores Medio, but not Martín-Santos. I remember asking one of them why they were not publishing *Tiempo de silencio*. I was astonished by my female informant's reply: it was, she said, an overly complex novel that the Soviet reader would not understand. I should have replied—since I did not at the time—that with such criteria literary and intellectual progress were impossible and the readership in her country would in the year 2000 still be legally underage and deprived of the most significant, enriching works.

When at one of the readings or cultural events in which I now participate, someone asks me the hackneyed question of why I write such sybilline, hermetic texts as *Conde Julián* or *Makbara* if an average reader cannot manage to comprehend them, I flourish this anecdote as a reminder of the real, deep contempt for possible improvements in public taste implicit in the paternalist, demagogic attitude of those who take it upon themselves to lower the creative level and arrogate the right to decide what the people understand or do not understand in matters artistic and literary. The history of literature—as of all manifestations of the human spirit—comprises a succession of difficult enterprises that often go unrecognized at the time of their conception: to be grasped in all its depth and complexity, any original, innovative work requires at times very lengthy lapses of time during which it will find a way through. An extreme example of this is the great poetry of Góngora, which has only become accessible to readers three centuries after being created. But one would merely have to extend the discriminating criterion adopted by the bureaucrats in the field of literature to the area of the sciences to reveal at

once the arrant nonsense of their position: since the people do not understand either, for example, the discoveries of physics, then the State should
logically ban them as well. If it does not, that is clearly, strictly a matter of
profitability: science, in its practical application, can be mobilized on its behalf; literature, on the other hand, cannot and will never be. Principles based
on the political-social function of art are the death of art itself. Of all the literary and artistic doctrines formulated over the last two centuries, that of socialist realism has one really exceptional distinguishing feature: it has not
produced a single work of value in fiction, poetry, music, or painting. When
Tvardovsky's collaborators asked me for my preferences in modern Russian
literature, they smiled at my list of writers—Blok, Essenin, Babel, Akhmatova, Mandelstam: all had composed their work outside and in the teeth
of official doctrine and some had paid with their lives for their audacity. The
magnitude of the punishment and risk immanent in any act of defiance explains the fact that both writers and readers in the USSR take literature extremely seriously. If the composition of a work different from that propounded by the state creed leads a writer to civil death and to being
ostracized; if the majority of printed books are mere moralizing tracts, a hybrid of conformism and propaganda, this situation sheds light on the eager-
ness of an alert, active minority for those works that are difficult to find even
on the black market and that, if they are published, disappear immediately
from the bookshop shelves. People in line in the street for a whole night to
buy a book of poetry, as happened months before my journey to the USSR
when a small selection of Akhmatova's poems were given authorization, is
one indication of the high value bestowed on literary creation by a ravenous
readership and, inversely, of the censors' justified fear of outbreaks of enthusiasm produced by their own absurd blind policy. The different status enjoyed by the artist in the Soviet sphere and in Western countries testifies to
the religious respect and admiration with which readers surround the figure
of a writer whose trajectory moves away from set canons and harnesses literary and artistic demands to uncorruptible moral rigor. The search for new
artistic forms of expression, the exploration of virgin linguistic territories
can be dubbed a game in the West; in the USSR, because of the external

sanction they incur, such matters assume in readers' eyes a surprising and shared gravity.

In the interval between my arrival and the date of Monique's flight, I also visited Agustín Manso's friends and the nucleus of Spaniards whose addresses Claudín had passed on to me. Some were Party members and were more or less integrated into the rigid, compartmentalized strata of the Soviet hierarchy; others, like the theater director Ángel Gutiérrez, encountered serious obstacles in their professions or lived entirely outside the hierarchy, like Dionisio García. The latter had recently been divorced from a gypsy and had lived a long time with the monks of Zagorsk, spent his time restoring icons and professed a real love of literature and philosophy, although his knowledge of the latter was minuscule: his ignorance of languages other than Spanish and Russian and the difficulty of obtaining a supply of related works in either language limited the range of his reading to a short, eccentric list of authors. I can remember his curiosity and interest in the works of Kierkegaard, Bergson, and Berdayeff, whose theories he knew only by hearsay, and his radical mistrust and contempt for politics. Thanks to him, I managed a few glimpses of aspects of Soviet reality that were different from, and even contradicted, those on show on official circuits: the flat he shared with several families or neighbors where he had only one modest room filled with books; the existence of anti-Semitic groups, where, as a Spaniard— from the home of the Holy Inquisition and the Catholic Monarchs—he was welcomed one day with a round of flattering applause. Although sentimentally inclined to things Russian—culture, customs, scenery—my new acquaintances revealed signs of a truly praiseworthy independence of ideas. They had a subtle, fair-minded vision of the USSR: they spoke affectionately about the country but did not hide its defects. My royalties, paid in nonconvertible rubles that I had consequently to spend on the spot, allowed me the luxury of inviting them to the most expensive restaurants. For the first and probably only time in my life, I had sufficient means to offer a group of friends a real banquet and, awaiting the day when Monique and Carole were to meet up with me, I fleetingly savored the pleasures of acting like a millionaire.

With her daughter and wearing a light white raincoat, Monique finally emerged from the passengers' arrival channel after going through police formalities. My companions did not suspect the deep emotion of that meeting nor the change wrought in our life by my letter. Her warm smile, tender manner and gestures really disguised her loneliness and uncertainty before the riddle I had set her. On that rainy but brightly luminous afternoon we took their suitcases to the Sovietskaya before going for a stroll around Red Square and the walls of the Kremlin. Irina and her colleagues at the Writers' Union had worked hard to smooth out all the problems and ensure we had a comfortable stay. Monique was delighted by the program for the holiday, which had been drawn up according to my wishes. The novelty of the perspective—friends, décor, pace of life—facilitated cautious mutual adaptation. Without the excitement of exploring that vast, alien, extreme world, things would have been different for both of us and probably more arduous.

My brief diary and notes on the USSR, worked out from Monique's diary, has only one aim, to restore the freshness of my impressions at the time, while adding indispensable later thoughts. Their deliberate superficiality and *parti pris* of carefree humor might upset both enemies and defenders of the Soviet system, but they reflect the vision of an observer like myself struggling to cast off the cobwebs of ideology. The fact that I was examining "real socialism" with the simplicity of a nursery child was not the fruit of some capricious decision or arbitrary point of view; it was part of a chain of circumstances that involved my break with the past and a desire to make a clean sweep of all that was stifling me in order to forge myself, counter to everybody—friends, enemies, those nearest to me—a new identity and, in conflict with myself, to impose a new direction on my life.

1

In the entrance to the Hotel Sovietskaya, Monique bumped into a friend with whom she had had dealings years before, for professional reasons. She too had just arrived in Moscow, knew no one in the city, and asked if we wouldn't mind taking her out for dinner. Monique said we wouldn't, and we agreed to pick her up later from her room. She was on a different floor, and at the agreed time I took to the stairs, walked past a stout woman who sat impassively at her small table looking after the keys to the bedrooms. I went down the corridor and knocked on the room door she had earlier indicated. However, for some unknown reason, my gesture infuriated the hall porter: she stood up immediately, shouted, ran toward me, and began to wave her arms threateningly. At that very moment Monique's friend opened her door, and the scene she surveyed astonished her; the matron repeated, "Nyet, nyet" and, not satisfied with that, suddenly pulled me by the sleeve.

"What's the matter? Has she gone mad?"

I said I didn't know, but the message was clear: unwittingly, I had committed a most serious crime. It was an unusual situation and we couldn't stop laughing. In order to bypass a trial of strength from which we would clearly emerge as losers, we agreed to meet up in the lobby. When I recounted the episode to Monique and my friends, there was general hilarity. Rather embarrassed, Agustín told me that the rules in some hotels prevented guests of a different sex from visiting each other, in order to stamp out immoral behavior.

Spanish Catholic Action, which I had met in my years at secondary school, would no doubt be proud to see the seeds of their preaching unexpectedly blooming on the distant shores of the Moskva!

2

The restaurant food was excellent, but the waiters seemed to be unaware of the notion of time and often remained absorbed in mysterious thoughts, not paying the slightest attention to a customer's futile signals and calls. An incredible interval could elapse from the moment one sat down at a table until one actually received a menu, and on the surface this did not seem to be justified by any other tasks.

My preferences went to the Uzbekistan and the Tibilisi, where the waiters seemed more awake and pocketed their tips without blinking. However, writers favored places reserved for their own guild, in which stars like Yevtushenko had a right to a table and could theatrically welcome the arrival of a distinguished visitor by throwing a glass of champagne to the floor. (The "distinguished visitor" writing these lines would be submitted to such an ordeal in the course of a second visit and would search in vain for a hole or corner in which to hide from the bard's flamboyant gesticulations.)

My hosts toasted the family reunion with vodka and white wine, and when it was time to get up and leave the drawing rooms of the Artists' Café, Monique and I felt cheerful, if slightly tipsy.

Less fortunate than restaurant-goers, ordinary people got drunk standing up, in solitude. During our first tour of Moscow, my friends pointed out a line of silent men, vaguely sad and unkempt like Salvation Army regulars, outside a liquor store. As I noticed on other occasions, the bottle of vodka was often paid for by two or three people who then swigged it down in the street without exchanging a word. The communion brought by alcohol was replaced by a ritual whose insularity I found disconcerting: the drinkers remained anonymous, and after briefly coming together to drink, each staggered off, pie-eyed, by himself. The price of vodka was relatively accessible to the pocket of the average citizen and, as I was informed, the system ensured that there was an uninterrupted supply.

3

Vidas Silunas offered us a sightseeing tour of Moscow with stops at the Kremlin, Red Square, Lenin's mausoleum, Gorki Street, the monument to Pushkin. At Dionisio's suggestion, we stopped off to visit the subway, built in the time of Stalin. Our guide led us to an imposing, cold, awe-inspiring station, with glass lamps in the ceiling and an escalator that went down to platforms adorned with statues of heroes of the Revolution; these had been cast in bronze, were larger than life, and represented soldiers, sailors, commissars, militiamen in impetuous, bellicose, triumphal poses. Uniforms, belts, and boots were reproduced faithfully to the tiniest detail, and one fine figure even waved a real revolver in a monstrous attack of rage. We decided to go for a ride and with Vidas got on one of the trains.

The train cars seemed more spacious, more comfortable, and cleaner than those of the Paris métro, and the passengers, who were few, given the time of day, went in and out easily, serious, patient, disciplined. We sat down in a row, both curious and the object of the curiosity of those seated opposite: villagy women in head-scarves, middle-aged ruddy-faced men, almost always wearing a hat or cap. One of the former's perverse stare in Monique's direction suddenly attracted my atten-tion: just as I was about to mention it to her, the woman suddenly got up and, without uttering a word, pulled down the edge of Monique's skirt until her knees were completely covered. The gesture left us tongue-tied and Vidas Silunas was quick to pacify us: peasant women, he said, were not used to foreigners' ways of dressing; any anomaly, however innocent, clashed with their exaggerated sense of modesty.

On successive days we would have occasion to verify that widespread mixture of harshness, warmth, and brusque behavior of the Russian people: the driver of the vehicle that took us to Suzdal showed a lively interest in us, bombarded us with questions through the interpreter, laughed like a child at our candor, and contin-ually turned round to look at us, to the point that we feared he would let go of the steering wheel and crash into a tree. Monique went with her daughter to the GUM department store to buy some small keepsakes; the customers, she said, pushed and elbowed their way through with incredible brutality. Later, in the Crimea, when she went one day to the bathroom in a pharmacy or a shop, an em-ployee slipped in with her and without ceremony seized the opportunity to ex-amine her underwear, ask her about and comment on the origin and quality of her bras.

4

A visit to Vladimir: the city had just been opened up to foreigners and my Spanish friends urged me to go. We went by train, with Vidas Silunas, and for two or three hours we passed through a land of oaks, firs, and birches. When we arrived at the station, a small group of men and women were waiting con-spicuously on the platform with bunches of flowers. Fears that I was the victim of such a glorious welcome were confirmed at once: forewarned by Moscow, the lo-cal organizers of the Writers' Union had come en masse to welcome us. Monique,

Carole, and I greeted our respective bouquets amid smiles and bows. I handed mine to Vidas and asked him whether they had confused me with Aragon or Alberti.

A journey to the hotel, where a banquet awaited us. For more than an hour we remained seated in a small drawing room with our hosts. The usual vodka was inexplicably delayed, and we all kept ceremonially silent in an attitude of stiff awkwardness. To bring some relief to the heavy atmosphere I was forced to ask a few questions: How long had the provincial branch of the Union been in existence? How many members or affiliates did it have? What literary genres did they cultivate? How did artistic life proceed? What were their main activities? Their replies were detailed, mechanical, and boring, and when the translation was broken off and the silence thickened, my questions again steered toward gratuitous extravagance and inanity: When was the library opened? How many volumes did it contain? What kind of books did readers prefer? The figures floated about, useless, unreal, absurd, and when I was about to discover the number of cultural— or philatelic, or financial—magazines they subscribed to, the announcement that the table was ready fortunately brought the nightmare to a close. The Siberian gastronomic speciality heralded by the president turned out to be a kind of ravioli. But the vodka finally arrived, and with their mouths full, nobody felt obliged to prolong the incongruous dialogue.

After bidding farewell to that lethal group of writers, we walked out into the street. It was a Sunday or a holiday and the pavements were packed with people: introspective, gloomy, inert, they brought to mind those described by Jovellanos in his upsetting, unforgettable pages on the atmosphere of exhaustion, sadness, and desolation in the villages of Castile. The men and women we saw looked more like a pack of soldiers suddenly abandoned by their officers. Street-sellers wandered along the main avenue and gathered around some enormous billboards inscribed with the names and photographs of the most meritorious workers of the month. The contemplation of this display appeared to be the only diversion in the city and kept attracting new groups of spectators. Nobody laughed, joked, or spoke in a loud voice: silence was obligatory. From time to time, music from a transistor radio ephemerally broke the almost physical density of that hybrid of alienation, lethargy, and monotony.

The churches were splendid and, as they were celebrating worship, full of the faithful. The canticles of the priests, smell of incense, solemn ritual of the offices created a strange counterpoint to the grayness and conformity outside. The massive church attendance did not necessarily reflect, however, the religious feeling of the population: as far as I could see, Vladimir was without cafés, cinemas, or other places for recreation. In such circumstances, any novelty inevitably attracts people's attention and, like our appearance and clothing, becomes a source of distraction and curiosity.

5

We continued to trawl churches and monasteries in the region. Their architecture was noble and majestic, though slender and light in design. The gold of the Byzantine domes stood out in its purity against the compliant blue of the sky.

In Suzdal we spied in the distance a pitched battle fought by hundreds of horsemen. We were not too surprised by the anachronism; however, we stopped to inquire. As we got out of the vehicle in which we were traveling, Vidas approached a group of technicians and drivers involved in the shooting of the film. As he then told us, they were filming Tarkovsky's now-famous film on the life of Andrei Rublev. The preparations for the scene, with great movements of the masses and deployment of armies, were harmoniously integrated into countryside that seemed to have changed very little since the time of that famous painter of icons.

These rapid incursions into "deep Russia" revealed, however, the disturbing backwardness of agriculture; the survival of conditions and ways of life profusely described in literature from the times of Gogol, Turgenev, and Tolstoy. The small isbas with their stoves and indoor plants fitted quite easily into the scenery in Tarkovsky's film and, almost fifty years after the Revolution, were probably still the same as they had been centuries ago. When I went to Uzbekistan and the Caucasus, that apathy and immobility, the almost mildewy existence of peasants only two hours by car from the capital would seem even more intriguing. It would be unjust and mistaken to blame everything on the Soviet régime, which had witnessed spectacular improvements in the standard of living of Georgians and Uzbekis, which was now much higher than under their former masters and occu-

piers. Rather than being a colonizer, the Russian peasant gave the impression he was vegetating, poverty-stricken and colonized. The peculiar features of his history would perhaps clarify such a striking contrast and the tenacious attachment that numerous layers of the population of the Socialist republic, in towns and in the country, had to traditional norms and practices.

A tendency to make the countryside a place to escape to: all my acquaintances, both Spaniards and native Russians, spoke blissfully of the forests of larches, oaks, and birches, to which they fled as often as possible and that apparently contained the decanted quintessence of all they identified as Russia. They were filled with emotion by the evocation of firs, snow, sledges. The disparity between my tastes and theirs was as abrupt as it was extreme: when I told them I was an urban animal capable of walking dozens of kilometers through the streets of a city that excited me, but incapable of taking a step in a setting whose peacefulness irritated me, they looked surprised and incredulous. Didn't the quiet and silence of the countryside favor work and inspiration? Without any desire to be paradoxical, I retorted that the latter were associated, in my case, with the lively bustle of the city: while the urban hum and fury hardly bothered me, the gentle rustle of leaves or the trill of a bird distracted me and made concentration impossible. Didn't any kind of scenery appeal to me? The desert, I replied; I found lush vegetation depressing and appreciated greenness only when it was sparse and bare, when placed against mineral splendor, the creation of arduous, laborious toil. A few fig, olive, or almond trees in a parched landscape, the persistent wavy hedge of oleanders along the dry bed of a stream move me much more than sixty thousand square miles of Siberian natural park. That mutual insensitivity to our respective preferred haunts finally made us laugh. Dionisio told me—in reference to his recent reading of Campos de Níjar—*that I had become an incorrigible specimen of Almería man.*

6

Visit to Leningrad: we stroll tirelessly around the streets near the beautiful Winter Palace, the age-old, now self-absorbed aristocratic districts, the bridges and banks of the Neva, the quayside where the Aurora *was still moored next to the dark, intimidating fortress of Peter and Paul.*

We enjoyed the sweet suspension of time, the ethereal subtlety, penetrating lu-minosity of the white nights in the company of two intellectuals living in the city, both former volunteers with the International Brigades: Dr. Pritkere, professor of Spanish at the university and a Larra specialist, and Ruth Zernova, a Jewish translator who had an equal command of Spanish and French and whose mother—whom we visited for a few moments in her tiny central flat—happened to be an old Bolshevik who had divorced Karl Radek before he fell in one of the purges and was executed by Stalin. Both Ruth and the professor displayed a warmth and spontaneity that were unusual in that hardened, scaly intellectual world, and we immediately felt a wave of mutual sympathy. When we interro-gated them on the period of the terror, the Spanish civil war, the siege and resis-tance to the Nazis, their replies were direct and honest. We visited the Pushkin mu-seum with them; walked along the gardens belonging to Yussopov Palace, where Rasputin was killed; we followed the route of Raskolnikov, drawn with such de-tail by Dostoevsky. Ancient Petersburg, beautiful and mournful as Venice some-times is, watched over us in an unreal heady atmosphere of fading light; our pres-ence seemed oneiric and false. Tenuous, lifeless, tired, the sun finally hid at midnight behind a panorama of sleeping palaces and deserted squares. From the hotel window we would see it reappear, still through mists and yellow haze, at half-past three in the morning.

7

As we knew from Paris, Sartre and Simone de Beauvoir were also in Leningrad, in the company of Lénina Zónina, a young attractive woman with whom Sartre had a discreet, emotional relationship for a number of years. Mo-nique, Carole, and I visited them in the Hotel Astoria and dined with Castor and Lénina in a Caucasian restaurant. Sartre had another engagement, but had lunch with us the day after and related some salacious anecdotes on the phobia of China: at one of the meetings of the World Council for Peace, to whose leading or advisory committee he belonged, one of his Soviet hosts, who was apparently rather drunk, had jokingly whispered to him that although peace was of course extremely desir-able, a small hydrogen bomb aimed at Peking, close to Mao's residence, would not be a totally bad idea. This bitter animosity—so accurately forecast by my fa-

ther—*was not limited to the well-known anti-imperialist rhetoric of official circles: on the contrary, as we were able to ascertain throughout our journey, it embraced the whole population. The number of anti-Chinese jokes, gags, stories that we heard was unending: while the average Soviet displayed a mixture of envy, admiration, and indulgence toward North Americans, they reserved scorn, sarcasm, and hatred for their comrades in the East. When a heroine in the world of the Guermantes sighed "la Chine m'inquiète" in one of her society gatherings, she could not imagine that half a century later her opinions would be shared by a huge country whose official doctrine would be none other than so-called proletarian internationalism.*

As we were eating dessert, we had an unexpected visitor. Luis Miguel Dominguín was on a business trip to the USSR and, having learned from a third party that we were there, he came to say hello. I knew his brother Domingo and his brother-in-law and rival Antonio Ordóñez: the time I went to Nîmes with Monique, during the period we saw something of Hemingway, they took me to Spain with them, and the frontier police were so intent on their rapturous welcome for the bullfighter that they didn't bother to find out who was in the car or to stamp my passport. On the journey to Barcelona, perhaps to keep sleep at bay, Domingo and Ordóñez had sustained an amusing political discussion. The former, at the time his brother-in-law's manager, insisted on converting him to his Communist ideas, but the bullfighter was not at all convinced and counterattacked with ad hominem arguments: if he was so proud of being red, why did he keep charging him a 10 percent commission? Was that not a form of bourgeois exploitation? Of course it was, Domingo answered. The capitalist's only moral rule was to appropriate the surplus value of others. The more he exploited, the more he would help to dissipate reformist illusions and objectively nourish revolutionary consciousness. Class collaboration, social democratic fudging would lead to the revisionist vices so severely condemned by Lenin. Ordóñez's arm would not be twisted and he burst out laughing: What the hell, you're no Communist! You're just on the make. Domingo's attitude—that I would later see reflected in the language and behavior of some Latin American magnates as they opened up their luxury umbrellas under the luminous firmament of Mexico or Caracas the moment they heard it rained in Moscow—was a characteristic product of the Manichaeism and confusion of those years and expressed very clearly the contradictions and shortcomings in our political and cultural world. Dominguín had hardly gone when I related the anecdote to Sartre, who laughed heartily. As Monique later reminded me, both he and his friends maintained an attitude of reserve toward bullfighting, if not of discreet moral disapproval, as was the case with his companion. Fortunately, neither introduced that issue, and as we said goodbye we agreed we would meet up again in Moscow on our return from the Crimea and Uzbekistan.

8

Luis Miguel invited us out to dinner, and we went with Vidas and Ruth Zernova to the Europa Hotel, where he had reserved a small drawing room. The bullfighter traveled with a tiny retinue of Spaniards, including Lucía Bosé, elegantly dressed in red and more beautiful than in her early films. Despite the vodka and champagne from the Caucasus, conversation languished, but Estela, a Soviet interpreter and translator of our social poets, unknowingly took responsibility for enlivening it. With that burden of moral sentiments often exhibited by the comic characters in Chekhov, she asked the bullfighter if the Spanish people were suffering a lot under the chains of an oppressive régime like Franco's. "What on earth have they got to suffer about? It couldn't be happier!" "Happy?" exclaimed Estela. "Yes, happy, the Spanish adore Franco and so do I." "But Franco has killed lots of people, he's very cruel and unjust . . ." "All governments kill people and are cruel and unjust: if the people obey them, what difference does it make?" "I thought the masses in Spain . . ." "Look, miss: the masses follow those who give them orders and quite right, too; who gives the orders in Russia? Is it the Communist Party?" Estela said it was, but then she got mixed up and had to get it right: well, it was really the Supreme Soviet. "If I were Russian, I would go along with the Supreme Soviet; but as I am Spanish and Franco's in charge in my country, I'm a supporter of Francoism." "But that's terrible," mumbled the upset Estela, "your views are selfish and cynical . . ." "Exactly," he agreed, "that's exactly right, cynical, yes sir, cynical."

We were cheered up by the exchange: Dominguín's sarcastic aplomb and Es-

tela's consternation delighted the party, especially those who were forced to put up with the funereal gravity of official speeches and their usual stock references to humanist values. Laughter plays a liberating role, and where the suffocating orthodoxy of a political or religious doctrine reigns supreme—as Bahktin taught me years later in relation to the world of Rabelais—the truths of the jester are like a breath of fresh air, the escape valve thanks to which life becomes more bearable.

9

Our stay in Leningrad—the walks along the streets of a somnambulant, sleeping-beauty city, in an atmosphere of hazy luminous tranquillity—seemed too short. The Petersburg, or Petrograd, that is so wonderfully described in literature survived specterlike on those white nights steeped in nostalgic memories. The desolate splendor of the city, the uncertain brightness of the night suddenly immersed the traveler in the atmosphere of the Russian novel. We decided to reread Pushkin, Dostoevsky, Tolstoy. Biely was little more than a name to me at the time: the decadent writer Trotsky fulminated against. But my efforts to meet Akhmatova would not bear fruit: they told me she was getting over a long illness and had gone for a few weeks' rest far from the city.

In the airport, after checking our luggage, we had a drink with Vidas while waiting for our plane to depart. We became entangled in a discussion of Soviet sexuality and did not notice the time go by until our guide was startled by a loudspeaker announcement demanding we present ourselves immediately on the runway. We ran after him to the foot of a small staircase where a dozen people were packed together, hoping to secure empty seats at the last minute. Our untimely arrival frustrated their attempt, and there was a chorus of muffled shouts, bad-tempered expressions. To make way for us amid those who hadn't yet given up and were waiting in vain for a miracle, a couple of militiamen pushed them aside with uncalled-for brutality: some of them lost their balance and thudded to the floor. Surprisingly, the expeditious intervention of the forces of law and order provoked no reaction. The disappointed travelers moved back, and we slipped between them and our protectors with heads lowered in shame. Such a scene would perhaps not be shocking in Calcutta or Bombay but, given the context in which it took place, Monique and I were filled with vague, if persistent, disquiet.

10

*We spent a day in Moscow, en route to Tashkent. Agustín, Ángel,
Dionisio came to see us in our hotel, and Monique pursued with them her survey
of Soviet youth. What's happening to couples? What are their moral attitudes?
Was the puritanical restraint that dominated press, television, books, and films a
relic of the old peasant tradition or did it reflect customs and social codes as well?*

*Although censorship excised any reference or allusion to the sexual act, my
friends said, the attitude of boys and girls was fairly lax. According to them, the
greatest obstacle to intimate relationships was rooted in the penury and packed nature of housing, a lack of space. In summer, people copulated in the woods, but in
winter only the fortunate owner of a private room could allow himself the luxury
of enjoying himself alone with his partner; everyone else had to be satisfied with
the occasional loan of room keys from their more fortunate colleagues. Those who
had influence or means also used the cabins on the boats that plied the Volga or the
sleeping cars on the train to Leningrad. As to homosexuality—on which Monique playfully insisted—their response could not have been more disappointing;
they had all heard about it as something way-out and extravagant, but declared
that they personally knew no "perverts."*

*Apart from these exchanges of opinions with my Spanish friends and excep-
tional personalities like Ruth Zernova, conversations with Soviet intellectuals
who were accessible to foreigners very soon became a painful ritual. Forced to
keep quiet on essentials—their absolute dependence on the system that lodged,
dressed, fed, and found work for them and, in cases of good behavior, granted them
the privileges of daschas, cars, and permission to travel—in their dialogue with
Westerners they pursued a continuous exercise in reserve, trivial comment, and
avoidance of the truth. Knowing they could say only what they ought to say, they
strove to compensate for their individual barrenness with a series of declarations
exuding vitality or vague, general, humanitarian political propositions. Their
propensity to sudden raucous laughter, in slightly more strident tones than normal; their recourse to rhetorical clichés and facile sentimentality; the habit of relating anodyne jokes about the régime as proof of their illusory independence; the
need to rapidly drown in alcohol any attempt at potentially dangerous commu-*

nication—all these tendencies betrayed a self-censorship or inner repression that gave their slightest gesture or movement an air of forced stiffness. Contact or acquaintance with one of them allowed one to spot the syndrome in all the rest. As I would verify years later, these marks stay with even those who have had the courage to break with the system and, still in exile, display the scars and traces of their traumatic apprenticeship and cultivation of mental wariness and restraint.

11

First impressions on leaving the airplane: bustle, warmth, sensuality, immediacy of human relations; a greater variety of faces, clothes, colors; sudden increase in temperature; refreshing stereophonic voices.

The cavernous, imposing Writers' Union car thundered along the dusty road, passed and left behind a motley succession of vehicles of all shapes and sizes. The Uzbeki driver, wearing a kind of biretta, seemed to be driving happily along, following the musical rhythms on the radio: an intense, warm, heart-rending Turkish-style melody I then heard for the first time. His steering wheel and windshield were decorated with rosary beads, photos, and lucky charms, just like those of his Arab colleagues. He sometimes greeted a friend through the window and laughed to himself, either at the chance encounter or the wit of his own words. On the journey we contemplated family scenes or set pieces, open-air cafés shadowed by vines, customers stretched out lazily on rush mats. Some were crouching, lost in their tea tray or game of checkers. Idleness was a way of life. I felt that I was, I am an integral part of that scene.

Tashkent looked like a modern city, with its functional, graceless architecture; but the contrast of its inhabitants' temperament and character with those of their Russian comrades could not be more extreme. The aura of alienation and gloom that enveloped the pedestrian masses in Moscow or Vladimir was dissipated here by the dual impact of Islam and the sun. The population's standard of living was clearly what it ought to be. If Russian ethnocentrism existed, as I would later see myself, Uzbekistan had not, on the other hand, been beset by the devastation and thieving of the booty-hunting régimes of the old Western protectorates and colonies. Poverty had been efficiently swept aside: people dressed better than in Moscow, notably with greater variety and imagination. No beggar was there to upset

visitors, unlike in Moslem countries. Their indolence was not the fruit of desti-
tution but of a particular relaxed casual style of life. An almost unique example
among peoples subject to capitis diminutio, *the Uzbekis could pride themselves*
on material conditions far superior to those in the distant but all-powerful me-
tropolis.

This dip into a nation of Islamic culture, annexed by force of arms by the czars
and then inserted against its will into the multiracial conglomerate of the USSR,
would allow me on my return to Moscow to distinguish the purely Soviet from the
Russian and not repeat the mistake made years earlier in Cuba when I erroneously
attributed to the Revolution elements of happiness, spontaneity, and dissipation
in fact inherent in the Cuban people. The oppression, melancholy, silence that
startle the visitor to Tula or Vladimir cannot be attributed, as one might think at
first sight, only to the hermetic immobility of the régime, but also to a centuries-
old tradition and experience; the creation as much of Ivan, Peter, and Catherine
as of Lenin and Stalin. After an open-air party, when we went for a walk with
Vidas and Valeri, the Uzbeki guide, amid gardens, pavilions, meadows, and ponds
in a municipal park full of families, couples, bathers, chess or checkers players, a
vague sense of well-being impregnated the atmosphere and finally intoxicated us
with a gentle, frivolous felicity. The heat was extremely dry and healthy: Mo-
nique's persistent rheumatism, a result of her winter bathing in Saint-Tropez,
would disappear within hours of her stay in Uzbekistan. At night the temperature
drove sleep away, but after showering a dozen times all in vain, I finally nodded
off like Marat in the bath, nibbling the slices of watermelon that we had provi-
dentially bought in a market.

12

Vidas's tact and care reduced our official contacts to the necessary
minimum: nevertheless, I was the first Spanish writer, apart from Alberti, to visit
the country, and we could not avoid a natural feeling of friendly curiosity toward
us. The leaders of the Writers' Union proudly showed me several brochures of po-
litical tourist propaganda in Spanish and inquired after the rigor and accuracy of
the translation. I politely examined the pages of one of them—The Progress of
Uzbeki Woman Under Socialism—*and had to make an effort not to burst out*

laughing. Rather than a traitor, the genial translator seemed to be a fan of Ionesco and his dialogues in La Cantatrice chauve. *Threading together like beads the unknown words extracted from the dictionary, his dronelike activity had created a stodgy, amphibious prose—subject to the breaks and dislocations of a fierce torturing steed—but one that was also incredibly comic. Referring to the traditional Islamic custom of wearing the veil, abolished by the Soviets, he had produced an inspired phrase that verged on the sublime: "The women would walk along upheld by their impenetrable velaments." When I read the most amusing Cervantine chapter in* Tres tristes tigres *devoted to translation, I remembered that anonymous though elegant rival to Riné Leal and her ineffable adaptation of the story of Mr. Campbell and his walking stick . . .*

The same strand would be repeated soon afterwards in the hotel dining room with an overdressed folkloric singer who was also anxious to try out on me the tuneful perfections his Brazilian or Caribbean accent. As I gathered on the journey, a number of Uzbekis were aware of the diplomatic mission of Ruy González de Clavijo, Henry IV's envoy to the court of Tamerlane: the words Spain, Castile *had then a familiar and exotic ring in their ears. However, days later a youth who looked like a peasant sat next to me in the airplane, stared, and then spoke to me. His brief dialogue with Vidas, whose help I sought, went something like this:*

"Which country are you from?"

"From Spain."

"Where did you say?"

"Spain."

"Spain, Spain . . . Whereabouts is that in the Soviet Union?"

13

We were dazzled by our arrival in Samarkand: although a great number of mosques and medresses were in ruins, the city as a whole was splendid and confirmed my presentiments of immediacy, familiarity, and harmony with the old Moslem civilization. Tall slender minarets, gilded domes, gloriously blue mosaic façades blended together with effortless symmetry; street life was dense and full of bustle, a subtle invitation to wander. On foot we visited the various markets sheltered from the sun by awnings and shades; we entered one of the few mosques still devoted to worship. The faithful were few and, generally, very old. Valeri, our local guide, commented that young people did not usually go. His explanation— "they don't have the time"—was not entirely convincing and was soon corrected by another Uzbeki youth who whispered in our ear in English, "Believers can't get into university."

We visited one of Tamerlane's palaces. The cicerone *responsible, stuffing us with her profuse historical knowledge, was a middle-aged Russian woman, dowdy and expressionless, wearing a hat-cum-parasol, her face covered in a thick layer of powder. She halted at every step in the heat of the sun to explain in her monotonous, dull voice unimportant anecdotes in the life and customs of the Mongolian emperor, his love of letters and astronomy, the number of his wives and concubines, his frequent after-dinner conversations with his astrologers. The heat was unbearable, and I looked in vain for a shadowy tree to stand under. The lady kept on speechifying at us, obviously something learned by heart, breaking off from time to time only to enable Vidas to continue his slow, deadly translation. A mini-lecture on the different turquoise shades of the* zellijes, *or tiles, lasted for several minutes: in the days of Tamerlane there were only eleven; now, thanks to the progress of Soviet industry, there were forty-three. Or was it a hundred and twenty-three? On the brink of committing a criminal act, I looked at that white, jellyfish mask whose pallid lips kept articulating that flow of inane, vacuous, incomprehensible words. Would she ever stop? She seemed not to notice the symptoms of my impatience and launched into a prolix story about Tamerlane's favorite wife, of which I can remember a few words translated by Vidas: doe, ankle, fall. Able to contain myself no longer, I pointed at the inexorable, hieratic face. Tell her to shut her trap, I snarled at the guide. Vidas obeyed and his translation clearly did not beat about the bush: the woman looked at me in amazement, and suddenly a double river of tears streamed down her cardboard cheeks. Monique was upset, turned to me indignantly: I had just humiliated that poor woman, who was only doing her duty; I was an odious Spanish snob. Ashamed of myself, embarrassed by the tears, I begged her through our guide to continue her fascinating talk. The woman gathered herself together at once, wiped her face with a handkerchief, and resumed the anecdote of the wife injured when playing with the doe, exactly where she had left off. The glare of the sun was like a real furnace; even the air seemed to catch alight and flame up. Almost ready to melt, I tolerated the were on our way. Our friend spoke to the Intourist woman, and from the sharp, lively tone of the exchange I deduced that she had refused. Her assignment was to accompany us to the airport, she said, not to show us the city. Fed up, impatient, I told her we had caught the plane to see Bukhara, not to put up with her bad manners and hysteria. Vidas translated my words literally and the impact was devastating: the woman ordered the driver to stop and got out of the minibus shouting and gesticulating. We also shouted and gesticulated, and while the driver drove off, abandoning her on the pavement, we celebrated our delightful victory with an outburst of general hilarity. The Uzbeki driver gave signs of appreciating our daring and took us amid laughter to half a dozen abandoned or deserted mosques whose ashen, withered beauty will always be with me: a pure, intense emotion that I relived years later in Cairo, in the symmetrical, desolate splendor of Ibn Tulun.*

We had a cheerful return to Tashkent: accustomed to escorting gray bureaucrats or gullible sympathizers, Vidas was obviously enjoying himself and confessed that he had never suspected till he met us that writers existed who were as irreverent and undisciplined as we were. Did all French or Spanish people behave like us, or were we an exception? He had innocently thought he was looking after an exemplary progressive family and suddenly discovered that we were very dangerous anarchists!

As our departure date for the Crimea drew nearer, Valeri looked somber and gloomy. During our stay he had become infatuated with the beauty of Carole, who at thirteen was heading for puberty with alarmingly attractive allure: he wanted to ask for her hand, invite us home, introduce us to his family. When we said goodbye to him, we had to console him. We had been captivated by Uzbekistan and would return again to Bukhara, we promised, but without the hassles or setbacks of that first, incident-prone visit.

15

On 23 July we flew to the Crimea and landed at Simferopol. As it was nighttime, we took ourselves to a motel near the airport. The Intourist car fetched us early and we traveled by road to Yalta, through a lush green landscape whose inhabitants seemed to be soaked in the warm caress of the sun.

Yalta had all the appearance of an antiquated city on the Riviera, with villas

imperturbable gymnast, hands on hips, absorbed in his repeated loosening-up ex-
ercises, did he write as well? After a brief gossip around, Vidas informed us he was
in the militia. What on earth was a militiaman doing in the writers' rest home? It
was a swap, he explained: a novelist wanted to write a novel devoted to the exploits
of the militia and, to get the right atmosphere, he requested a stay in their rest cen-
ter; in exchange, with that strict, fussy symmetry of engineers, ideologues, and geo-
metricians, the militia sent one of their own to the writers' mansion. The dreamy
Japanese of the striped pajamas was in fact, in contrast, a specimen of a most rare
species: the official bard of a country, the Yakut, situated in a remote confine of
Siberia and whose language had yet to be codified. He had been writing a gram-
mar or dictionary for years and was preparing to write a poem with thousands of
lines on the mythology and history of his people: their Odyssey, *their* Iliad.
Weighed down by that giant responsibility, the Yakut Homer wandered in a day-
dream along the paths in the park, in his anachronistic pajamas and incurable
gloom. I was frightened by his unusual fate, and when I came across him I imag-
ined the blind poet and his pathetic jarring reincarnation in this pleasant Chekho-
vian theatrical setting in which text, production, and actors took us back unwit-
tingly to the world of Kafka.

16

When the afternoon bus came to pick us up, we got on with fifty-
odd fellow writers who rushed to sit down and exchange noisy jokes as the vehicle
panted slowly down a winding road till it finally came to halt in a pleasantly treey
square. We got out and I walked to the beach with Monique and Carole, but the
group of matrons in front waved at me, signaling I shouldn't go on. The place I
was going was for women only; to reach the men's beach I should go in the other
direction. Confused by such an unexpected event—not yet understanding that
rigorous segregation worthy of our ultramontane bishops—I was forced to desert
them and look out with my peers onto a rocky shore, covered by a uniform mass
of pallid, naked, paunchy bathers. Rather than a concentration camp for nudists,
the place looked like a colony of penguins with protruding bellies, flashy glasses,
rubber sandals; the uneven ground strewn with pebbles and crops of rock hin-
dered even more their waddling movements; penises and testicles hung down

sadly, flaccid, lifeless, and unprotected. The spectacle evoked the prints of both Bosch and Doré, heightened by some surrealist touch: while dozens of individuals plunged and surfaced walruslike in the water, others stayed motionless on the side, their arms stretched out in the sun as if in surrender or worship, with their plastic eyeshades and goggles. Was this limbo a nightmare, a hallucination, a forerunner of a future extraterrestrial society of Selenites and Martians? Where were the slender, taut, athletic youths, the splendidly formed Tadzios immortalized by Thomas Mann? On the other side of the wire fence separating the beaches I spotted Monique and Carole, who had laughed themselves silly and had come to console me. The vision in their patch, they told me, was not any more comforting: Soviet men and women were unaware of dieting, and once youth had passed by, there was physical flab in abundance.

Back at the residence, we communicated our comic misfortune to Vidas, and after several calls and consultations, we obtained a special pass to the difficult, sought-after artists' beach where, he assured us, we could swim together. Dinner was served at six, and with no appetite we resigned ourselves to the same strenuous, tasteless menu we had suffered at midday. Monique timidly requested Crimean wine, but we were told there wasn't any. A drop of Moldavian or Caucasian wine? The establishment does not dispense alcoholic drinks, translated Vidas: writers came there precisely to dry out. We were not alcoholics, we objected. Our polite observations were of no use: the regulation was unbendable. Dinner was over at once, and as it was still daylight we went out into the garden. The pajamaed Homer, materfamilias, readers of Pravda, *the brave militiaman were engaged in their usual occupations, already part of the scenery. Not knowing what to do—there were no cafés in the vicinity and it was not time to read in bed—we also wandered through the park, talking about Chekhov and Kafka. A distinguished, elegant man wearing a panama hat and simply dressed in white came along arm-in-arm with his wife from the other direction, and as he passed us gently nodded at us. His discreet manner and style—the opposite of the other guests in the residence—intrigued and whetted our curiosity. When we met up with Vidas, we found out that he was a well-known translator from Spanish and French who had rendered nothing less than the* Quixote *and the work of Rabelais. In corroboration, his two children came to say hello and welcome us on his behalf, to express his pleasure at seeing us there. In our innocence, we thought that their embassy was the prelude to a visit, but that was not to be. Despite his mastery of the languages we spoke, the translator would content himself with distant greetings and communication with us through his offspring. Boris, the boy, was the same age as Carole, and during our stay and even after he chatted to her in English about books and poetry. Thanks to those conversations, we would discover that his father had translated À la recherche du temps perdu knowing that it would be accepted by no publishing house. From various references in their adult conversation, well beyond their years, we deduced that "he has had problems." But neither Carole nor myself dared question him. The day someone mentioned his past imprisonment by Stalin we would finally see behind his wariness: knowing that he was being watched by one of his so-called colleagues, he preferred to smile at us from afar and thus avoid running the risk of a relationship with a foreigner without the corresponding permission from the authorities.*

17

*   The artists' beach did not offer the same depressing spectacle as the day before had: the majority of the bathers were young, and some slim, attractive girls, apparently dancers, were going through rhythmic, gymnastic exercises at the edge of the sea. By the empty space where we stretched out, a group of actors were silently listening to a lean, dark colleague, oozing in suntan lotion, mercilessly declaim a speech or press editorial. A bit further away, Vidas told me, there were half a dozen Egyptian Communists just released from Nasser's prisons: they had brought with them a fair number of books in their beachbags and, as I walked past them to dive in, I looked out of the corner of my eye and made out several novels in French.*

*   Seaside passenger boats, like the old pleasure boats in the port of Barcelona, slowly edged along the coast, linking up the different spa stations; the next day, rather than staying on the beach, we boarded one of them and went along several miles of shore, contemplating from a distance the crowds of vacationers who splashed on the bank like a shoal of sardines. As Vidas explained, the different trade unions and professional associations availed themselves of their respective beaches, reserved for their own exclusive use. In between the two monumental workers'*

residences was an almost deserted fenced-off area occasionally dotted with awn-
ings and sunshades. With the help of binoculars, we made out small bands of
bathers comfortably spread along the coast: it was the beach for the Party hier-
archy and foreign guests of honor, the same perhaps where, two or three years ear-
lier, my friends Claudín and Semprún, then still members of the Politbureau, had
consoled themselves in the sun for the Party's failure and difficulty in adapting to
the new, disconcerting realities of structural change in Spain.

The stay at the writers' rest home was in all ways becoming unbearable: the
diet, times of meals, park stuffed with bureaucrats and materfamilias, indirect, al-
most clandestine communication with Boris's parents were injecting drop by drop
a mood of claustrophobia, and we decided with Monique to have a change of air,
break the daily monotony, escape for a few hours, in a word, breathe. Airports, ho-
tels, Intourist offices displayed striking posters with alluring invitations to visit Se-
bastopol, la ville héroïque. *Although unenthusiastic about patriotic tours, we*
begged Vidas to organize the excursion. It seemed a simple project that in principle
posed no problems, but our friend returned downcast from Intourist: traffic be-
tween Yalta and Sebastopol was provisionally halted by roadwork on a stretch of
the road and, for the moment, it was impossible to go. We were rather incredulous
but discussed other possible trips when, on looking at the map of the Crimea, I re-
alized that another road going inland linked the two cities. I communicated my
discovery to Vidas and accompanied him to the Intourist offices. He had a few
minutes' discussion with the female agent before coming back crestfallen: the in-
land route was also cut off. We would go by boat, I said: there was a jetfoil service.
Another brusque half-whispered exchange with the representative: the timetable
had been suspended! Annoyed by the amazing accumulation of obstacles, I asked
Vidas to ask her frankly why on earth she did not want us to go to Sebastopol. Our
friend translated my words and her only response was to fold her arms haughtily
in an eloquent mixture of anger and disapproval.

Days later, in Moscow, when commenting on this strange episode with Sartre
and Simone de Beauvoir, we were amused to discover that on their earlier journey
to the Crimea they had had exactly the same experience: they too, despite their in-
sistence, could not reach Sebastopol. There was probably a new regulation for-
bidding foreigners access to the town; but if that were the case, what was both in-

triguing and beyond explanation was the abundance of polyglot posters inviting you to visit. The gap between reality and propaganda defied any rational or logical schema. What was the secret of this city? What was behind that ridiculous contradiction? The most plausible of the hypotheses offered by Sartre was the possible secret dispatch of arms to Cuba. However, twenty years after these events, this I never got to Sebastopol *is and will continue to be one of the enigmas of the trip that, I fear, I will never manage to solve.*

18

The prospect of spending one more day in the aseptic "writers'" residence forced us into new schemes and strategies for escape: a drive through the outskirts of Yalta, a visit to the Livadia gardens, where Roosevelt, Churchill, and Stalin agreed on the redistribution and future of the world. Fortunately, Vidas mentioned to us the nearby presence of Nicolai Tomashevsky, whom I had met with Nekrassov in Florence, at a COMES congress: a son of one of the founders of the famous formalist school of Brik, Jakobson, Shklovsky, and Tynyanov, the young Tomashevsky had been a Russian lector in Naples, spoke Spanish perfectly, and brimming with vitality was fond of a drink; his spontaneous, frank character was a million miles from the reserve and officiousness of the majority of his colleagues. Tomashevsky was taking his summer holiday near Yalta and laughed heartily when he found out we were staying with those most cultured, intelligent bureaucrats of literature. With the exception of Boris's family, he said, not one of the guests in that place wrote anything but bureaucratic reports or really liked reading: what evil Trotskyite agent had had the perverse idea of sending us there?

Piloted by him, we went up to a beautiful mountain spot and sat down to have a drink in a picnic area. What's happened to the famous white wine of the Crimea? asked Monique. The wine of the Crimea is no more, he said: in the old days the Tartars used to produce it, but after their deportation they were replaced by Ukrainians, and the secret of its exquisite bouquet was lost. The present wine was on the bitter side and he did not advise it. Although connoisseurs now drank wine from the Caucasus, the favorite wine of czarist times belonged exclusively to the world of myth. Relaxing in a clearing in the wood, we spoke at length about literature. Tomashevsky admired as I did the work of Svevo and Gadda and spoke very enthusiastically about two Russian writers who had just emerged from the long purgatory where they had been kept under Stalin and Zhdanov and were beginning to dribble through the publishers but had not yet been translated—Platonov and Bulgakov. He was not generally inspired with great respect for the work of his contemporaries: Voznesensky had written some decent poetry, but was the victim of provincial snobbery and a love of fame; the poetry of Bella Akhmadoulina, the author of a delicate evocation of Pushkin and Danthès, the translation of which in Les Lettres Françaises *impressed me, connected, according to him, with the best Russian lyric tradition without, however, reaching the depth and poignancy of Tsvetaeva and Akhmatova. Nonchalantly, trying not to reveal my irony, I asked him about Yevtushenko. Well, he smiled, he was something like our Zorrilla. I remembered Eugenio d'Ors's gloss on him and quoted it from memory: "a pianola; and as he's the one who gets tired of pedaling . . ." "Oh," exclaimed Tomashevsky, "the worst thing is he never gets tired. His readers do, but he never does!"*

The conversation and wine had put us in a good mood: neither of us wanted to go back, and Tomashevsky suggested a visit to an old Tartar cemetery. We went along a mountain road that had sudden views of the Black Sea until we came out at a village with pretty rustic houses not as yet spoiled by modernity. The Ottoman mezarlek *was a miniature reproduction of those I would later look at in Turkey; the memorial stones on the grave monuments, with or without a turban at the top, indicated the sex of those buried, and the symmetrical disposition of the tombs pointing toward Mecca provided a quiet scene, imbued with gentle calm. But something there, alongside the theatrical ploys of twilight, accentuated the feeling of melancholy and surreptitiously added a pathetic, desolate note: the total absence of the living. Transferred thousands of miles away, the Tartars could not come and meditate by the tombs of their forebears, which were decaying in their solitary abandon, covered in grass and moss. Deprived of their community, erased from memory, the dead lived there a second definitive death: no curious visitor even managed to decipher their names cut in Arabic characters. On my return to Paris, I would add the lines scrawled hurriedly on the journey, Cernuda's simple lines:*

No es el juicio aún, muertos anónimos.
Sosegaos, dormid; dormid si es que podéis.
*Acaso Dios también se olvida de vosotros.**

19

Although we stayed in another hotel, our third stop in Moscow
followed a by now familiar framework, in line with well-established but flam-
boyant rituals: cheerful dinners at one of our favorite eating-houses, evenings
with Sartre and Simone de Beauvoir at the Prague restaurant or in the lounges at
the National, strolls with Agustín, Ángel, and Dionisio.

Agustín related to me an anecdote illustrating the recent conflict of factions
within the Spanish CP leadership and its bizarre repercussions in the field of lit-
erature: Two years earlier, he had been advising the editors of an anthology of
Peninsular authors to be published in Russian; the editors were visited by a Span-
ish "cadre" who demanded to examine the list of those selected. He scolded them
severely: "Why haven't you included Jorge Semprún? He must be included at
once!" None of the compilers then knew who my friend was, but they managed
to have sent to them from Paris the galleys of his novel, hastily translated a chapter
of Le Long Voyage, *and incorporated it into the volume. After a few months the*
book was ready, and the same person returned for a second time. He consulted the
contents page again and a look of angry surprise came to his face: "What on earth
is Jorge Semprún doing here? He must be eliminated immediately!" Neither
Agustín nor his Soviet comrade had understood that nonsensical succession of
contradictory orders until through some CP militants they discovered the identity
of the mysterious Federico Sánchez, first praised to the sky by his colleague and
then thrown into the dustbin of history with equal conviction.

We went for a walk with a group of Spaniards around the side streets off cen-
tral Gorki Street, where there were gathered more or less furtively the sellers of
secondhand books that did not carry the nihil obstat *of the authorities. They*

---

*You're not to be judged yet, you nameless dead.
  Calm down, go to sleep; that's if you can.
  Perhaps God has forgotten you as well.

drifted through looking conspiratorial, and when they met an eventual buyer mumbled the password for their merchandise. I heard one fair-haired romantic youth, in a tight-fitting threadbare mackintosh, repeat quietly: Pasternak, Pasternak. The area looked strangely like a spot for picking up males or clandestinely selling drugs: but instead, hash was, to advantage, replaced by authors outside the canon or glowing with the aura of the forbidden. They told me the most sought-after and expensive title was Salvador Dalí's Secret Life. *A fact that ought to be food for thought for future Hispanic censors concerning the imponderable marvels of their stimulating, beneficent trade!*

As we could see from many small pointers, the country had been biding its time ever since the fall of Khrushchev. The personalities and intentions of the new leaders were still unknown factors: the writers I spoke to were not sure whether the timid thaw Krushchev had begun was to be prolonged or whether they were headed, on the contrary, for harsher times. Strangely, while Stalin's name was still wrapped in a halo of fear and respect, his successor was earning the most surprising, ridiculous criticisms and reproaches: he was having thrown back at him his rudeness, his vulgar attitude the day he hit the rostrum at the United Nations with his shoe. Almost no one seemed to grant him any recognition for having freed hundreds of thousands of prisoners and for his denunciation of the crimes and persecutions of Stalin, from which I would deduce correctly that the winds blowing from above and inspiring the supposedly personal comments from the more or less "official" colleagues with whom I had dealings indicated a phase of greater ideological rigidity and a return to the sacrosanct principles of Leninism.

20

As our departure date drew near, the comrades in the Writers' Union and other cultural entities multiplied their friendly overtures. Tanya—the efficient adviser to the Foreign Literature Review—*Irina, always very warm and sensitive, Hispanists, and translators of my books came to our hotel, went shopping with us, tried to make life easy while Boris took Carole out and initiated her in the study of Russian.*

Four weeks at Monique's side had softened bit by bit the blow dealt by my letter, and in various scenarios and moments on the trip we had recovered gestures we thought had died, resumed familiar communication, reached physical intimacy with the same disturbing novelty as on our first encounter in Barcelona. The Soviet Union—model or Aunt Sally for so many writers—had filled us with neither enthusiasm nor horror. Our stay there had been initiatory, warm, and sometimes friendly. Anyhow, our glimpses and taste of the society of the future had injected us with a healthy skepticism in relation to the state planning of happiness and had sharpened, perhaps involuntarily, our sense of humor.

F OURTEEN MONTHS LATER, at the end of summer in
1966, I would repeat the journey under very different
circumstances. I had been invited to the festivities commemorating the cen-
tenary of a stupendous Caucasian poet—whom I had never heard of before
those events and whom I would never hear mentioned again afterwards—
and went as part of a group of foreign guests who were mainly French,
Communist Party sympathizers or members. The year gone by had been
rich in developments not only in relation to my private life—my first stay in
Tangier, emotional distancing from Spain, return to Paris with Monique—
but also my political connections and feelings of ambivalence toward the
USSR: the Sovietization of the revolutionary process in Cuba, the arrest of
the writers Daniel and Siniavsky, the abrupt end to hopes of a gradual cultural thaw. In August Carole had spent several weeks at Tanya's house in
Moscow and had made great progress in Russian thanks to Boris and his
friends. I thought at first I would politely decline the invitation, but the
friendly insistence of the Soviets and the short length of the trip filled me
with doubts. Rightly convinced that this would be my last visit if I published,
as was my intention, a kind of diary of the previous tour, I thought it rather
senseless to squander the opportunity to set my impressions against the reality that had produced them. Although I shelved the publishing idea months
later, as much through a passing lack of interest in the issue as from fear that
my criticisms might be used by Francoism, the argument about testing out
my attitude of conscious subjectivism finally persuaded me to accept.

My affinity with nascent Soviet dissidents, my condemnation of the military occupation of Czechoslovakia—where I went, immediately after the
invasion, as a guest of the Czech Union of Writers, to work on an article that

would appear in *Les Temps Modernes*—would finally terminate my rather ambiguous relationship with the official world of the USSR. The certainty that the crushing of the "Prague spring" was in no way different from the sending of marines to Santo Domingo would in the future enforce upon me a double-edged, more complex militancy in respect to Palestinians, Afghans, and the victims of Castro's dictatorship and the criminal juntas of Central America and the Southern Cone. The cardinal discovery of the last decades, as Maxime Rodinson has seen very clearly, is that revolutions are relative and that the final struggle moves ever away, as we think we get closer, inasmuch as "existing socialism" never by a long shot puts an end to exploitation or oppression but transforms them and sometimes intensifies them; consequently, the methods, objectives, and programs of real or would-be revolutionary states or movements should be examined with a clear-thinking caution. "Unconditional adherence often leads one to approve mistakes and, often, real barbarity." Such experiences, full of setbacks, disillusion, strokes of luck, and relapses, would gradually take me to the conclusion formulated years later in a university session with arts students in Sevilla: that I prefer making my own mistakes to following the right slogan.

Since saying farewell to the Soviet Union in 1966, I have fleetingly seen some of the friends who have appeared on these pages or have found out indirectly about them: Agustín Manso is still in Moscow, busy working as a translator; Dionisio keeps himself rather on the fringes and apparently supports the nationalist and anti-Semitic ideological currents set out in Alexander Zinoviev's latest startling interviews; Ángel, having become a rabid anti-Communist, returned to Spain and works or worked for the Russian service of Radio Free Europe; Lénina Zónina spent brief periods in Paris, faithful to her old friendship with Sartre and Castor, and I am filled with sadness and emotion as I receive news of her death in Moscow as I sit writing these lines; Vidas works in the university and goes about with the usual friends; Ruth Zernova emigrated to Israel when her mother died, and the night she dined in Paris with Monique and myself posed strange arguments—coming from a former volunteer to the International Brigades—against my defense of the right of Palestinians to self-determination . . .

Several times over recent years I have dreamed that I am back in the USSR: the oneiric intrigue is not oppressive or anxious but develops generally in a pleasant and rather unreal atmosphere. A vague awareness of returning to a dead and unrepeatable past that launches me afresh into remembering my journeys and, subliminally and indirectly, to the tardy discovery of how ridiculously happy I was there.

CHAPTER VII

All That Glitters Isn't Moorish

THE NEWCOMER GREETED the concierge for the block and exchanged a few polite phrases: an old woman with her white hair tucked up in a bun and a strong southern accent. Madame had warned her he was coming and given her the keys. The flat's on the first floor; a young man like him, she says, better take the stairs, not the elevator. She apologizes for not going with him; she can't leave the porter's room unattended and the imagined hint of a smell of some dish perhaps indicates that the old lady has also got her coal or gas cooker on the burn.

The foreigner accepted her excuses with an understanding smile: in spite of the pleasant or neutral look on his face, the absentminded re-creator of the scene could imagine that there was even a glint of satisfaction. Perhaps he would rather no third person share his initial glance at what will be his home for some time: the exclusive first fruits of that vision. Perhaps he also wants to keep to himself those gestures that betray his clumsiness, the difficult relationship between his hands and the tiniest objects of everyday use: the inevitable confusion over the keys until he hits the hole corresponding to the lock and the bolt, possibly then stumbling into something as he gropes for the light switch, a less than glorious skirmish with the blind-pull warped with damp. The flat, as he will see, comprises two spacious rooms, bathroom, and kitchen. The furniture is comfortable but impersonal: a suite upholstered perhaps in green, dining room table and chairs, a double bed already made up, more chairs, built-in wardrobes, refrigerator, small framed prints and engravings, standard lamps, a table suitable for writing. The foreigner inspects things as if adapting to them and assessing their exact shape and size before taking them over. For the first time in his life he is settling down in a city that he does not know and where he in turn is a total stranger. He is pleased by the anonymity of the home he agrees to rent hours later: after thirty-odd years of life *en famille*, he is relieved by the idea of camping down amid furniture that lacks history. Appropriation will be cautious, in stages; check that the water heater for the bath is working, that plugs and bulbs are in good order. The objects and clothes he has brought with him fit in a medium-sized suitcase: before nightfall, he hangs up jackets and trousers, puts shirts and underwear on their shelves; inkpot, pen, books, paper on the small table. The refrigerator will continue to be empty and disconnected: the new tenant knows his limits and it doesn't even occur to him to use it. Crockery, saucepans, cutlery will stay clean and tidy, piled up on the cupboard shelves or lined up along the rack. When he draws a summary conclusion to his move, he finds that the flat has not lost its cold, battered look; his presence there is to be anodyne and slight, just a passing visitor. The dining room window, at the front, looks out on a dull block of flats in the unmistakable architectural style that marked his childhood in the forties; a plot surrounded by ruined walls, covered in rubbish and weeds, acts as a store or hiding-place, he later notices, for European and indigenous junkdealers and kids; from the back balcony adjacent to his bedroom, the newcomer can glimpse, hemmed in between two buildings, a small patch of the port, with breakwater and cranes and, in the distance, like a whitish, misty scar, the blurred coastline of his distant and despised country.

At first sight, the new tenant is a man of sober habits, neat and elegant to an extreme: he gets up early, showers, shaves, and goes out straightaway to stretch his legs and purchase for a few cents some tatty esoteric local newspaper. About fifty meters from home he has discovered a café belonging to a compatriot and has decided to adopt it for the moment, while awaiting a better solution. In midmorning, after writing an extensive letter and sticking stamps on it, he checks all is in order and equips himself with the necessary items for his program of exploration: a conversation manual bought at an airport kiosk, a short tourist guide to the city. Although the manual is not much help and the guidebook doesn't include a map of the small streets in the district that interests him, he embarks daily on his rambler's route armed with them, like some tiny derisory protective barrier. A decision that is all the more absurd given that the expatriate—like his wife years later in Roscoff*—does not really wish to preserve himself from anything and, on the contrary, gives himself over to the adventure with the incentive of total availability. For the first time in his life he too has no timetable or work schedules; his stay in the town is the same as any ordinary gentleman of leisure attracted there—like the tourists he comes across on his way down to the seafront—by the typical, proverbial local color or the chance enjoyment of evasive, impregnating luminosity. Usually, he stops on the terrace of some café near the bus stop and station, asks for the same aromatic infusion as his neighbors, unobtrusively follows their conversation and from time to time scribbles down a word on a cigarette box or in the margins of his conversation manual. Later on, as he loses his diffidence and feels more on home ground, he speaks to the locals, although after an elementary exchange of phrases on weather, nationality, or origins, he is forced to give up his efforts unless, as sometimes happens, his interlocutor speaks his language or, to his greater mortification, responds directly in French.

In retrospect, the expatriate seems like a topographer in his detailed taming of this exotic world. Day after day he wanders through the labyrinth of narrow streets, copies down the trilingual sign in each of them, draws and corrects maps, redoes routes, checks his accuracy.

His meanderings are both obsessive and erratic, as if he were following in someone's footsteps or, in reverse, was being tracked by someone he was trying to throw off course. In truth, he is behaving in the city as circumspectly as he had initially behaved in the flat. He often gives the impression that he feels a need to encompass and measure the space he moves around in in order to fit himself in: before entering the small cafés that attract him, immersed in those shadowy, silent, narrow streets, he explores the nooks and crannies of the alleyways, sketches in beforehand a brief outline of place. His

*See Monique Lange, *Les Cabines de bain*, Paris 1982.

persistence in overcoming his manifest insecurity finally earns its reward: the most arduous, unyielding bastions surrender in turn to his curiosity. He gradually gets acclimated, is recognized by the waiter or owner, savors his infusion, smokes a pipe or two, alternates reading and notetaking with a scrutiny of everything happening about him. Given the lack of the sought-after understanding of language, he strives like a deaf-mute to observe expressions and gestures. The aim is to familiarize himself, melt into this milieu, acquire the privileged impunity of a chameleon.

Daily observation of the expatriate allows one to establish a timetable for his activities that, even though subject to modifications and imponderables, nonetheless pinpoints his basic propensity toward routine: he never leaves home before the mail arrives, then goes down to the porter's minutes later, and when the old lady hands him the awaited letter, he separates it out from the others, the ones that are less important, and keeps it in a jacket pocket so as to read it unhurriedly in one of the cafés on his walk, where he usually sits down before climbing the slope and taking on the steep steps that lead to the old quarter of the medina. If the reply from his correspondent is delayed and the postman has no new ones, rather than rereading the old ones, he heads for the main post office, joins the line for a telephone, and when it's his turn asks for a long-distance call to Saint-Tropez. Apart from that brief, sporadic incursion into the modern quarter, largely inhabited by Europeans, his walks take him exclusively to the small cafés and terraces that he has become attached to: he has lunch by himself in an eating-house, greets or smiles timidly at the waiter, stops to drink an infusion at the crossroads in the old quarter, turns down the labyrinth of alleyways that he trawls doggedly with growing aplomb and confidence. His conversation manual, with its imprecise and even misleading phonetic transcriptions, is now full of words, corrections, and crossings-out. This interest in getting a command of the language contrasts with his slowness or difficulty in finding someone to share it with. Whether in the seaview cafés set in the city wall, the dingy backrooms where he crouches on a rush mat, or the place from which he enjoys a view of the flat roofs and domes of the city, he goes in and out unaccompanied and, often unaware of the voices of the lotto players and the noise of the

dominoes, he tries to memorize a phrase he has just learned or the complicated conjugation of some verb. He is satisfied by the novelty of all he sees,
hears, touches, tastes, breathes. Unlike other journeys he has been on, he is
not seeking to confirm a theory or validate his own knowledge. The ideological monolith where he once lived has given way to a fertile range of petty
kingdoms. The vast, changing nature of the area excludes facile assimilation
and he prefers gradual annexation, like someone scaling a fortress or walled
keep. Only mental appropriation of that world can enable him to forget old
errors and learn from new ones, the task of casting off the oppressive experience of the past, the need to extend to himself the investigation he has till
then urged on everyone else. The expatriate is convalescing from an afflic-
tion that does not appear in any dictionary and against which no medicine
can be prescribed. His rejection of all that marks him out assumes the dimensions of an allergy: proximity to his fellow countrymen irritates him
and, as far as possible, he flees from their presence. When he returns home,
he transcribes in an exercise book the lexis acquired during the day and
strives to express his effervescent ideas on notepaper that he sends to his wife.

Although the correspondence is not dated, the content of the letters allows
you quite accurately to establish the correct chronological sequence.

> When my bedroom is bathed in sunlight, it's as hot as in summer. I feel
> happy, I walk around for ten hours a day, I'm seeing Haro [Tecglen] and
> his wife, I'm not going to bed with anyone and I look at Spain from afar,
> full of intellectual excitement.
>   I need to be here: I couldn't stay in Saint-Tropez with no ideas and no
> will to write and I predict that in Tangier I will recover both. This is what
> really matters to me, not sex.

> One observation that will interest you: while European homosexuals
> usually reveal themselves by imitating women, here, in contrast, they take
> on an extra layer of exaggerated virility. That's what attracts me to them
> and helps me to distinguish them without fail, since naturally there are
> plenty who aren't.

A little while ago, I was watching and listening to Spanish television (you can pick it up here). Its cretinism and the profanation of our language made an incredible impression on me.

I'm dying to get writing, and I'm not sure yet what about.

I really miss you, but I am afraid to return to Saint-Tropez and get upset. I admit life with me is difficult and you have had to swallow a lot since we came back from Moscow; but in Saint-Tropez, I just don't exist if I'm not involved in something more tangible. Although I detest Spain, this feeling has its positive side: it's useful to me since it helps when it comes to writing. In Saint-Tropez, and I insist that this has nothing to do with you, I'm not in or opposite Spain and I cannot look at her as I can from here in a *new way*. If I'm not working, I'm just growing older in a pleasant climate. I'm not making any moral or intellectual progress.

I have just received your three letters all together: I love you a little–a lot–passionately totally. As I read them in amorous crescendo, I felt happy. But I have since seen that the real order was in reverse. Having said this, you're right and I'll try to be more explicit. You must believe me when I say that if I'm staying here for a while that it has no bearing at all on you. I miss you and I seem to have been without you for a long time; but I've no wish to return to Saint-Tropez to feel fucked up, get drunk, and then blame it on you. I would rather you got annoyed with me than that I feel rancorous toward you. The idea I'm working on is based on the vision of the Spanish coast from Tangier: I want to start off from this image and write something beautiful, that goes well beyond anything I've written so far. Tangier is still indispensable [for] this daily struggle with a theme that is still hazy. [At the moment] I'm immersed in Golden Age literature.

I've just received a letter from Luis. Eulalia died three days ago and she was buried on the second of January.* They preferred me not to go since she remembered me arriving when Dad and Grandfather were in their death agony, and she thought that if I didn't go that meant her illness was not serious and she wasn't at death's door.

---

*See *Forbidden Territory*, pages 108–11. This letter was written after my sister-in-law's telegram reached me in Fez.

Perhaps it's all been for the best, but despite the predictability of what was coming, the news had a terrible effect on me. Neither Luis nor I have anyone behind us now—as regards the past and the family—nor in front—in relation to death. The umbilical cord's been cut and we're on the waiting list.

The expatriate has found a friend. Their eyes had met the day before on a café terrace in the main square, and he bumped into him again crossing the road on the way to the post office. The stranger said hello without more ado in his garbled Moorish Spanish: he's wearing a blue woollen hat, and trousers and overcoat in the same color. He looks like a fisherman or a sailor, but isn't; he has worked for several years in the port with Spaniards, he explains; there he learned to get about in the language of Cantinflas and Joselito. After drinking tea together, they went to buy wine in a Jewish shop and quietly closed themselves off in the flat on the rue Molière.

Although the farmhand is about as old as our hero, his appearance is totally different: his rough, solid face and tough, coarse complexion make him look like an oarsman, a sturdy, muscular fighter. His untamed intelligence and uncouth ways are not without their humor or mischievous appeal. When he's talking he laughs, showing off his teeth beneath his thick mustache; his half-shifty, half-confused manner remind the expatriate of Alfredo, the deceased Torrentbó cropper. There's nothing better than wine, he assures him, to lose his sense of shame with him; he makes out he hasn't tasted any for months and gulps it down while answering his questions, your questions, naked by now, but still wearing his cap.

From then on—the end of November—the man from the wilds will often visit your house and escort you with the somber looks of a bodyguard in your trawl of the medina; he usually walks with you up to the small cafés by the Alcazaba, helps you unthread and mix the leaves, initiates you in your fruitful incursion into maashun: thanks to him and his robust protection, you forced entry into the toughest dives and discovered the pleasure of smoking a pipe or two in the hanging garden of the Khafita, scrutinizing the enemy coast from your watchtower or vantage point. After supper, your guide prefers the attributes of the modern city and a thirsty visit to the English bars, in one of which he had worked as a doorman or, more precisely, as a bouncer. Infected by his excesses and nocturnal fury, you will also down alcohol with maashun and grass, you will make up for the deceptive austerity of your first days with the seer's search for the abyss or precipice. You have hit upon the perfect inductive agent and only await the moment that will spark it off. The inexorable gravitation it sets off is light-bringing, horizon-opening. Only by yielding to it will you attain the fullness of the mental space hinted at: raw, cooked, consumed acts paralleling the word as it is purified to the marrow.

It's an evening like any other, just like the others, following your headstrong, worrying wandering path: to and from the Alcazaba, pipes of shared kef, televised course in Spanishry, a rushed meal in Hammadi, nocturnal bustle in a taxi, cheerful disembarking with your guard and mentor on the usual entertaining circuit: out-of-the-way dives and quaysides, Rolling Stones background music, conniving little grins, waltzing around like an African queen, finicky queens, Oxonian accents of some broken-down noble or su-perannuated lord: cheerful libations in the half-dark, never-satisfied thirst, the expansive euphoria of my Hispanarabic wildman, the obsessive repeti-tion of old stories of Nasride, trailing in the rear, and the last Abencerraje a navy-blue cap, perhaps pulled down tight, thick, hircine brows, primitive nose, sylvane mustache, voracious lips, energetic, crushing jaws, determined to serve him forever, he swears again and again, such a good understanding companion, guide him through the city, ensure his rest and safety, attend night and day to the exact fulfillment of his desires, wash and cook for him, go daily to the market, accompany him to the baths, prevent any trouble, in-cident, or danger, ready for anything to satisfy his friend, drink a few com-forting glasses of wine with him, make up his joints, have a look around the bars far from the dirt and the rabble without faith, religion, or trust, intent only on robbing and kicking their peers up the backside, he's a man to be trusted, his only dream is to get to know Spain one day, to cross the accursed Straits, to clear off forever from Tangier and all these thieves and bastards on the loose, to travel with his friend, greet those friendly Spaniards who toiled with him in the port, loading and unloading oranges, sixty, even eighty kilos of oranges on their back, just touch his body to see it's true, he's not a braggart and a liar like everybody else

he's raised his voice, begun to strip so as to show off the tough sinewy muscles of his arms or perhaps it's later, in another setting or, more likely, in the bed-room?

you don't know and will never know because everything is misty and unreal and the imagined exchange is the one you heard or will hear afterwards from his lips, stammered out as night advances and the empty bottles of Bou-laouane pile up: fifteen years in the service of those bastards, from dawn to dusk, never complaining, then suddenly they shut the firm and throw him out on the fucking street like a cigarette butt, no bonuses or compensation, just a letter of recommendation, look at it, twenty liters of olive oil, a pair of new boots, and a bag of flour, how the hell was he going to feed and look after his mother and sisters with that, suddenly quiet, calmed down, taught a les-son by what happened tonight, ready to laugh or cry, depends how the mood catches him, yes, that's life, brother, time to down another glass and stare at you, on the brink of laughter and tears

still in the bar, the cushions and the buzz of the bar, surrounded by evasive presences, anxious creatures fleeing from the light, adding up, perhaps to hold onto something, the alarming way the glasses are replaced, gin cognac vodka, perhaps everything's mixed up, both lost in thick, dark foliage, paths tracks shortcuts simply rubbed out, no memory of them after the storm blowing down and buffeting you, picks you off, pulls you up, kicks you out on foot or by taxi? but finally in the flat, unsure how you have arrived or why you are arguing, did you start it, as he'll say later when facing up to the con-sequences of the scene, a hidden desire to kindle his fury till you drove him out of his mind? to reach the bitter raw truth in your bitter garden of de-lights? veiled images, opacity broken by the glaring lightning flash of vio-lence, your stunning communication of energy, the bruising damage of the blow, fall, painfully get up, brutal order to stretch out on the bed, intermit-tent flashes of consciousness, shriveled up, weighed down, drowsy while he stalks the room like a caged beast, looks for alcohol in the kitchen, drinks from the bottle, fires threats and muffled accusations at you, at the city, at lousy life, stands there not taking his eyes off you, grim alert like a brutal guard, nodding off for minutes hours in the chair till sleep overcomes you and him and, when you wake up, you can see him there lying on the floor, inert, spread-eagled, snoring in the middle of the ravaged room, clothes scattered everywhere, upturned chairs, dirty, unmade bed, gradual perception of the tense scene around you, cruel aggression of day, accusing upside-down time of day, mental and material disorder, painful effort to get up, go to the bathroom, look at oneself incredulously in the mirror and find a face that is not yours, transmuted as well into the fierce whirlwind of the night, still incapable of thought, of understanding what has happened, the chance spark that set off that sudden outburst of virulence

get washed, shaved, hide the swelling behind merciful sunglasses, open the window wide to let the fresh air in and wake up your befuddled guard, he in turn gets up, goes for a lengthy piss in the bathroom, reappears looking flustered, his mustache lank and contrite like a child who has just broken his toy; mumbling pitiful excuses, wishing to make it up, make friends with his friend who is so well-behaved, so kind, a real brother who looks after him and helps him when he hasn't got any money, daintier than lace, softer than cotton, ready to reach the bottom of the pit of self-abasement just like the lover caught erring so beautifully and sharply described by Ibn Hazm

but you want to be alone, to digest what has happened, distance yourself, transform humiliation into yeast, rage into power: reach that point of fusion in which the war waged against yourself symbolically transcends, augurs in morals and literature a new departure, vindicates the reason for the mishap, the cataclysm both sought and feared: stern imposition of destiny whose prize will be the written word, the blight or grace of creation.

On the same day you arrived in Marrakesh on a flight initially planned for both of you but that you alone took: a threadbare image of dusk over the palm forest and the ocher land, insensitive, in your state at the time, to the beauty, radiant abundance of a city that in the future will grant you the magnificent gift of the word. Closeted in your hotel room, between Kutubia and Djemaa el Fna, you experienced moments of solitude, elation, and madness, conscious you had broken the cortex round your burning center, reached the depths from which bubbled, poured out, the magma of filth, burnt matter. The sudden, violent exhilaration, the bright, destructive lash glimpsed from childhood had ceased to be a secretive vision, panting to become real: a force tied to your peculiar experience of sex, the animal gravitation of bodies that you had to experience and integrate in the body of your text with the same disenchanted lucidity and calm fatalism with which Fernando de Rojas, the student from Puebla de Montalbán, laid out, for the lovers in *La Celestina*, the recondite laws of their intimate, substantial vulcanology.

Not the same as happened in Madrid years before, that evening you got drunk with Lucho, moral disaster has become a vital source of self-knowledge. Beyond the personal sphere, it reveals, renders diaphanous the latent mechanisms within society, exhumes and rescues from the bone marrow the energy that will propel the devastating invasion you propose: that work not yet written in our language, against it, to its greater glory, to destroy and pay homage, to profane and bring offerings, schizophrenic, oneiric, alienated aggression, integral alliance of imagination and reason, as Malraux says of Goya, beneath the lying appearance of delirium. Strings of resolutions forged dizzily from your flight to the city where today you evoke and transfix on the page what has happened: penetrate the real history of the country from which you felt inexorably proscribed; immersion in a lustral bath of its classics; sieve through the totality of its literary corpus with the same painstaking frenzy as you daily trawled the chaos of Tangier; place the humanistic mass of the epoch—linguistics, poetics, historiography—at the disposal of such an enterprise; reach down to the roots of the civil death you have had to live through; bring out into the light the demons and fears crouching in the depths of your consciousness. Days, hours, privileged moments, lush richness unequaled since, brooding on your anger, insults, thirst for revenge on those windmills or giants by the name of religion-fatherland-family-past-childhood. The mental spring set off by the taunts of your

guard proliferates, spreads out: it presents out-of-the-way corners, shady
spots, rough edges, a vast field to sound out and explore. For a time, your
proximity to the initiator is indispensable and, back in Tangier, you submit
to the magnetism of his blind, repellent labors.

Antagonistic parallelisms and schemas: topographic appropriation of the
urban nucleus where you have taken refuge and distancing overseas from
the land glimpsed as receding outline; clumsy, childish apprenticeship in the
new language and irresistible pull of the old, entranced and forever captivated by the incandescent splendor of the word; renunciation of a broad
alien space and gradual immersion in the strata of its history and culture; purification, decanting, refining of an extreme, diamantine language against
the sterilizing monopoly of an arrogant, all-embracing caste.

Ritual wanderings after spying from your window the arrival of the messenger with news from Saint-Tropez or of Eulalia's cancer, accompanied
not just by the conversation manual and gradually amended map but also a
modest, dog-eared copy of *Soledades*. Your close, attentive, almost obses-
sional reading of the text, its rich leafy bowers and twisting tracks inter-
woven with the pauses and fantasies of kef. Sitting in one of the cafés that
you like, you break off your siege of the poem to rise up at will, watch over
minarets, flat roofs, and white domes, scrutinize the faded scar of a repudiated, hostile land. Góngora indissolubly linked in your memory to the
changing capricious sky of Tangier, as Juan Ruiz will be years later to the
bustling forum of Djemaa el Fna: line after line joined together like cherries,
metaphors of wily, insidious beauty, enjoyment, subtle beatitude. Waking
up at midnight with a quotation on your lips as if you had commended your
dreams to the Poet: immediacy, outpouring, impregnation of writing that
supplants the world to your advantage, acts as a reference point and, like a
lighthouse, beams its light toward you in the midst of the chaos.

Only later, much later, will you establish the existence of a cartography and
speleology common to mystic and lover alike that, by transcending and gen-
eralizing what you thought was particular to you, will free you of guilt but

will also strip you of your precious strangeness: a similarity of experiences translated in identical throbbing images, tightness and breadth, pain and joy, harshness, flame, consummation: the universal law of the subsoil, complementing the discoveries of Kant and Descartes, Marx and Bakunin, Humboldt, Rousseau, thanks to San Juan de la Cruz and Mawlana, Eckhart and Al Hallax, the Marquis de Sade and the obscure Masoch.

Like Mlle. de Vinteuil next to the paternal photo in the love scene, you will incorporate Eulalia's dreaded imagined death agony into the peaks, ups and downs, precipices of your perverse frame: illuminating assumption of the center and its igneous reality: extending, unraveling, intensifying the friction till you are dizzy associating it with the original nodule of anguish: counterpointing conflicting visions, slow devouring by opened jaws, a pallid, worn-out face, sanctified by pain: enigmatic relationship between the intrusive, inductive image, the stubborn dipping into glorious suffering and the brusque syncopated swoon: magmatic eruptivity, red-hot volcanic slag surging out of your own Gehenna: duality, ambivalence, Zoroastrian love and profanation, generating spark of a secret alternative current.

One meager, greedy January day, winter harshens, Eulalia has died and the expatriate has digested the news in his way, walked up without his guard to one of the small cafés by the Alcazaba, dissolved a good dose of maashun in his glass of mint tea, been delirious, sobbed, moaned for hours his guilt out in the open, fulfilling the millenary, funereal, anthropophagous rite of the final missing explanation. His stay in the city is coming to an end and he has written a few lines to Saint-Tropez announcing his return.* He now has a familiar relationship with his environment: he recognizes spaces and players and, gradually, in turn, feels accepted and recognized. He daily retraces his steps with all possible variants, stopping to drink tea or smoke a pipe in the same places, he reads a few lines of *Soledades*, notes down words or phrases in the margins of his conversation manual.

The air of Tangier, imbued with gentle light, stimulates him. Under its

*Letter of 10 January 1966.

caress people and things acquire relief and liveliness, the street bustle un-
winds in an atmosphere of dense plasticity. Wrapped in their djellabas, bur-
nooses, or hooded cloaks, women and men move through the shadowy side
street as if it were a theatrical set, the salty damp of the Straits impregnates
the whitewashed walls, light and shadow combine their effect with subtle
skilled harmony. The man of leisure can spend minutes or hours absorbed
in the contemplation of the clouds or following, almost hypnotized, the cautious movements, in a patio or on a flat roof visible from his lookout post, of
a little old woman wrapped round in a towel near a minute coal stove. The
morning gust of breeze transmits and scatters round voices and messages:
greetings, shouts, bits of music, noises and echoes of craftsmen, the simultaneous invocation of the muezzin calling the faithful to prayer. The mobile
flight of the birds, their anxious hovering seem to obey secret, indecipherable
signals: the pigeons that were dotted over the minaret of the nearby mosque
abandon it with noisy conviction and fly off in a whirl of white patches to the
ancient town walls. Visions beyond grasp, fleeting images, drenched in sun
and mist: trumpets and drums of a mountain marriage, a procession of religious brotherhoods with their dingy oriflammes, flashy polyglot flocks after the red fez of their shepherd.

The expatriate guided his steps through the labyrinth of the Alcazaba
through gardens and green spaces in the Marshan, till he reaches the Square
of Motherhood and zigzags up to the haughty vantage point of the Khafita.
A warm, indulgent sun invites him to sit at the tables set on the slope along
the flowering terraces: thickly verdant nests sheltered from indiscreet gazes,
in which loners, groups, couples smoke, read, converse, savor mint tea curled
up in a ball of lazy warmth. The coastal scarp is precipitous, and from these
heights can be surveyed the panorama of the Tarifa Strait to Gebel Tariq, the
bellicose succession of waves that in slow suicidal majesty break and die in
foam at the foot of the cliff: repeated realization of the distance separating
him from the other shore, the kernel of his aggressive anxiety and vehement
desire for betrayal. Gripping his falcon-mentor's book, he awaits the sharp
flash whose blinding light will transfigure him; but from Lermontov, and
not from Góngora, from a poor Spanish translation read by chance months

before, will leap like a hare the refrain in lines that will engrave themselves with their devastating truth: *goodbye, filthy Stepmother, country of masters and slaves / goodbye three-cornered leather hats, and you, the people that put up with them.* New excitement and emotion entrance him at once, fire him with the intoxication of someone who has solved the riddle. The poem he has just adapted to his own obsession is a dawn to something: the feverishly noted phrase triggers off, drives on, the generative furrow of writing.

The one who sees and the one who is seen are one within yourself, says Mawlana; but the expatriate you now bid farewell to is *another*, and when he packs his case and disappears from the city to which he came quietly in the ephemeral sweetness of autumn he could exclaim, à la Flaubert, in the fever of his undertaking, totally at one with the felon in the distant legend: don Julián, *c'est moi*.

Memory, wrote Walter Benjamin, cannot transfix the flow of time or en-compass the infinite dimension of space: it is restricted to re-creating set scenes, encapsulating privileged moments, arranging memories and images in a syntactic order that word by word will shape into a book. The unbridge-able distance between act and written word, the laws and requirements of the narrative text will insidiously transmute faithfulness to reality into artis-tic exercise, attempted sincerity into virtuosity, moral rigor into aesthetics. No possibility of escape from the dilemma; the reconstruction of the past will always be certain betrayal as far as it is endowed with later coherence, stiffened with clever continuity of plot. Put your pen down, break off the narrative, prudently limit the damage: silence, silence alone will keep intact a pure sterile illusion of truth.

Design by David Bullen
Typeset in Mergenthaler Granjon
with Weiss display
by Wilsted & Taylor
Printed by Maple-Vail
on acid-free paper